Problems in Organizing Library Collections

PROBLEMS IN ORGANIZING LIBRARY COLLECTIONS

· ·

by Doralyn J. Hickey

R. R. BOWKER COMPANY

New York & London, 1972

Published by R.R. Bowker Co. (A Xerox Company)
1180 Avenue of the Americas, New York, N.Y. 10036

Copyright © 1972 by Xerox Corporation
International Standard Book Number: 0-8352-0539-8
Library of Congress Catalog Card Number: 74-39692

Printed and bound in the United States of America.

CONTENTS

• • • • • • • • • •

   The bibliographic search unit in a university library has failed to discover a Library of Congress card for a book on which a cataloger has spent considerable time.

   A school librarian disagrees with her supervisor about the need to record each newly received item in a loose-leaf accession volume.

   In an attempt to provide more in-depth analysis of the collection, the cataloger in a public library decides to add analytics and divide the file into author, title, and subject sections, thereby confusing some of the library patrons.

   A new library school graduate accepts a cataloging position in a research institute library, only to discover that much of her work will involve the typing of cards and other records.

and discovers that his own book has been given a wrong classification number and subject entry.

discovers that he cannot retrieve it quickly from his wife, to whom he had taken it over the weekend.

FOREWORD

• • • • • • • • • •

No area of the library school curriculum has been the subject of more frequent or more severe criticism than the introductory courses in cataloging and classification. Students complain that course content is either excessively theoretical or not theoretical enough. Alumni report that they were taught all of the wrong things about cataloging and none of the right ones, while employers grumble that recent graduates know either too little or too much to adapt readily to the requirements and pace of an ongoing technical services operation.

Doralyn Hickey's *Problems in Organizing Library Collections* opens a new and significant direction to both teachers and those responsible for the continuing education of librarians in the technical services. This book makes available, for the first time, a substantial body of case materials for use by those who have become impatient with the limitations of traditional approaches to instruction. These case studies, designed to bridge the gap between the idealism of the classroom and the inescapable, if sometimes harsh, reality of the world of library practice, challenge the reader's ability to modify and adapt concepts and principles in order to resolve a variety of complex and subtle problems. At the same time, the cases themselves provide the best illustration of that most useful, if most often overlooked, of all principles: "the organization of library materials never takes place in a vacuum."

Professor Hickey's casebook is the fourth volume to be published in the Bowker "Problem-Centered Approaches to Librarianship" series. As such, it marks the extension of this series into an entirely new curricular area; one in which the need for innovative teaching approaches has been particularly urgent. Future titles in this series will continue to reflect the aim of enlarging the body of available case materials for instructional use, while at the same time demonstrating the value of the case approach in the analysis of professional problems in libraries and information centers. As series editor, it is a matter of particular pride to have had a part in making this provocative book by a well-known and highly respected teacher available to students and librarians.

THOMAS J. GALVIN
SERIES EDITOR

PREFACE

● ● ● ● ● ● ● ● ●

A common complaint heard among librarians is that young people do not want to be catalogers anymore. Further, when suitable candidates for cataloging positions are located, they often appear to be unable to perform their jobs without considerable in-service training. Both of these problems are, it is sometimes asserted, the result of inadequate library school education, the implication being that if the schools were meeting their obligations, catalogers would be in good supply and initially well trained to cope with all eventualities.

This series of case studies will not, of itself, overcome either of these problems. The unique contribution of formal education in librarianship lies in its ability to provide the student with an overview of the profession and introduce him to the range of solutions available for coping with a particular job situation. The local library must accept the responsibility of creating work opportunities which are attractive to the library school graduate and of training him in the procedures associated with his assignment.

A more important problem, perhaps, is the gap which exists between the ideals expressed in the classroom and the realities of the local library situation. In school, the student may learn what his instructor considers the best way to organize a collection; on the job, he must adapt to traditions and pre-established routines which sometimes go counter to his educational experience. To bridge the gap, library educators have turned to the use of realistic case studies through which the student is provided with a dramatic glimpse into the definitely human world of the working library, while at the same time he is afforded the opportunity to analyze the structure and operation of that world.

In the area of library work often called "cataloging" and, more broadly, "technical services," the student may fall into two errors: that of assuming that all such work is strictly routine and mechanical, and that of viewing the tasks of organizing a library collection as self-contained. One purpose of the case studies here presented is to help correct both these errors, and to do so by illuminating some of the ways in which interpersonal relations affect the character of the routines and by setting the organizational tasks in the broader context of the total library situation.

There is still another attitude which may be disturbed by the reading and analysis of these studies, namely that of viewing the organization of library materials as a dull occupation. The contemporary catalog department is an insecure place. Its once remote and quiet world of scholarly books has been stirred and enlivened by new media—films, recordings, microforms, computer-based data banks—which must be identified and categorized if they are to be meaningful to future generations. The mere assertion that there is excitement in the contemporary cataloging function is insufficient; hopefully, these case studies will help to bring alive the image of the cataloger's life as an interesting, demanding, and ever-changing one, without which the effort to secure information in today's complex society would be severely impeded, if not made futile.

The thirty cases comprising this volume are drawn from incidents which have actually transpired or were reported to have occurred in approximately the manner described. Considerable liberty has been taken in reworking them to provide a reasonable time sequence and to make some of the interpersonal relationships clearer. Cases have been drawn from all types of libraries: school, public, college, university, and special; they represent problems related to cataloging records, classification decisions, the handling of specialized materials, and the relation of public to technical services.

In selecting an order for the cases, an attempt has been made to move from somewhat less complex problems to more encompassing ones, and to vary the type of library and type of problem discussed. In this way, it will be possible to read the studies sequentially, if desired. Two of the studies (Cases 29 and 30) are supplemented by a student's analysis, followed by the author's more comprehensive treatment of the situation.

The names of persons, places, and institutions used in these cases have been chosen from the author's own imagination. In no instance does a name used refer to a real person or an existing locality. There was a deliberate attempt, however, to select names which would seem natural to the reader; in so doing, the author risks, perhaps, offending someone whose name is coincidentally the same as that used in a case study.

To acknowledge all the help provided by the many people who have been interested in and supportive to the work represented by this volume would require dozens of pages. Colleagues and students have suggested incidents; others have asked repeatedly that a book of "cataloging cases" be provided for classroom and in-service training use. Let it suffice to say that everyone whom the author has known has made a contribution, either through his comments or simply through his impact as a person.

INTRODUCTION

· · · · · · · · · · · · ·

The use of the case study as a teaching device has been well documented, and its success is almost taken for granted among educators in the various professional disciplines. The ability of a student to place himself within an imaginary context and decide how he would behave is indicative, it is believed, of his potential competence when faced with such a situation in his later professional life. There is some danger, however, in allowing a volume of case studies to be read by an individual student as merely a series of incomplete short stories; for educators have also learned that the full dimensions of a case study are best revealed within group discussion rather than through individual analysis.

Because this series of case studies is designed more for group analysis than for individual reading pleasure, it may be useful to discuss briefly the problems relating to the introduction of the case method within the context of traditional courses in cataloging and classification, organization of library materials, and bibliographic control of library materials. Such courses frequently center upon the techniques of cataloging and may pay some attention to management analysis, work flow, and task distribution within the library's processing area. In recent years, cataloging instructors have attempted to correct an overemphasis on skills and routines by introducing more theoretical elements: reasons for cataloging, basic bibliographic units common to all list-making projects, theory of classification, and systems analysis related to information storage and retrieval programs.

Often missing from even the newer version of the cataloging course has been the human element. Of course, this can be inserted by the instructor anecdotally during his lectures or by the student as he observes the actual workings of a library selected for a course project. The prevailing impression, however, conveyed to most students seems to be that cataloging, of necessity, embodies an antisocial element.

Practicing librarians, on the other hand, know full well that the organizational function of the library is at heart a social one and that the design and operation of a library catalog department requires as much skill in interpersonal relations as it does in the construction of flow charts or the preparation of a catalog card. They also know that the failure to recognize the impact of the cataloger's personality upon his colleagues and upon the library's public can be disastrous, for even the most logically designed procedure is often thwarted by the human being who is charged with implementing it.

Surprisingly, cataloging instructors seem to have been slow to utilize the case method in their courses. Part of the reluctance may lie in their unfamiliarity with the technique or in the fact that few case studies in cataloging have been available. More fundamentally, however, there is a question as to the ability of students to analyze a case study intelligently when they have not been previously grounded in the skills and procedures which are part of every cataloging situation.

So far as can be determined at the moment, no cataloging course has been taught using the case method exclusively. It seems reasonable to suggest that a course could be so taught if training in the skills of cataloging could be acquired elsewhere, perhaps through programmed learning sequences. For those schools in which the basic technical services course concentrates upon learning how to construct a catalog card, select a classification number and subject heading, and reproduce the cataloging record for the library, the case study may offer an adjunct learning technique. For those, on the other hand, which concentrate the practical work in a laboratory or other out-of-class experience, the total case method approach might be recommended as a way of overcoming the recognized hiatus between practice and theory.

The particular cases in this volume represent an attempt to reflect the contemporary situation in a variety of libraries facing many different problems. It is tempting to view the cases as short stories of "the lady or the tiger" type. This is not, however, their purpose. They are designed to project the student into a realistic setting and force him to make a commitment to that situation. He must endure it with all its mistakes, ill-considered actions, emotionalism, and complexity, although he may also profitably specify ways in which a particularly unfortunate experience might have been avoided.

Practing librarians may quarrel with some of the statements made in the cases as being incongruent with the facts. A particular example of this may be noted in one of the cases selected for analysis: "Make More Title Added Entries, Please." There is a discrepancy between the interpretation by a cataloging assistant of a portion of the *Anglo-American Cataloging Rules* and what the pertinent rule actually says. The case study, in this instance, reflects a common misconception about the rules. It is the student's responsibility to check the accuracy of any statements made by the people quoted in the study, and it is the instructor's obligation to point out such discrepancies when the students miss them.

This suggests the need to analyze the cases in the light of published information on the topic, rather than to limit discussion to speculations about what might have happened and why it might have occurred. Again, the group analysis technique is likely to be more satisfactory in this regard, because the participation of many students acts as a corrective on the biases of a particular student or of the instructor. It should be admitted, nonetheless, that the technical nature of some of the issues demands the presence of a knowledgeable and experienced discussion leader who can discern the errors or half-truths expressed in the cases. For this reason, many of the cases might also prove interesting as a basis for discussion among practicing librarians, who are more likely to spot the subtle issues embodied in them.

Although no index has been provided to the themes of the cases, it may be helpful here to specify the type of library orientation of each. Cases 5, 14, and 29 are set in college libraries; cases 1, 6, 9, 12, 16, 17, 19, 20, 22, 23, 26, and 27 in university libraries; cases 3, 7, 10, 13, 18, 21, and 25 in public libraries; cases 2, 8, and 30 in school libraries; cases 4, 11, 15, 24, and 28 in special libraries or specialized situations. The titles of the studies have been deliberately chosen to try to convey the type of problem being considered.

In general, the cases are arranged in order of ascending complexity of issues, although in most instances there are buried issues in even the simplest-looking case. One theme, however, recurs: the organization of library materials never takes place in a vacuum. Thus each case will be found to carry enough information about the library system as a whole to enable a student to understand something of the context in which a problem arises. Further, the people in each study are given some chance to reveal their personality traits so that the analyst can base his recommendations upon human as well as technical considerations.

One difficulty almost inevitably arises in using case studies, but it is especially annoying in those dealing with technical problems: not enough details of a statistical or a procedural nature can be included to permit an informed, thoroughgoing redesign of the system. Experience in the use of case studies with cataloging students has revealed, however, that no system can be satisfactorily redesigned on the basis of a paper description. Even without exhaustive statistical and procedural details, the basic issues can be discerned and alternative courses of action projected. This delineation of issues, with the accompanying ascertainment of the truth of the data presented and an analysis of the interpersonal relationships discovered, is precisely the point of engaging in case study. Out of such discernment, real life situations may be effectively analyzed and understood, so that systems redesign will proceed more intelligently and more humanely.

Problems in Organizing Library Collections

1.
An Elusive
Library of Congress Card

· · · · · · · · · · · · · ·

"But there's a perfectly good LC card for this book," complained Ruth. "Here I've spent thirty minutes checking subject headings and looking up class numbers, and what do I find when I start doing the authority work? There was an LC card for it all the time under another entry!"

Joanne Hayden, Ruth's nearest neighbor in the Catalog Department, tried to think of something sympathetic to say, while Ruth rushed on in her diatribe.

"You know, this is the third time in a month that I've had this happen. I do all the work and then at the last minute find out there's an LC card. This wouldn't happen if those searchers in the Order Department were doing their jobs right!"

Although she understood how Ruth felt, Joanne had worked in the Catalog Department of Randell University Library long enough to know that this kind of occurrence was not uncommon. Joanne no longer got upset when it happened, but she could well remember her reaction during her first couple of years on the job. She had been a young, idealistic, library school graduate, master's degree in hand, all primed to save the library world by applying the principles of scientific management. But every time she had made a suggestion for change, someone had always come up with a reason why it couldn't be done. However, as Joanne began to understand the situation more clearly, she learned to accept the fact that even though some procedural alterations looked good on paper, they would only meet with stiff resistance from some of the workers.

"I know how annoyed you must be," she commented to Ruth. "When I was first here I used to go home with a headache night after night, just from frustration. You have to put things in perspective though. Ask yourself how important this is in the whole picture."

"Well it may seem unimportant to *you*," Ruth countered, "but my time is worth more than the searchers' time. And I think this has got to be settled once and for all."

Joanne had expected Ruth to talk out her anger and then let the matter drop, but Ruth had a different solution. Before Joanne even realized what was happening, Ruth had grabbed up the book and the order slips, and was heading for the bibliography section.

"Who did the search on this book?" she demanded as she entered the area.

"What book are you talking about?" responded Rob Hendrix, who happened to be the first searcher in her path.

"This book!"

"If you'll stop waving it in front of my face and let me look at the initials on the slip, I can tell you."

"The initials are REH."

"Then I guess you've found your man. What's the trouble?"

"There's an LC card for this book under another entry. After I spent more than thirty minutes working on this title, I found the card. It looks to me like you did a pretty sloppy job of searching it."

Although Rob was working only part-time in the library while he completed his master's degree in political science, he had never felt particularly inferior to the professional staff. He was especially unimpressed by the catalogers, who seemed to him to be complaining about something all the time.

"How do you know," he demanded of Ruth, "that the LC card was in print when I searched the title several months ago?"

Ruth Jabbock had, for the first time, apparently, met someone who could think as fast as she. In that one brief exchange, she had lost the initiative in the argument, and she knew it. "You and I both know I can't prove the card was there. But you're not going to get off that easily. This is the third time this month this has happened. I'm getting pretty tired of having to do the searchers' work over again."

"Were they all ones that I did?" asked Rob.

How should I know? All I know is that they were done wrong and somebody needs to see that this stops."

"What needs to stop," interrupted Jean Andrews, the chief bibliographer, "is this conversation! You're disturbing everyone in the area and embarrassing the library. If you want to continue the discussion, it had better be in my office."

"I'm sorry, Mrs. Andrews," Rob responded. "I guess we did get a little noisy, but this cataloger is giving me a hard time about my work."

"That's obvious enough from the conversation," answered Mrs. Andrews. She turned to Ruth. "Let's see, I'm not sure I know your name."

"I'm Ruth Jabbock. And I'm sorry I lost my temper. As you can probably see, I'm still pretty angry about the whole thing. I've got work to do. Maybe we'd better talk about it later."

Before Mrs. Andrews or Rob could respond, Ruth whirled and walked rapidly toward the Catalog Department. "What was that really about, Rob?" Mrs. Andrews wanted to know.

"Oh, she thinks I did a bad job searching that book. She says she found an LC card for it that I missed. She may be right; I don't know. But we do the best we can. I really get angry when those catalogers take it upon themselves to tell us how to do our work."

"I guess I'd better go talk to the head cataloger about this," said Mrs. Andrews. "You go on back to work, and don't worry about it."

Although Jean Andrews recognized that she could be accused of violating protocol by going directly to Constance Gordon, she expected no repercussions. She and Connie had been classmates in library school, and their relationship on the job had never been strained by the fact that Connie was technically one step above Jean in the hierarchy. In fact, Jean's administrative superior, Arlene Miller, had encouraged direct communication between the staff of the Acquisitions Department—of which the bibliographic unit was a part—and the Catalog Department.

As Jean approached Connie Gordon's office, she was relieved to note that Connie was not being visited by anyone else at the moment. Finding the head cataloger alone was not easy.

"Hi, Jean. What can I do for you today?" Connie asked cheerfully.

"I seem to have a problem on my hands."

"Come now, you never have problems. You run that section like a machine."

"When you have six distinctly different individuals in that machine, it sometimes gets out of whack."

"I take it you have a personnel problem with one of those individuals."

"I guess you'd call it an interpersonal relationship problem. Rob Hendrix and Ruth Jabbock just had a round of angry words. It seems that Mrs. Jabbock—I think it's 'Mrs.' though I've never really paid much attention to her until today—anyhow, she came roaring into the bibliography area. She accused Rob of not having found the LC card for the book she was catalog-

ing. He got angry about her accusation. I honestly don't know who was
right or wrong, but they were really going at each other."

"Were there other people around at the time?"

"Yes, quite a few. People using indexes and such. I was mainly just
plain embarrassed for the library. I'm not sure what I want you to do,
maybe nothing, but I wish there were some way to keep the catalogers from
creating a disturbance in a public area."

"I can see to that, all right. But what about the argument they were
having?"

"Oh, this comes up all the time—though not usually quite so dramat-
ically. For various reasons the searchers can miss finding an LC card. The
catalogers always seem to think it shows incompetence, but surely you know
that it's something that often can't be helped."

"I suppose so, but I wonder if we shouldn't try to eliminate the cause
of the disturbance, too."

"I'll leave that up to you. But if Mrs. Jabbock has any more complaints, I'd be grateful if she'd bring them to *me*—and somewhat more quietly, if possible!"

"We'll see to that, certainly. Thanks for telling me."

After Jean Andrews had left, Miss Gordon dispatched her secretary to
find Ruth Jabbock. As Ruth entered the office, Miss Gordon closed the door
and recounted to her what Mrs. Andrews had reported.

"Certainly you must realize, Ruth," Miss Gordon concluded, "that we
can't permit such outbursts to continue. No matter how justified you were in
your anger, you simply ought not to have rushed in that way. I don't mean
to be harsh, but in the future you are to bring all such matters to me. Is that
clear?"

"Yes, ma'am. But what about the basic problem? Are we just going to
let the searchers keep on doing their sloppy job?"

"Frankly, that's not your problem. It's mine. How much evidence can
you produce to show they've been sloppy?"

"This kind of thing has happened with at least three books this
month."

"Do you have a copy of the order slip or anything to identify which
books they were?"

"No. I didn't think about it at the time."

"Then there's nothing to go on. It seems to me that you'd better keep still until you can produce some evidence to back up your claims. Anything else?"

"No, ma'am. I guess that's all I've got to say."

"Then you may go back to work now. But remember that there are to be no such scenes in the future."

When Ruth emerged from Miss Gordon's office, it was nearly five o'clock. Joanne watched her as she headed straight for her own desk, put the cards and workslips back into the books she had been cataloging, stacked the volumes on a booktruck, picked up her purse, and left without a word to anyone.

At almost the same moment, Connie Gordon came up to Joanne's desk. "Ruth tells me that there are problems with the searchers' work. She was wrong to try to take matters into her own hands, but if the searchers are really doing a poor job, I ought to know about it."

"Actually, Miss Gordon . . ." Joanne hesitated, "well, you know I've been here for a long time now. I'm kind of immune to some of the problems that bother Ruth so much. But this time she's probably right—about the errors, I mean. There really do seem to be more mistakes than usual. When we're so rushed, we get sort of frantic when we find we've wasted time on a book that already has an LC card."

"I understand the feeling, but there just isn't any proof that it's the searchers' fault. Maybe the LC cards were just slow in showing up."

"I know that's possible. But—well, I remember one that I did just yesterday. The book was five years old, and I found it under a corporate entry in last year's *NUC.* The searcher ought to have found it, but maybe he didn't understand about corporate entries."

"I see what you mean, but we still don't have enough evidence to make a case. Oh well, it's obvious that we can't do anything more about it today. And everyone else seems to have gone home."

As Joanne gathered her things to leave, Miss Gordon had another thought. "Joanne, I'm really up to my neck right now in budget preparations. Why don't you take this on as a project and see what's really happening?"

• • • • •

Despite the fact that Ruth's approach to the problem was undiplomatic, she provoked a confrontation and moved Connie Gordon to some action. In what other ways might the problem have been called to Miss Gordon's attention so as to promote some positive action?

If you were Joanne, what would be your strategy in trying to attack the problem? What strains, if any, will be likely to result from the fact that Joanne, not Ruth, has been entrusted with this investigation?

2.
The Battle
of the Accession Book

· · · · · · · · · · · · ·

When Anna Williamsten actually signed her name to the contract which designated her as "librarian" for the West Hills Elementary School, she experienced a brief moment of terror. This was Anna's first employment contract, and she found herself doubting her ability to do the job for which she had been hired. "What do I really know about running a school library?" she asked herself.

The first few days of the new school term were, to put it mildly, hectic. The West Hills Library had been closed all summer. When Anna opened it, prior to the start of school, she discovered that her predecessor had not completed the cataloging of the materials received the previous year. There were little piles of books all over the workroom, filmstrips in various places on the workroom shelves, and several apparently unopened packages. She searched in vain for any trace of a procedure manual, although she did find some notes in the books waiting for cataloging, an order file of sorts, and a looseleaf notebook which she recognized as an accession book.

During the next few days, Anna unpacked the boxes, checked the items through the order file, and tried to determine what still needed to be done to the books and filmstrips which were scattered about the workroom. Some of the materials obviously presented problems which she could not quickly solve, and she contented herself with getting the reading areas in order and readying the circulation files for the fall onslaught. "If these things have waited a year to be cataloged, I guess they can wait a few days longer," she rationalized.

Once the students began arriving, Anna realized that the uncataloged items might have to wait considerably longer than a few days. Several of the teachers spoke to her about bringing their classes to the library on a regular schedule each week. She needed to recruit student assistants from the upper grades. And even though many of the children were brought to school on

buses, they had time to come to the library for a brief period before and after classes.

Anna also had a number of ideas about ways in which the collection
could be made more useful to the teachers and students. Despite the fact
that the library was designated as a media center, many of the audiovisual
materials were dispersed throughout the building, and Anna very much
wanted to find out, at the very least, what these materials were and where
they could be located, even if she were unable to claim them for the library.

After the end of each full day, Anna was haunted by the ghost of those
uncataloged books and filmstrips. She had talked several times with the supervisor of the city school system about procedures relating to the ordering
and cataloging of materials, and Miss Johnson had been extremely helpful in
working with Anna as she planned her schedule. In fact, Priscilla Johnson
had come out to the West Hills School and spent the better part of two days
simply working through the routines with Anna.

Although it was often difficult to find the needed minutes, Anna finally
put herself on a timetable: at least one hour a day (after school, if necessary)
would be devoted to ordering, cataloging, or processing library materials.
Fortunately, Jack Thomas, a sixth-grade student who had been a library assistant during the previous year, was available to help her with the processing and other clerical jobs. The two of them working together gradually reduced the cataloging backlog to manageable proportions.

One of the more annoying tasks related to the processing routines,
Anna discovered, was the maintenance of the accession book. Although she
had heard about such records, she had never actually seen one before. Anna
vaguely remembered something from library school about the accession book
being a thing of the past; unfortunately, she could not remember precisely
why.

The routine connected with the accession process was simple enough:
author's name, title, date of publication or copyright, price, source,
classification number, and copy number were to be recorded in the accession
volume. The price and the source were also written on the item being cataloged, together with the accession number. Actually the accession number
was stamped into the accession book and onto the material being cataloged,
using a repeating sequential numbering machine. Everything else was handwritten, using pencil for the information put onto the material and pen for
that recorded in the accession book.

Miss Johnson had been through the process with Anna and had remarked that the previous librarian had not kept the accession book in very good condition. "I wish that the librarians would type the information into the accession book. That's why we decided to make it looseleaf. But many of the librarians seem to find this hard to do, so I've agreed to let them hand-write it. But I do wish they'd print! Some of the entries here are almost illegible."

Anna heeded the comments and duly printed all the accession book entries. She toyed with the idea of typing the entries, but she really wasn't a very good typist and felt that it would waste more time than it would save. However, she discovered that Jack was a good typist, and she thought that he would be able to take care of the accession book. When she suggested this to him, he protested a bit: "Mrs. Allendale always said that the accession book was something *she* had to keep. She wouldn't even let me touch it! Are you sure it's all right for me to do it now?"

Anna assured Jack that he need not worry. "Mrs. Allendale was only doing what she thought was right, but I don't see any reason why you can't type the information onto the accession sheet. It'll be neater than my printing, and faster, too. And you'll be careful to do it correctly, won't you?"

"Yes, ma'am, I will, if you want me to," said Jack. And that settled the matter. Jack typed the information on the sheet; then Anna checked it quickly and stamped the accession number onto the sheet and into the material being processed.

This seemed to solve the problem for the moment, but Anna kept wondering why it was really necessary to keep the accession book at all. As the year progressed, she found that she had absolutely no occasion to refer to the book except to determine what the next accession number should be. "I wonder what would happen," she mused, "if I just stopped keeping it." The idea pleased her, although she was wise enough to recognize that the decision was not hers alone to make. "Next time I see Miss Johnson, I'll ask her about it."

Anna was hardly prepared for the reaction which her question evoked from Miss Johnson. An onlooker might have thought that Anna had suggested doing away with the library, or something equally drastic. "It's quite obvious," bristled Miss Johnson, "that you don't understand much about school library procedures. For one thing, you are required by the laws of this state to maintain an accession book. What is more, there is a lot of valuable information in that book. What would you do if a book were lost and you needed to know how much it cost? You'd look in the accession book, of course. And what if the principal or the PTA president wants to know what new books you've added this year? How would you show them without the accession book?''

Truly astonished by Miss Johnson's reaction, Anna apologized for making such a rash suggestion. For the remainder of her time with Miss Johnson, the atmosphere was negatively charged: very little communication took place that day.

The matter of the accession book still bothered Anna. She even went back to her library school notes to look for the references to the accession process. And she found a clear-cut statement: "Most modern libraries have eliminated the accession book, although some still use accession numbers."

A little further along in the notes she found a list of reasons for having an accession book. Each reason was accompanied by a suggestion for providing the desired information in some other way. Prices, for example, could be recorded on the shelflist card, rather than in the accession book. As for providing a list of new materials, the librarian could maintain a new book shelf, prepare a list of new titles for distribution to faculty, students, and parents, or simply put out a display two or three times a year.

Despite all these counter-arguments, Anna realized that the "clincher" was the state law. She could, perhaps, work to have the law changed; but Miss Johnson's attitude—and probably that of other supervisors in the state—would have to be altered first. And such a miracle did not seem to be in the offing.

At a meeting of the city school librarians, Anna mentioned her frustration to a colleague who had been in the local school system for almost ten years. "Oh, Johnson got you on that one, did she!" laughed Eugenia James. "Every new librarian in this system must have asked the same question for the past five years—and received the same answer. I keep telling Priscilla that one day we're going to call her hand on that 'state law' bit. In case you don't know, the law says that an 'accession record' must be maintained; it doesn't say anything about a book. Other states have the same regulation, and some of them have interpreted it to mean that you have to have a record of some sort, but even a shelflist will do the job."

After this exchange, Anna was even more frustrated. "If I really don't have to keep the silly old record, why don't I just throw it away? O.K., let's face it: I'm chicken! I don't want to make Miss Johnson mad. She probably wouldn't fire me, but she could really make things uncomfortable. But it still makes me angry to think of all those librarians poring over their miserable accession books and wasting all that time they could be spending with the students."

Anna was still fuming at dinner that night. Her husband, Jim, could hardly ignore the mood she was in."All right, let's have it: what's wrong?"

"Oh, it's that stupid accession book." And she hastily ran through all the history of her discussions with Miss Johnson and Eugenia.

When she had finished, Jim yawned and commented, "I think you're getting yourself all worked up about nothing. So the accession book's stupid, so what? After all, it's just a small part of your job, and you won't be here forever anyhow. Let Jack type it up to please the old bat, and you go ahead and work with the kids. You like that part of it—you ought to be able to put up with the rest. When *you* get to be supervisor, you can burn all the accession books!"

• • • • •

What are the arguments, pro and con, relating to the maintenance of an accession book? To what degree are the arguments which Anna found in her library school notes an adequate summary of the discussion embodied in library literature? If the accession *book* were abandoned, how important would it be to record elsewhere such information as source, price, and date of receipt? What purposes does an accession *number* serve, even when an accession *book* is not kept?

If Anna adopts the attitude which her husband is recommending, will this solve her problem? What other problems might it create?

Supposing that Anna decides to keep the battle going, how should she proceed? What kinds of reactions might she expect from the supervisor and from her colleagues in the system?

3.
Is a Divided Catalog
a More Useful Catalog?

. . . .

The Wellvale Public Library was small, and its staff members were proud of the fact that its very smallness enabled them to give custom service to their users. Gerald Price, Librarian, knew all the arguments against maintaining public library service of the type provided at Wellvale. The community could not adequately support a professional staff of more than two people; a new building would not have been even contemplated without the assured contributions of a wealthy local patron; the collection, limited by meager financial resources, would probably never contain more than 20,000 volumes. The new acquisitions each year numbered fewer than 1,000, of which almost 20 percent were gifts.

The Wellvale Library had, however, aggressively avoided anything more than a cooperative liaison with the county library, which was in turn part of a regional system. The local Board of Trustees and the Council of Alderman preferred "home rule"; if the citizens of Wellvale needed resources beyond those offered by their own library, then they could pay a fee for the use of the regional system. That way, the leaders reasoned, their constituents could never complain that they were being forced to subsidize a service which they didn't need. Those who required materials elsewhere would be the ones who paid, not the whole community.

Gerald accepted the fact that his library could be viewed as reactionary, failing to change with the times. But, as he told his Assistant Librarian, Arthur Burton, "I think networks are fine, so long as the people who don't need them and can't afford them are not forced to pay for them."

Gerald's plan was to utilize the local collection to the maximum and to tap the resources of the regional system only in rare instances. Thus he concentrated on careful selection of materials, particularly reference books, and on the exploitation of those materials through a more elaborate cataloging system than might be expected for a library of Wellvale's size.

The cataloging procedures came under Arthur Burton's control. Gerald had recruited Arthur particularly because Arthur was interested in creating a catalog which would be a very nearly complete index to the collection. In fact, before coming to Wellvale, Arthur had been a professional indexer of periodical literature. He agreed to the change, at a small decrease in salary, because he was dissatisfied with the fact that he never actually got to see the user of his product. He wanted a chance to measure user response and viewed the small, self-contained library at Wellvale as the ideal place for experimental work in bibliographic control.

Although Gerald was particularly pleased to have Arthur's services, he was initially a bit worried that Arthur's ideas would be too advanced or esoteric for a community as ordinary as Wellvale. To his satisfaction, however, Arthur seemed to have the common touch, in addition to indexing experience. He spent a great deal of time during his first months at Wellvale talking with all types of library patrons—small children, teenagers, the elderly, business men, housewives, laborers—trying to find out what they wanted from the library and projecting cataloging and indexing devices that might make the library more responsive.

"There are some rather ordinary things we can do to improve the catalog," Arthur had reported to Gerald, after his initial survey had been concluded. "Some of the high school students are in need of specific information about various literary figures, or they have to find the text of a particular play or short story. We could help them a great deal by doing author-title analytics for the plays, for instance. And we can do subject analytics for all the collective biographies we buy."

"That sounds good, in many ways," Gerald acknowledged. "I thought there were printed indexes to do that kind of thing, though."

"Sure. We know that, but our patrons don't. And we don't have enough money to get a reference librarian to spend time showing them such sources. Besides, I'd be surprised if it turned out that we have even a third of the books indexed in things like *Short Story Index*. So they find the reference there and then discover we don't have it anyhow. Wouldn't it be better for them to look in just one place and to know immediately whether we have what they want?"

"I can't quarrel with your logic there, but can we afford to do indexing at that depth? Won't you have to go back and redo a lot of the old stuff?"

"We can begin with the new books, at least. And, speaking quite honestly, the collection needs a bit of weeding anyhow. Over the next few years we can work our way through it systematically, recommend that some books be discarded, and do the indexing on those we decide to keep."

"I don't know about that, Arthur. I don't think the Library Board would ever approve throwing anything away, especially since we have so few materials in the first place."

"Well, we can keep them if you want. But there'd be no point in indexing stuff that's badly out of date. If we can't throw an item out, then we can simply leave it on the shelves but not bother to do any analytics."

"O.K., I'd go along with that modification. But I still wonder where you're going to find time to do all this and still do the other things."

"A lot of the chore work can be done by the clerks. And there are a couple of local women's groups that have volunteered to help out in the library whenever we need them. Some of their members are probably good typists and could do the new cards. And, of course, we can use our offset card duplicator whenever we have a whole set of cards to be done."

"The idea of using volunteers might not be too bad. In fact, it might create some local interest in the inner workings of the library. It's easy enough to find some individuals who'll give money for books or even for a new building, but most of them aren't interested when you go after support for new staff members. Maybe if some of the women worked here as volunteers for a while, they'd see the need for adding some paid staff."

"It might work that way. I don't know too much about that angle, though. What I want to do is make this catalog a model of effectiveness."

With ingenuity, persistence, and thoroughgoing dedication, Arthur pursued his goal for the next six months. He caused one minor crisis during that time by announcing to Gerald that the catalog cases were getting too crowded. Fortunately, however, Gerald was able to find a generous member of the Library Board who was willing to contribute the money to purchase a new case.

As the card catalog began to reflect Arthur's efforts, another strain manifested itself—filing problems. Arthur described the situation to Gerald: "The file is in much worse condition than I had realized. There are a lot of out-and-out mistakes. But the worst thing is the inconsistency. There are some sections that have all main entries separated from added entries for the same name, and then the subject entries following them. In other places, the main and added entries are interfiled and subarranged by the title of the book, with the subjects in a separate group, subarranged by author. But in still other sections, the added entries and subjects are interfiled, but all the main entries are in front. The whole file is really in a mess—and I haven't even mentioned the inconsistencies found in the form of an author's name or the problems connected with place-name entries."

"Hey, stop! I give up! I haven't the slightest idea what you're talking about, but I'll take your word for it. If you say it's bad, then it's bad. So what do you plan to do about it?"

"Well, it's clear the whole catalog needs to be gone over, card by card. But if we're going to do that, I think we might as well go ahead at this point and divide the catalog."

"Divide it? Why?"

"Well, if you stop and think about it, you'll realize that most bibliographies are divided into sections. Even if there's only one main section, it's usually arranged by subject or classification, with author and title indexes. Only a few bibliographies and indexes are arranged in dictionary fashion anymore, and most of them are ones that were started in the nineteenth century."

"Come to think of it, you're probably right. But what does that have to do with our library? We don't have that big a file. It seems sort of silly to divide it."

"Even though it isn't very big now, by the time we finish recataloging and doing all the analytics and cross-references we need, we'll have a sizable group of cards. Besides, it's not so much size as it is the complexity of the structure. People using the public library aren't very sophisticated about cataloging procedures. If we divided the file into three parts—author, title, and subject—each section would be easier to use and the patrons wouldn't have to wade through so much extraneous material trying to find what they want."

"I think you've convinced me. Anyway, I don't see that it can do too much harm. We can try it and see how it goes."

"Once you see it in all its divided glory, I'll bet money that you won't want it recombined."

Thus, with Gerald's approval, Arthur began the construction of a three-part divided catalog. Despite Arthur's indexing experience, he discovered a few problems he had not expected. The first was what to do with subject entries of the author-title form. If the library acquired a volume written to criticize or analyze a particular literary work, that volume was given a subject heading consisting of the name of the author of the work criticized, plus the name of the title of the work. If such cards were transferred to the subject file, then they would be separated from the text of the work criticized. Despite this slight illogicality, Arthur ruled that *all* subject cards would go into the subject file, regardless of significance. Then he had to decide whether "SHAKESPEARE, WILLIAM. HAMLET." should precede or follow "SHAKESPEARE, WILLIAM—BIBLIOGRAPHIES." His choice this time was for a straight alphabetical sequence, disregarding punctuation.

The next dilemma related to the practice of entering autobiographies. Since the author and the subject of an autobiography are the same, only a card under author had been made for the dictionary-style catalog. This meant that the autobiography would not be represented in the subject portion of the divided catalog unless another card were made. In this case, Arthur decided to have an entry typed up to insert in the subject section; otherwise, a valuable source of information about the author would not be listed in the subject catalog.

Arthur had anticipated the third major difficulty. The rules for construction of a dictionary catalog stipulate that if the title of the work is identical with the subject heading to be assigned to it (or identical with a subject cross-reference), a title card will not be made. In the divided catalog, then, title cards would not appear for such works, despite the fact that the section of the catalog labeled "Titles" might be expected to be complete. Again, in order not to mislead the patrons, Arthur decided to have a title added entry card typed up whenever such situations were encountered. He worried a bit that some of them might be missed, for it meant examining the tracing on each main card; but he reasoned that it would be better to catch as many as possible, even if a few were overlooked.

In addition to the various policy decisions which were occasioned by dividing the catalog, the discovery of a number of typographic errors and of the need for inserting certain cross-references and guide cards somewhat prolonged the process. Within five months, nonetheless, the division stood complete: three clearly-labeled sections of the catalog—one each for authors, titles, and subjects. Arthur was truly proud of his accomplishment, as were his assistants. Even Gerald had to admit that, in terms of good looks and apparent efficiency, the divided catalog rated high.

For the next month, so far as Gerald and Arthur were aware, the catalog lived up to its advance notices. The staff members seemed to like the arrangement, and Arthur found that less time was being devoted to filing since sequencing decisions were not so complex among the various types of cards, once they were separated. The question of the public's reaction was moot, however. No complaints had been voiced, but neither had any comments of approval been heard. In fact, what would seem to be a major readjustment had, if anything, received only casual attention from the library users.

Although the lack of reaction from the public disappointed Arthur, he recognized that users are not so likely to voice praise as they are to let their objections be known. He had just begun to feel comfortable with the divided format and to conclude that the patrons were happy with it, when he overheard part of an exchange between a user and the circulation desk attendant.

"I would like to enter a complaint," said a feminine voice. Arthur could not see the patron, but the tone of annoyance was clear.

"Yes, ma'am," answered the assistant at the desk. "What is your problem?"

"It's that catalog. For years I've been able to find what I wanted without a lot of bother. Everything was in a nice alphabetical list. But now I don't know where I am half the time. When I start looking for a book, I can't just look under the author or the title or whatever I know about it; I have to go to one section if I have the author and another if I have the title. And I haven't the foggiest notion of what's in the subject section. It's all very confusing. I don't know why people have to go changing things. I was happy with it just like it was."

These comments were audible throughout the library entrance area, and Arthur felt compelled to speak to the unhappy user. She appeared to be about sixty years old and was well dressed and groomed. "Excuse me," he said as he approached the desk, "but I couldn't help overhearing what you said to Miss Cade. I'm Arthur Burton, and it was mainly my decision to change the catalog. I thought maybe I might be able to explain why we did it."

"I'm sure you had very good reasons," the woman countered. "However, that doesn't change the fact that I don't like the new arrangement."

"But maybe I could show you ways in which the present arrangement would be more useful."

"Young man, I don't want to argue about the matter. I'm getting too old to adjust to things like this. I've been a faithful library user for years, and if it weren't for my help you wouldn't have that new catalog case over there. But when you go and change things that are working perfectly well and just make them confusing, I feel I've been betrayed. It should be obvious to you that this is making me angry. I think the best thing to do is to terminate this conversation right now."

• • • • •

What should Arthur do at this point? How seriously should he take the woman's complaint?

Review the steps taken before the decision to divide the catalog was made. Is there a consensus in published literature about the value of a divided catalog in a small public library? What does the literature say about the basic decision made in this library to turn the card catalog into an in-depth index to the collection? What are the advantages and disadvantages of making so many analytics in a relatively small public library?

To what degree is the card catalog normally used by the patrons of a small public library? How might Gerald or Arthur have learned in advance whether investing so much time and money in the catalog could be justified in terms of increased use? To what extent might someone with Arthur's indexing background be utilized at Wellvale in some type of library service other than cataloging?

4.
"Is This Supposed to Be a Professional Position?"

. . . .

The Metropolitan Research Institute had been organized as an independent group of social and life scientists who were ready to contract with educational and business institutions for the completion of specific, usually short-term, projects. No limit was placed upon the type of project, length, or staff required. Elton Whitehall, Director of the Institute, subscribed to the proposition that "if we don't have anyone in MRI who can do the job, then we'll hire somebody."

MRI selected its location with the purpose in mind of easily securing such expert assistance. Two major universities, one state-owned and one privately endowed, were located within a fifty-mile radius of MRI; and MRI itself was situated in an industrial park. One of the prime factors attracting MRI to the area, other than the fact that the land would be provided free of charge, was the convenient access it afforded to library collections of research depth in all major subject fields. At the outset, it had been agreed that MRI would not attempt to duplicate the collections maintained by the two universities. The presidents of both institutions had promised that MRI staff would have free access to their libraries, and the librarians at both campuses had also agreed.

After ten years, MRI had, despite the initial plan, begun to gather a library collection of noticeable proportions. At first the materials were simply housed in the researchers' offices. Later, especially after a project was completed, the books and technical reports acquired to support the research would be boxed up and sent to a storage area in the building. Periodically, some researcher would comment to a colleague, "We ought to do something about all that stuff gathering dust in the storeroom," but no plan had emerged.

When Arlin Karliff, head of the MRI statistical unit, began to work on a new project for the local textiles manufacturer, the materials storage prob-

19

lem took on crisis proportions. Karliff knew that the operations research unit had done a study three years earlier on work flow in the textile industry. To Arlin, it seemed highly probable that some of the reports gathered to support that project would also be relevant to his current area of research. But where were those reports?

The OR staff, like most of the others at MRI, had a high rate of turnover. The director of the earlier project had left to become a plant manager for one of the fiber manufacturers, and only one of the team members could be identified as still associated with MRI. When Arlin questioned him about the disposition of the materials collected during the research, all he got was a vague indication that "the stuff is stored down the hall someplace."

The chief secretary in OR had been somewhat more helpful. She showed Arlin to the room in question, where he was able to unearth a group of reports and governmental documents relating to textile manufacturing. For Arlin, this intolerable situation had been allowed to continue too long. Using this particular instance as a dramatic example of wasted time and money, he took his case to the Institute Director.

Whitehall was sympathetic to Arlin's concern: "I've had this problem on my mind for a long time. I guess the reason we've never done anything about it is that it's never cost us much. The materials have either been purchased with money brought in by the contract agreement or picked up gratis from governmental agencies."

"It's not so much the money as it is the time involved," countered Arlin. "When I know that we ought to have some stuff and can't find it, I start hunting. Even that's easier than starting all over again trying to find out what kind of supporting documents we need. It just looks to me like we ought to have a library so we can pull all this stuff together and get some idea of what we have."

"Well, we'd have to take the money for it out of overhead. We can't charge a library off to a contract."

"Yes, I know. But couldn't you pull somebody out of the information services unit and put him on the job for, say, six months? He could set things up and then we could get someone to keep it going."

Whitehall liked the idea well enough to bring it before the rest of the administrative staff and then take it to the governing board. Austin Henry, from information services, was asked to take on the project. Both staff and governing board approved the establishment of a central MRI Library, and Austin began work shortly thereafter.

Although Austin had no library training or experience, he was acquainted with the reference staff at both of the nearby universities. He used these contacts to help him get the information he needed to begin the library operation. In fact, he enjoyed the work so much that he asked Whitehall if MRI would consider transferring him to the job permanently. Whitehall approached the governing board again and found them quite willing to approve this arrangement.

As the months went on, Austin found himself more and more involved in designing programs to support the rather wide-ranging information needs of the research staff. He put an SDI system into effect for alerting the researchers to items of interest found in current periodicals. In addition, he scanned all the major publications lists and current awareness services so that he could call relevant materials to the attention of the various project directors. His principal ambition was, however, to draw as many of the literature search operations as possible under his jurisdiction. Austin recognized that most of the MRI staff were no more skilled in bibliographic searching than he had been when he was first put in charge of the library. Certain now that he could do a better job than they, he decided to try to take control of this phase of the research process.

Austin's plan was to persuade Whitehall to employ a second "professional" in the library. "We need a library school graduate," he told the director, "someone who can take over the day-to-day operations of the library and leave me free to expand our information services."

"I should have known I was creating a monster when I let you take on the library as a permanent assignment! I guess there's no one to blame but myself. If you weren't doing such a good job, I'd probably balk. But the staff are all very happy with your work. I may have to scrounge a bit, but I think I can come up with enough money to add another staff position. You go ahead and look for someone and don't worry about it. Whatever the going rate is for librarians, we'll match it."

On the advice of his reference librarian friends, Austin made a trip to the nearest school with an accredited library program, to recruit applicants for the new position. He talked with several promising students, each of whom responded positively to the interview. One in particular, Frances Olson, seemed to have ideal qualifications. She had majored in statistics, had done some computer programing during her undergraduate days, and was taking her library courses in the information services area. In addition, she had been a student assistant in the catalog department of the university

which she had attended as an undergraduate. Her placement dossier included excellent recommendations from the faculty members; they praised
her for her cooperative spirit as well as her high intellectual caliber.

After reviewing the credentials of the other applicants, Austin decided
that Frances had, by far, the best qualifications. With Whitehall's approval,
he offered her the job, and she accepted it enthusiastically.

As Austin had described it to Frances, the position at MRI would involve the management of the basic library operation. She would supervise
the work of one clerk, and she could call upon the services of the secretarial
pool for typing, mimeographing, and photocopying. Insofar as time permitted, Frances might also participate in the literature search program which
Austin intended to establish. They agreed, however, that supervision of the
"housekeeping" work of the library would be her prime responsibility.

By "housekeeping" was meant the ordinary activities associated with
the securing of materials recommended by the MRI staff—writing up the
purchase order, finding missing order information, and keeping the various
records of items on order or in process—and with the preparing of those
materials for circulation, once they arrived. Austin had told Frances that she
would have a full-time clerk who was skilled in the various routines entailed
by the ordering and processing of library materials. He assured her that the
clerk would complete all the procedures associated with typing the purchase
orders and preparing catalog cards, but Frances would be expected to put
together the order information and the catalog copy which the clerk would
then transcribe into the proper form.

Frances would have prime responsibility for deciding whether an order
needed to be searched and what sources should be consulted. She was also to
prepare a workslip showing the essentials of the descriptive and subject cataloging decisions to be incorporated into the catalog card. The clerk was then
to type a draft of the main card, which Frances would check and have corrected if necessary. As time permitted, Frances would be expected to try to
reduce the backlog of materials in storage, as well as keep up with the current acquisitions. Austin assured her that he wanted her to continue to follow the standard cataloging procedures (i.e., Library of Congress style) which
he had established.

When Frances arrived for her first day of work, she was introduced to
the various people with whom she would be associated. In particular, she
met Ida Marlin, the supervisor of the secretarial pool, and, of course, Rick
Valdese, her clerk.

For the first few days, Frances and Rick worked closely together so that she could learn the routines connected with ordering and cataloging new materials. On Friday of the first week, however, Rick dropped a bombshell: "I don't quite know how to tell you this, Miss Olson, but I'm going to be leaving MRI after next week. I've got a chance at a job that'll pay me more money, and I want to go back to college next fall. I can't afford to pass it up."

"I can't blame you, Rick. But this really comes as a blow to me. Does Mr. Henry know you're leaving?"

"Oh sure; I have to give two weeks' notice. He asked me to tell you. I guess I've been stalling a little. I sort of hated to tell you when you'd just started."

Frances knew that such resignations were to be expected, but it seemed like a cruel trick to have it happen so quickly. On the following Monday, she attempted to talk the matter over with Austin.

"Do you know where Mr. Henry is?" she asked Ida.

"I haven't seen him at all this morning. Let me call the main office and see if they've heard anything. I need to see him too."

A few minutes later, Ida came into the library. "They tell me downstairs that Mr. Henry won't be in today. In fact, they're not sure when he'll be back. His wife's been taken sick, and he had to take her to the hospital in Greensburg. From the word I get, he's going to have to stay with her for at least this week and maybe longer. He said he'd try to call in sometime today or tomorrow."

"Oh, great. Rick's getting ready to leave, and I don't know when I'll get a replacement. And I'm not even sure what I'm supposed to be doing."

"Why don't you go downstairs and talk to the girls in the office? They'll probably know whether anyone's been hired to take Rick's place."

"O.K., I could at least do that, I guess. Thanks."

The word from the office staff was negative. No one had any information about a replacement for Rick, and so far as they could tell, no one had been interviewed for the job. When Austin Henry finally called in on Tuesday, he confirmed the fact that Rick's position would have to remain unfilled for awhile. "In fact," Austin added, "I'm not sure whether they'll be willing to replace him at all. Whitehall is on something of an economy kick, and I think he's going to try to cut out that position."

"Then what will I do for an assistant?"

"After Rick leaves, you'll just have to use the secretarial pool, I guess.

I'm sorry—I know this isn't exactly what you had in mind when you took
the job, but I don't know what else to tell you. Maybe when Sarah is better
and I get back to work, we can do something about all this."

Frances felt depressed and generally discouraged as she hung up the
telephone. Rick helped all that he could for the remainder of the week, but
the following week proved to be a very difficult one. Frances received a carton of new documents ordered from the Government Printing Office, and
one of the researchers came back from a symposium with a suitcase full of
reports, preprints, and reprints of papers written by the speakers. She tried
to keep abreast of the cataloging, as well as place orders for new documents
as they were requested. By Thursday, she had several stacks of books ready
for catalog cards to be typed and another carton of new materials waiting
unopened on her work table.

Although she rather dreaded the prospect of trying to teach one of the
secretaries the special format and spacing required for catalog cards, Frances
realized that she could delay the ordeal no longer. Shortly after 9 A.M. on
Thursday, she presented herself at Ida Marlin's desk.

"I need to claim one of your typists, please," she began. But Ida interrupted her quickly.

"Sorry, I won't be able to oblige you today, dear."

"But. . . . I don't understand. Mr. Henry said I could use one of the
typists anytime. I thought all I had to do was let you know when I needed
her."

"That would have been true last week. But this week and next, we
have to put everybody we can spare on getting out a big report for the OR
people. If I take anybody off that job, I'll get my head chopped off. Now you
wouldn't want that to happen to me!"

Frances was too frustrated and angry to answer. She marched out of
the room and back to her own quarters without another word. She didn't
really know anyone in the administrative structure well enough to go over
Ida's head, and she wasn't even sure it would do her any good. Deciding to
try to work out her annoyance, Frances set about to type the catalog cards
herself. Her anger didn't help her accuracy very much; but, by Friday afternoon, despite some false starts, she was finished with the pile of books on
her desk.

Frances's mood was not particularly improved by Ida's carefree call as
she passed the door: "Quitting time! Everybody out!" The unopened box
remained on the work table, and Frances decided to stay an extra hour to
unpack it and get that much ahead on Monday's work. At least she didn't

have to face the Friday afternoon traffic jam when she finally got away sometime after six o'clock.

The next week brought no relief. Austin Henry called on Monday to say that he was taking two more weeks' leave to be able to stay with his children while his wife had an operation. Frances explained to the various researchers that she could not hope to take over Austin's work, but that she would try to keep the new materials coming through and place orders for any documents they needed.

For the next ten work days, Frances did almost nothing but clerical jobs. The only "professional" part of her activity was the making of decisions about catalog entries, subject headings, and classification numbers. Everything else was mere typing and order verification work. By the time Austin returned, she was nearly frantic.

"I really am sorry this had to happen," he said apologetically. "I should have told you that you can't always count on the secretarial pool. Even if somebody were available, say today, there's no assurance that you'd get the same girl tomorrow."

"What are the chances of my getting an assistant anytime soon?"

"Well, as I told you over the phone, I can't guarantee anything. I'd hoped to talk to Whitehall, but his secretary says he'll be away—out of the country—for three weeks. And the Personnel Manager doesn't have any authorization to fill Rick's position while Whitehall's gone. I know I sound like an idiot to keep saying I'm sorry, but that's about all I can do. I wish I could be more optimistic, but I guess we'll just have to make the best of it."

• • • • •

The job at MRI has certainly not turned out to be what Frances expected when she was employed. How could she have investigated the situation in advance so that she might have obtained a more realistic picture?

If Whitehall refuses to authorize the employment of a replacement for Rick, what should Frances do? What are Austin Henry's responsibilities, if such is the decision?

Supposing that Frances is left to do her own clerical work, what steps might she consider taking to reduce the amount of time required for these duties? To what extent might she be able to utilize the secretarial pool, given the fact that she will not always be able to count on securing their services when they are needed?

5.
"How Will I Know What to Charge for a Lost Book?"

• •

The procedures for handling lost books had always been the same at West-brook College, at least as long as Calvin Stillwell, Chief of Circulation, could remember: get the price from the shelflist card, add to it the current "processing fee," and charge the offending borrower the total. Cal knew, of course, that there were a lot of exceptions. Sometimes a book wasn't really lost, just misplaced; and any patron who insisted he had returned the volume was given the benefit of the doubt. Most annoying, however, were the cases in which the shelflist carried no price: gifts, exchanges, and bound volumes of serials, for example.

Despite the exceptions, the lost book routine was quite clear and relatively simple to follow. On Cal's desk, however, was a memo from Jackson Barbor, Librarian at Westbrook, which might change all that:

> In an effort to reduce the extremely high costs of processing materials, the Catalog Department is attempting to eliminate all unnecessary routines. One suggestion is that the recording of source information and price be dropped from the shelflist card.

> I know that the Circulation Department sometimes uses such information in working with lost books. For that reason, I am suggesting that we have a meeting to discuss the suggestion.

> The meeting will be held in my office on Wednesday, at 3:00 P.M. If this time is a poor one for you, please let me know right away.

Cal assumed that Dorothy Wilson, Chief of Cataloging, would also be at the meeting. He knew her to be a fair and reasonable person who did not propose changes irresponsibly, nor was she likely to cling to an outdated procedure simply because "we've always done it that way." Although the idea of dropping the price from the shelflist seemed absurd from the circulation viewpoint, Cal was prepared to agree that the rest of the information could be eliminated.

At the meeting on Wednesday, Mr. Barbor began by asking Cal for his opinion of the proposed change. In response, Cal offered his compromise position: "The circulation staff uses the price quite frequently in determining what to charge for lost books. Very seldom, however, do we use any of the other information—in fact, I'm not even sure what all goes on the shelflist besides the price."

"We add price, date of order, and fund to each shelflist card," Dorothy Wilson interjected.

"O.K.," Cal responded. "Then why not drop the date and fund, but retain the price."

"Then we might as well forget the whole thing," Dorothy replied quickly.

"I don't see how that follows," Cal retorted.

"It's simple: if we have to put the shelflist card into the typewriter to add the price, we might as well do date and fund too. The whole point is to avoid an extra keyboarding operation, so the card can go directly to the filer after the set is photoduplicated. But if the price has to go on, nothing's been accomplished."

Although he could see the logic in Dorothy's argument, Cal was still convinced that the work of the circulation staff would be impeded by the loss of price data. "What will we do," he countered, "when a book is lost and we need to know what to charge for it?"

"Can't you look it up in *CBI* or *BIP?*" asked Dorothy. "Surely you can manage to find it—or make a good estimate—some other way than by looking at the shelflist."

"I suppose we could, at least for some things. But that takes a lot of time—a lot more than just looking it up on the shelflist. All that scheme does is save time at your end while you're adding it at mine. What kind of economy is that?"

Dorothy turned to Mr. Barbor: "Honestly, I don't know what to do! Every time I try to cut costs, somebody objects."

"Come on, now, Dorothy." countered Mr. Barbor. "We want to do all we can to help, but Cal does have a point."

"Maybe I'm not up on your operations," Cal added, "but I thought there were some cases when you had to add copy or volume information to the shelflist card."

"Sure, there are a few. But we've decided we can put the holdings statements on the shelflist card in pencil, just as we do on the main card. After the master card is photoduplicated, the holdings information has to be transferred by a clerk to the main card; it won't add anything to the routine if we just tell her to do it a second time to produce a shelflist. And of course you know we have a completely separate system for handling the serials holdings. This change won't affect them at all."

"Well, I see your point, certainly," Cal admitted. "But I still have to stick with the fact that while you'll be doing less work, I'll be doing more."

Once again Dorothy looked helplessly at Mr. Barbor. "You see how it goes," she complained. "No matter what I suggest, I get a complaint. I give up!" And with that, she quite unceremoniously left the room.

This outburst was so uncharacteristic of Dorothy, that Cal was un-nerved. "What happened?" he asked Mr. Barbor. "I thought we were having a calm, sensible discussion, and all of a sudden it fell apart. Did I say something wrong?"

"No, I don't think so, Cal. Dorothy's been feeling a lot of pressure re-cently. Her husband is ill, and the doctors can't seem to find out what's wrong with him. Then, to make matters worse, she's lost three clerks and two catalogers this year. That's almost half her staff.

"Yeah, I guess it's been pretty rough."

"It wouldn't have been so bad if we weren't also buying a lot of new material in the Romance languages and literature area, to support that new major. She had no sooner eliminated the backlog she inherited when she came to Westbrook than it began to build again. Dorothy tells me there are already about 1500 volumes waiting to be cataloged, and the number's grow-ing."

"Can't the library get her some help?"

"Unfortunately, the word from the president is that we won't get any extra money for staff this year, and probably not next. My reliable sources in the administration building tell me that anyone who asks for more staff will be told he has to have a management survey done first."

"Would it be so bad to do one? It might actually help convince the president that we need more people."

"I wouldn't mind so much if we could be sure we'd get to select the members of the survey team, but the college already has a contract with a firm that's almost totally business oriented in its experience. According to what I hear from other libraries, a team like that can wreck staff morale. And they usually wind up telling you that you need less staff, not more."

Feeling that Mr. Barbor was not likely to take his side in the argument with Dorothy, Cal decided not to pursue the question any further at that juncture. He excused himself and returned to the circulation area where the paper work was beginning to pile up on his desk. The first item to attract his attention, ironically, represented a problem relating to a lost book. One of Cal's assistants had written him a note about the difficulty.

Mr. Stillwell:
  The book listed on the attached call slip has been lost by the student who borrowed it. He's willing to pay for it, but I haven't been able to find out how much to charge him. The shelflist card just says "gift," but the book is in German and I don't know where to look for a price. What now?

Jerry

This was exactly the type of problem which Cal feared would multiply indefinitely if the price were dropped from the shelflist card. It was bad enough at present coping with gifts and exchanges, but to have to do this for all lost books seemed to Cal to be impossible.

Not desiring a further confrontation with Dorothy in her present mood, Cal took his evidence to Mr. Barbor the next morning. "Here's a good example of the problems we face," he explained to the librarian. "If the price data are dropped from the shelflist, we'll have to go through this for everything! I can't see that the library will be saved any money in the long run."

"I really am sympathetic to your point of view," responded Mr. Barbor. "You may remember that I worked in Circulation for a number of years before I became librarian. But, to put it bluntly, I'm a whole lot more likely to be able to wangle some extra money to add some more student assistants in Circulation than I will be to get more staff for Dorothy. I don't like to play politics, but I think it'll be a shrewd thing to shift some costs out of the cataloging area, even if they have to be added somewhere else."

Barbor's logic was convincing enough to send Cal away resigned to the fact that prices would no longer appear on shelflist cards. As he reflected on the matter throughout the remainder of the day, however, he found that he was still emotionally unconvinced. "It's not simply a matter of shifting costs," he argued with himself. "It's a question of whose time is better spent doing this. Jerry's not equipped to find prices for books in German, and neither am I. The people in Cataloging do searching of that type all the time: they can do it faster and better. I guess we never would have done it at all if it hadn't been so easy to find prices on shelflist cards."

The upshot of this conversation with himself was that Cal decided to continue the fight. This time, however, he would try a memorandum. While he was busily typing out his thoughts, one of the circulation assistants interrupted him. "Say," she commented, "I was just talking to one of my friends back in Cataloging. She says they're not putting the price of the books on the shelflist anymore."

"It looks like that might be true, unless I can come up with some convincing arguments to stop it."

"Well, from what I hear, you'd better hurry up. The way Amy tells it, they've already started leaving it off. She said the revised procedure went into effect yesterday."

"It sounds like I'd better look into this; I didn't know the decision was final."

Cal quickly headed for the cataloging area to look for Dorothy Wilson, though he dreaded a confrontation. To his relief, Dorothy was out of her office, but Grace Parsons, her first assistant, was nearby.

"The grapevine tells me that Cataloging has decided to omit source information from the shelflist cards these days. Am I right?"

"Absolutely," answered Grace cheerfully. "I've been nagging Dorothy to do that for years, but she never would till now. I guess it just goes to show you: if you hang on long enough, things finally do happen."

"Yeah, I guess that's what it shows, all right," muttered Cal, as he turned away.

• • • • •

What recourse, if any, does Cal have now? If he continues writing his memorandum, what should he say?

What steps could Cal take to counter the arguments presented by Barbor? How could he determine whether it would really cost more to have prices searched out by circulation assistants rather than by cataloging assistants?

What other ways are there, if any, to determine what to charge a borrower who has lost a book? What have other libraries suggested as alternative procedures?

6.
Too Much Conversation in the Catalog Department

· · · · · · · · · · · · · · · · · · ·

When George Davies accepted the position as Chief of Cataloging at Wilburn University, he knew that his job would not be an easy one. Dr. Gwendolyn Arams, Director of Libraries, had written to him to ask if he would be interested in the position. He had spent two days at Wilburn at her invitation so that he could look over the Catalog Department and the Catalog Department could look him over.

"You know how hard it is to really tell much in two days," George told his wife, Ellen, after the visit. "But it looks as though the cataloging staff is friendly enough—maybe a little too friendly. While I was around, there seemed to be an awful lot of socializing. I think I'll check the production statistics for the last few years."

Dr. Arams had sent George a copy of the two most recent annual reports of the director. Fortunately, the library in which George was currently working had a good collection of library reports and statistics. From the data available on college and university libraries, he was able to piece together what seemed to be a fairly accurate picture of the Wilburn Library's cataloging output for the last five years.

The resulting profile was not particularly encouraging. Wilburn employed seven professional catalogers, in addition to the chief. These were assisted by six subprofessional staff members and four clerk-typists. By asking questions while on campus, George had learned that the professional component had been the same, in terms of numbers, for three years. Before that, there had been only five professionals, plus the chief, for some three or four years. One clerk-typist had been added two years ago, and two subprofessional positions had been created, one each year during the last two years.

Although George was not completely certain that all the budgeted cataloging positions had remained filled throughout each of the five years, the statistics still looked odd. He constructed a table, just to make sure he was not misreading the situation (see Table 1). The data array confirmed what he had already seen on casual inspection of the figures.

TABLE 1

Year	No. of Staff			Titles Cataloged	Vols. Cataloged
	Professional	Subprof.	Clerk		
Most recent	8	6	4	18,696	23,969
Two years ago	8	5	4	19,101	23,854
Three years ago	8	4	3	18,454	23,201
Four years ago	6	4	3	16,722	20,436
Five years ago	6	4	3	16,259	20,003

George had learned to expect that in a university library, the professional cataloging staff—on the average—should be able to send through 3,000 titles per cataloger. In terms of volumes, they ought to account for at least 5,000. Applying these figures to Wilburn, the Wilburn Library should have been producing something like 24,000 new titles and perhaps 40,000 volumes. Although George knew that such figures would have to be adjusted to local conditions, and that the volume count which he was projecting was probably especially unrealistic for a university library which did not buy multiple copies heavily, the fact that eight professional catalogers supported by ten nonprofessionals could catalog no more than 19,000 titles in one year was distressing.

To make matters worse, the staff had actually handled fewer titles with eighteen workers than they had in the previous year, with only seventeen. Further, the addition of two professionals had raised production by less than 2,000 titles. Something was surely wrong.

When Wilburn offered George the position of Chief of Cataloging, he called Dr. Arams and told her what his investigation had revealed.

"Yes," she replied somewhat sadly, "that's one of the reasons we want to get someone like you into that job. The work is certainly not being done as efficiently as we think it ought to be. The former head of the department was pretty easygoing. He was reluctant to crack the whip, so things have slowed down and the staff isn't working up to capacity."

Since Dr. Arams's comments at this juncture merely reinforced the picture which had been painted for him during his visit, and since she and other members of the staff had alluded to the problem during several earlier conversations, George decided that, politically, he would be in a strong position at Wilburn to undertake a thoroughgoing procedural evaluation and revision. In a final telephone conversation with Dr. Arams, George asked if he would have her backing for such a study, and she assured him without hesitation that he would.

Three months later, George and Ellen Davies moved into an attractive home adjacent to the Wilburn campus. After the first week on his new job, George was full of ideas for improving the situation. "I thought my last job had a lot wrong with it, but Andrews's Catalog Department was a model of efficiency compared to this one!" he confided to Ellen one evening.

"Are you sorry you took the job?" she asked somewhat anxiously.

"No, not really. There's an awful lot of shaping up to do, but it could be fun. Besides, I've got a good staff and they seem willing to cooperate."

The experiences of the next four months did not fully support George in his optimism. His first tactic was to review procedures and eliminate duplication of effort. Some of his plans were carried out, but several key changes were blocked by the Chief of Acquisitions, Millicent Jamison, who objected to transformations which would, in effect, have combined the two departments in terms of work flow. George was understandably disappointed, yet he realized that the implications of his recommendations posed something of a threat to Millicent. And he knew, as well, that if the departments were combined—as he thought they ought to be—Millicent would probably wind up being his assistant instead of his equal in the administrative hierarchy. "I can hardly blame her for resisting, in view of what might happen," George acknowledged to Ellen. "I'd probably do the same thing if I were in her place."

By eliminating several unused files and combining a few others, George was able to redirect some of the staff efforts into areas that would, at least statistically, be more effective. He recognized that some retraining would be necessary and organized some seminars to help the staff adjust. He tried hard to encourage and reward his department members, publicly praising them for unusually good work and keeping the criticisms to a minimum. He was determined not to alienate the staff during this time of upheaval, for he well remembered his own experiences at Andrews when a new administrator arrived and began making changes without discussing them with the staff.

George watched the monthly production statistics with keen interest. Although he expected no major change during the first six months, especially in view of the procedural adjustments that had been underway, he believed that the remainder of the year should reveal significant improvement in the number of titles processed.

During the seventh, eighth, and ninth months, production stayed about where it had been. There was a slight improvement, but George knew it was not statistically significant. When the tenth month showed a decline, he began to despair. No one had been out sick; it was not a month for vacations. There was no reason why production should have decreased, so far as George could tell. There had been no extraordinary influx of items requiring original cataloging. In fact, if anything, there were fewer items being newly cataloged now than had been done in earlier months.

Despite the unpleasant news, George was not about to retire to lick his wounds. "But I really can't figure it," he reported to Ellen. "Staff morale is as high as ever, but fewer books are being cataloged. What am I doing wrong?"

"How about that problem you noticed when you were visiting; you know, before you took the job?" Ellen reminded him. "You thought maybe the staff was too friendly, and spending too much time talking to each other."

"That could be it, but I've been trying to convince myself that if the staff liked me, they'd work hard and quit talking so much."

"And have they?"

"No. I guess I've been kidding myself. Nothing has really changed since I came. Everything's so relaxed that nobody's feeling any pressure. What do I do about that?" George asked rhetorically.

By the next Monday morning, George had come to terms with the situation and had settled on a plan of action. Over the weekend he had debated with himself, reviewing and rejecting several courses of action. He had decided, for example, that posting a notice to his staff would be an easy way out, but ineffective. Nor could he see any particular advantage in speaking only to those workers who were the chief offenders. He decided, therefore, that he would try holding a staff meeting.

Since it was the first meeting attended by the entire department— usually someone was left in the cataloging area to answer the phone and field questions from other departments and from library users—the gathering was recognized as being special. George had even rehearsed his speech at home on Monday night.

As the staff gathered, he found he had a little trouble getting them settled. Chairs had to be brought in and the setting of the Conference Room rearranged to accommodate eighteen people instead of the usual ten. The fact that this meeting was unique seemed to stimulate conversation rather than subdue it. But, after a few clearings of the throat, George was finally able to bring the group to order.

"It's unusual, I know, for the entire Catalog Department to meet. But the matter that we have to consider is one that affects us all.

"As you know, since I came to Wilburn, I have been trying to improve the efficiency of the department. Although there is no cataloging backlog of any great significance, the departmental statistics are not in line with what might be expected from a staff of this size.

"Over the past few months, I have been working with many of you on redesigning the work flow. Many snags have been eliminated; some files have been combined, others phased out. Most of you have been pleased with the results—at least, no one has complained or threatened to resign. And some of you have even learned new jobs, without protesting.

"I think you know that I have been very grateful for your support and cooperation. I don't think any new department head could have asked for a nicer group. Unfortunately, however, the departmental statistics do not indicate that we have improved our efficiency very much. In fact, the most recent month shows a decline in the number of titles cataloged, even though we've been at full staff.

"The one factor which has not changed since my arrival seems to be the culprit. Putting it bluntly, there is too much idle conversation in the department. Coffee breaks are running to thirty minutes instead of fifteen; lunch hours are being extended by fifteen minutes or sometimes half an hour. It takes us over half an hour to get started in the morning, and we begin to close up almost an hour before quitting time. Staff members can be seen talking to each other at the public catalog for ten or fifteen minutes at a time. It is not even unusual to find one worker standing at another's desk for twenty or thirty minutes for no ostensible reason other than to share information about a recipe or look at the latest snapshots of the children.

"When the library pays your salaries, it expects a full day's work for a full day's pay. Spending so much time in activities which do not contribute to the library is really cheating the university, its students and faculty.

"Frankly, I'm not sure what I should do to solve the problem, though I have some ideas. I'd really rather you handled the matter yourselves, though. Are there any suggestions from any of you about what we should do?"

If George had seriously expected some response from his staff, he was

certainly disappointed. They simply sat there, looking embarrassed, and saying nothing. After several uncomfortable minutes of absolute silence, George
continued:

"Well, if you have no suggestions, then I guess I'll have to inject mine.

"First, all staff members will be expected to be at their desks and ready
to begin work at 8 A.M., not at 8:20 or 8:30.

"Second, coffee breaks—morning and afternoon—will be fifteen minutes
in length, no longer. And there will be one hour for lunch, no more.

"Third, staff members will discipline themselves to discuss only library
business while they are on duty. Personal matters will be discussed during
lunch and coffee breaks.

"Finally, there will be no congregating at the public catalog or at each
other's desks. If you wish to discuss a departmental problem with a colleague, you may both come to the Conference Room to talk it over. This will
prevent others from being disturbed and will, I hope, remind you that the
discussions should concentrate on library matters.

"There is one other item that I almost forgot. A good many of you are
spending an hour or more a day in telephone conversations relating to personal matters. The use of the phone should also be confined to library business, except in the case of emergencies. Please ask your relatives and friends
to call you at work only if some crisis arises.

"I don't want to have to police you on these matters. I expect each of
you to assume responsibility for his own actions. But if I see anyone violating these rules, I shall not hesitate to call it to his attention publicly.

"Does anyone want to make any comments at this point?"

Again, George's query elicited only silence. "I guess that's all then,"
he concluded. "You may return to your work now."

There was some whispering and a general air of uneasiness which per-
vaded the group as it dispersed. George felt that he had gotten his point
across, but he also realized that the pleasant, easygoing atmosphere of the
department had been effectively dispelled by his lecture. "I wonder if it's
possible to run a tight ship and still have people like you?" he mused. "It's
pretty clear that right now I'm just about the most unpopular person in the
place. But what else could I do?"

•   •   •   •   •

What else could George have done? How well did he handle the situation? What is likely to happen in the Catalog Department during the next few months?

To what degree was George's analysis of the situation adequate? What other reasons might have explained why the department's production did not increase despite the procedural adjustments? Should he have investigated the situation further before calling his meeting?

What management studies are available which might have helped George in diagnosing and solving his problem? What are the factors which affect productivity? To what extent is a happy staff likely to be a productive one?

7.
A Paperback Dilemma

· · · · · · · · · · · · · ·

"I don't know what this library's coming to!" exclaimed a middle-aged woman, as she stopped at the circulation desk to check out a couple of novels from the current fiction shelf. "It used to be a nice quiet place to read. Now it's overrun with children all the time. My friend, Mrs. Wilson, doesn't even come here anymore. I asked her why and she said she couldn't stand all the flurry and bother. You know what she did? She joined a book club and buys what she wants to read. I told her she was silly to do that. If she's been driven away from the public library, she ought to complain. After all, her taxes support it!"

The circulation desk attendant at Riverton Municipal Public Library listened politely but made no reply. Cindy Martinsen had long since learned that it didn't pay to try to argue with a patron like Mrs. Clelling.

"There are times, though," she told Anderson Kelley, Public Services Librarian, "when I'd like to answer people like her. All she cares about is herself. The fact that these kids are getting the benefit of a good library for a change doesn't mean a thing. Just so she gets her books; the rest of the world is supposed to keep out of her way."

Andy had heard Cindy sound off this way before, and he listened with a half-smile on his face.

"O.K.—yeah, I know. You've heard all this before," said Cindy. "But I wish these stupid people could see how much better the library is since you've been here. To them, it's just more noise, but at least there's some action. For years this place has been nothing more than a haven for little old ladies like her."

"You know I appreciate the testimonial, Cindy. But we aren't going to quit serving your 'little old ladies' just because we're trying to reach another group, too. Actually, I've been thinking of trying to set up a quiet reading area for our older patrons—one that's not so close to the main reading room.

We might be able to move some of the back periodical volumes upstairs and wall off a corner on the other side of this floor."

"Why don't you put our senior citizens upstairs?"

"Come now, Cindy, you know that some of them would never make it up a flight of stairs. And we can't count on the elevators to be working all the time."

"Sure, you're right. I guess I just don't really have much feeling for people like that Mrs. Clelling. She complains every time she comes in, and I get pretty tired of it."

"By the way, Cindy, have you thought any more about where we might put our paperback section? You've been around longer than any of the other circulation staff, and you ought to know the traffic patterns better than I do. What's the best location?"

"Oh, I didn't forget that you asked me. I've just been doing a little observation. I figure the kids are the ones most likely to use the paperbacks, but some of the adults will probably want to browse there too. Do you think we could . . .? Well, I know it sounds like heresy, but why don't we get rid of the exhibit cases in this area and put the paperbacks on several low shelves there—across from the desk. The space is wide enough so some people could browse and still not get in the way of the ones going in and out."

"I'm pretty sure you're right about that being the best location. I'm just not very confident I can get approval to move the exhibit cases. You and I know that nobody looks at them, but can we convince anybody else?"

"Maybe not. Still, you've been able to do some other weird things. I'll bet you could get even those useless exhibit cases moved."

"Well, I guess it's worth a try. Maybe I'll see if Mr. Kline is in his office."

Collin Kline had served as Director of the Riverton Public Library for almost twenty-five years. During that time, he had worked slowly and patiently to secure an adequate collection of materials, increase staff size, remodel the building, and open several branches in the suburbs. His colleagues recognized him as progressive but not rash. Andy Kelley had accepted the Riverton job primarily because of Kline's reputation. Although Andy was occasionally annoyed by what seemed to be a slow process of analysis applied by Kline to every suggested change, he had found the director to be open-minded and receptive to innovation.

"What can I do for you this morning?" Collin asked, as Andy entered the director's office.

"Collin, just how sacred are those exhibit cases in the circulation area?"

"Well, let me see. I think the bishop consecrated them in 1902. . . ."

"Oh come on now, don't give me a hard time! You know what I mean."

"Sure I do. So why don't you ask me what you really want to know: 'Can we get rid of those musty old cases?' Right?"

"I'll never learn not to spar with you. O.K., can we get rid of the exhibit cases?"

"Don't know why not. It may upset one of the local garden clubs a bit—they always have a display on flowers in the spring. The good exhibits usually wind up in the Children's Room, anyhow. And I think we could manage to find some space for the garden club somewhere, don't you?"

"If they like, I'll hold a rose in my teeth for a couple of weeks in April. How would that be?"

"Now who's being cute? So, what designs have you got on that space?"

"We want to set up a display of paperbacks there."

"Sounds interesting. What'll you put in it?"

"Well at first I think we'll stock it with some popular fiction and nonfiction. Maybe a few science fiction titles and some mysteries, too. Later we might try some quality paperbacks, if we see some demand for them."

"Sounds like it might be a gimmick to lure people into the library."

"Partly that. But I guess it's really something to brighten up the area and make it look more active. You know I've been trying to create a new atmosphere for the service areas in this building. This might help take away some of the stuffiness—at least I *hope* it will."

"I can't see why it wouldn't be feasible. But I am wondering where you plan to get the money to start this collection."

"I was counting on some help from my local friendly library director, sir."

"Ah ha, now the truth comes out. The exhibit cases were just a ruse to throw me off the scent!"

"So you found me out again. How about it? I'd only need a couple of hundred dollars."

"I almost hate to admit this, but one of the civic clubs has been wanting to do something for the library. I told their president that I'd find a good use for their money. And I think it would probably be a contribution of at least $150."

"You're a positive genius, boss. I must be off to start compiling a list of titles."

"Whoa there, friend. Take it easy. I don't have the money yet; and besides, there are some other things to consider. Like what kind of cataloging will these books get?"

"Cataloging? I don't see why they need to be cataloged. We'll just put them out for people to use."

"What if they start disappearing? It's easy to slip a paperback in your pocket or purse. The exit guard wouldn't catch that kind of theft."

"So they disappear, so what? We'll just get some new ones. At least it means people are reading."

"That's fine, but the money for buying new ones won't be so easy to come by. I was talking about a one-shot contribution, not an endowment!"

"Well, then we can get people to donate their own used paperbacks. No controls, just an exchange system."

"Maybe. But I think we need to plan this a little more carefully. I'll call a meeting with Barton Taylor and Carrie Jones. The Order Department and the Catalog Department may have a stake in this. Then we can sit down and talk through the implications before we get ourselves out on a weak limb."

Andy was not particularly pleased at the thought of having the technical processing people brought into the discussion. His relations with the Catalog Department and the Order Department heads had never been especially warm. Though no open hostility existed, Andy was sure that Barton Taylor did not like him. Carrie Jones had seemed cordial enough, but her general approach to life reminded him too much of Mrs. Clelling, his irate patron of the morning.

Collin Kline, though patient in working through the kind of problems that the paperback proposal created, was not one to postpone consideration of issues deemed important by his staff. A meeting of the heads of the Order, Catalog, and Public Services Departments was called for the next afternoon. When Andy arrived, Barton and Carrie were already there, deep in conversation. Carrie looked up to nod to Andy.

"Now that we're all here, we can get down to business," began Collin.

"Excuse me, Mr. Kline," interrupted Barton. "Before we get started, I'd like to mention the fact that I have an appointment with a representative of our main jobber in an hour and a half. I still have some things I need to pull together to show him, so if this meeting lasts much more than an hour, I may have to duck out."

"That's okay, Barton. If you have to leave, we'll understand. But Andy has raised a question—one that's likely to affect both the Order and the Catalog Departments. I think we ought to talk about it together. Andy, why don't you begin by describing briefly what you have in mind."

"All right. We've been talking about setting up a paperback section opposite the circulation desk so patrons can stop there to browse as they go in and out of the building."

"Won't that mean moving the exhibit cases?" Carrie interjected.

"Yes. Mr. Kline and I discussed that. We think they can probably be placed somewhere else in the building, or maybe put in storage."

"In storage? I hope you haven't forgotten that those cases were a gift from one of the founders of the library. You're likely to hear unhappy noises from the family if they are put into storage without asking permission."

"Yes, I do remember their history, Carrie," responded Collin. "But I think we can make arrangements to move them. And of course we'd only store them if the family approved. I suspect young Gerald and his wife don't feel much sentimentality for them now."

"Anyway," Andy continued, "we want to put a group of paperbacks in that area, and—"

"Who's going to handle the details of ordering them?" asked Barton suddenly.

"I guess your department would do the actual ordering," answered Andy. "Mr. Kline thinks he can get some extra money from one of the civic groups to defray the cost of buying the initial stock."

"Are they going to have to be cataloged, too?" Carrie asked somewhat anxiously. "You know we're trying to get that new branch collection ready, while we keep up with the regular acquisitions. Mr. Kline, I think we're really going to have to add another staff member if you want us to take on new projects like this."

"I don't think Andy had that in mind, Carrie," responded Collin, soothingly.

"No, Mrs. Jones, I wasn't expecting the paperbacks to be cataloged. It would only be a browsing collection."

"Then what happens when they get stolen?" asked Barton. "If you don't have some kind of catalog record, how will you know what's missing and needs to be replaced? And if there's no record, we might order duplicates needlessly."

Andy felt himself becoming annoyed. "I don't see why things have to get so complicated. This is just a simple browsing collection. It will make the library look more interesting to the patrons and maybe even lure a few kids into reading some books they'd never see otherwise. Do we have to make such a big deal out of it?"

"I appreciate what you're trying to do, Mr. Kelley, but I think you may have overlooked some of the problems such a collection can pose for the technical services people," responded Barton. "Although the idea has great merit, it could eventually cause trouble. If the library undertakes to set up a paperback section, it should be done responsibly. All of us are aware that this library is supported by tax monies. If we waste that money on maintaining a collection that's only going to disappear eventually, we might be rightly criticized. I really think we ought not to do anything until we can more fully explore the ramifications of such a plan."

"I agree with Barton." echoed Carrie. "Besides, the kind of collection Mr. Kelley is talking about might tend to clutter the entrance way. As well as being nice to look at, the exhibit cases help channel the traffic and keep people from getting in each other's way."

"I've just about had it!" Andy suddenly exploded. "I come in with an idea to help get this library off its rear end and into the twentieth century, and what do I get? A lot of half-baked reasons why it shouldn't be or can't be done. We all know there's nothing wrong with setting up a paperback collection. I could start it today, just with gifts from our patrons. No matter how good an idea it is, somebody will come up with a reason why it won't work. Why don't we just get really rash sometime and try something new without agonizing over all the possible 'ramifications'?"

"I'm afraid, Mr. Kline, this discussion is getting out of hand," commented Barton Taylor, with no show of emotion. "We don't seem to be making much progress, so, if you'll excuse me, I'll leave now. That jobber's representative will be arriving soon."

Without further comment, Barton departed. Carrie remained, looking embarrassed, but said nothing. Andy had not expected Barton's reaction and sat looking a bit surprised. "Perhaps we'd better postpone any further discussion until a more convenient time for everyone," Collin interposed, to break the awkward silence.

Carrie Jones left quickly, but Andy remained to talk further with Collin. "Does that mean I won't get my paperback collection?" he asked Collin anxiously.

"I honestly don't know at this point. I'll put it to you straight, Andy.

By making an emotional issue out of this, you haven't helped your case. One of my basic policies in administering this library system has been never to make a major change without getting at least the grudging approval of the department heads affected. Right now, I wouldn't take any bets on your getting Barton Taylor's approval. Would you?"

•   •   •   •   •

What should Andy do at this juncture? If he feels that the paperback collection is important, how might he proceed to try to persuade Barton and Carrie of its value?

If Andy had not let his emotions show, how might the discussion have proceeded? What arguments, if any, could have been presented to counter the points of objection raised by Barton and Carrie? What compromise might have been achieved?

What does the published literature recommend about the settting up and controlling of paperback collections in public libraries? Could Andy have justified his plan by referring to the experience of other libraries?

8.
The Lost Catalog Tray

· · · · · · · · · · · · · · · ·

"Mr. Carstens, do you know where the drawer is that has the first of the H's in it?" asked Ann Edwards. "I can't seem to find it, and I'm supposed to file some cards in it."

"No, Ann, I don't know where it is. I haven't taken it out of the catalog. But I'll check with Mrs. Watson. She's over in the processing room. Maybe she needed it for something."

Jack Carstens momentarily deserted his post in the main reading area of the Central High School Library and stuck his head through the door to the adjacent room in which Beverly Watson was working on a few knotty cataloging problems.

"Say, Beverly. There's a catalog tray missing. Know anything about it?"

"Sorry. I didn't bring one in here. But let me check around on the tables. One of the student assistants might have brought it in when I wasn't around. No, no sign of it. Maybe it's on one of the reading tables out there."

"Thanks. I'll check, but I didn't see it."

A quick circuit around the reading area, the adjacent shelves, and through the audiovisual room produced no results. Jack found himself distinctly baffled. After telling Ann to go ahead filing in the later sections of the alphabet, he returned to the processing room.

"That catalog tray doesn't seem to be anywhere in the library. What could have happened to it?"

"Oh, somebody must have taken it to a classroom. Knowing our principal's secretary, it might just be sitting on her desk right now because 'the boss wanted me to make a note of this book.' "

Jack laughed, for Beverly was an accomplished impersonator of Central High's secretary. Still, he couldn't imagine even the presumptuous Miss Wilkins appropriating a catalog drawer without asking someone.

"Why don't you just relax," continued Beverly. "I'm sure the wandering cards will soon be home."

"There are times, Beverly, when I think you don't take things seriously enough. But you're probably right. I mean, what can happen to a catalog tray, anyway?"

"I don't want to worry you, Jack," she answered in mock seriousness, "but I do remember reading in one of the library periodicals about a catalog drawer that someone had *found*. And nobody could figure out what library it belonged to. I say, sir, what identifying marks did this missing drawer have?"

"Always kidding, aren't you! Look, I've never lost a catalog tray before. I don't know the proper psychological reaction. But it has occurred to me that it would be no fun to try to replace it if it's really gone for good."

"You know I wouldn't tease you about it if I didn't think it would turn up eventually. After all, I'm the one who'll get stuck with the job of reconstructing it."

By the end of the week the catalog drawer still had not been returned. At least three of the students, in addition to the student assistants, had asked where it was, and several of the teachers had inquired about its location. When it was not found by Monday afternoon, Jack and Beverly began to worry.

"I think I'll ask Miss Wilkins if I can make an announcement to all the classes on the PA system," Jack said, as they began the routine of closing the library for the day.

"That might do some good. But I'm beginning to wonder whether someone took it as a joke, or to get even with us for not letting him scream in the library, or something."

"Possibly, but I honestly don't believe anything like that has happened. It's probably just someone with a weird sense of humor. And it's still possible that some teacher has it in a classroom. Anyhow, I'll try a general announcement and see if that gets any results."

"Jack, I just got a brilliant idea."

"What's that?"

"Why don't you let Ann make the announcement? I was trying to think through what you'd say, and no matter how you put it, it's going to come out sounding ridiculous: 'Ladies and gentlemen, the library needs your assistance. One of our catalog drawers is missing and unaccounted for. Its description is as follows: brown wooden exterior, with label reading H–HI;

white interior consisting of approximately 600 cards, three by five inches (that's 7.5 by 12.5 cm. for you science buffs); impaled in the drawer by one brass rod approximately fourteen inches in length. If you have seen this drawer or heard of its whereabouts, please notify your local friendly librarians. No questions asked.' "

"What, no reward?!"

"If you want to offer one out of your salary, be my guest."

"I don't know, maybe it'd be more effective to play it for laughs with the students. Instead of using Ann, why don't you just do it the way you did for me?"

"Me and my big mouth! But, O.K., I think maybe it might work. Book me for a public appearance tomorrow afternoon."

Beverly's PA debut proved to be an unquestioned success in terms of the notoriety it brought the library. It did not, however, produce the missing catalog drawer. By the end of the week, Jack was ready to tear the building apart to find the lost cards.

"Come on, Jack," countered Beverly. "I really think you're getting overanxious about this. How much trouble is it really causing, anyhow? If somebody comes in and needs a card in the H to HI section, we just tell them—we can even fix a neat sign to go in the hole—that the drawer is lost. If they were looking up an author, they can try under title. If it's a subject area, we can talk with them and show them the section of the shelves with books on that topic. I don't see why we can't work around it."

"Yeah, I know we can. But I have this feeling that we'll never see the drawer again. If that's true, then we ought to start trying to replace it."

"We both know that replacing those cards won't be easy. We've got our hands full just keeping up with the work waiting for us now. I move we table this problem."

"I don't know; I feel uneasy about—"

"Sorry, Jack, but a motion to table is not debatable. How do you vote?"

"O.K., we'll table the matter. But I think we're going to have to face this question again."

The search for the missing drawer continued, at least intermittently, for another two months. Both Jack and Beverly made it a point to look carefully in any classrooms or storage areas they had occasion to visit. They found nothing that resembled a catalog drawer, nor did anyone report having seen a drawer or cards being taken from the building. Whether done as a joke or maliciously, the removal of the drawer had been highly successful.

As the Christmas vacation period approached, Jack became visibly more annoyed by the absence of the H to HI cards.

"Look, Beverly, I'm not going away over the holidays. And this missing drawer is really getting to me. I think I'll begin to try to reconstruct it during the vacation period. It'll be quiet then, with no interruptions."

"But won't the school be closed? How'll you get in?"

"I've talked to the principal, and she says she'll authorize a key for me."

"But they don't keep the heat on when school's not in session, do they? You'll freeze to death."

"I've already thought of that. I can use a couple of electric heaters and wear a sweater. It won't be too bad."

"I wish I could help you, but Hank and I are going to his folks' place for Christmas. We'll be gone for almost the whole two weeks."

"Thanks. I knew you'd be away, but I just can't put this off any longer."

"How's Janet going to like having her husband working all through the holidays?"

"Actually, she said she'd help me. She says she's tired of hearing about that miserable catalog tray and is willing to work with me so she won't have to listen to me bitch about it anymore."

"All I can say is you've got a noble wife. So how are you planning to go about this reconstruction project?"

"That's where I need your help. You're the one who does most of the cataloging. What's the best procedure?"

"You know, Jack, when it comes right down to it, I don't know. I've been assuming that the crazy drawer would turn up eventually. Look, why don't you and Janet and I get together on Sunday afternoon and brainstorm about this? If she's going to be helping you, she might as well have some of the fun of planning the adventure."

"O.K., I'll check with her. If it's all right, we'll invite you and Hank over."

"Don't bother about Hank. He's off to the mountains for a camping trip with the boys this weekend."

"Well, unless Janet has some plans she hasn't told me about, you might as well come have Sunday supper with us. Then we can plot a strategy."

Sunday turned out to be a wet and rather gloomy day. "Just the kind of afternoon," Beverly announced as she closed her umbrella before entering the Carstens's house, "for strategizing. I just wish we were plotting something more exciting than the replacement of a lost catalog drawer."

"I just hope the two of you will be patient with me," said Janet about an hour later, as they settled in the living room with their after-dinner coffee. "Jack knows how little I understand about library matters. He tells me that being an avid reader is not the best qualification for replacing a bunch of lost cards."

"Maybe the easiest thing," Beverly began, "would be to just name aloud the kinds of cards that would have been in that drawer. Then we can figure out some way to recapture the information on them."

"That sounds reasonable," agreed Jack. "There would be author, title, and subject cards. Right?"

"Actually, from the cataloger's standpoint, you'd call them by different names. What you'd have would be main entry cards, subject cards, added entries, and cross-references. And of course, there'd be some guide cards, but they're not important right now. We can put them in at logical points when the drawer's finished."

"And we know that the letters covered are from the beginning of H to the end of the HI section," added Jack.

"But I don't see how you'll know what the cards were," countered Janet.

"Frankly, it looks to me like we're going to have to go through the rest of the catalog and look at the tracings on every main card," responded Beverly.

"Look at the what?" asked Janet.

"I knew I should have made you take those library school courses with me," Jack interjected impatiently. " 'Tracings,' my dear, are the list of headings under which a book appears in the catalog."

"What Jack means, Janet, is that we keep a record of all the cards we make for a book. This record is called the tracing, and it appears on the so-called main card for each book."

"Well maybe I'm just being stupid," answered Janet, "but I thought you said you didn't have the main cards—that some of them were lost too."

"That's quite right," agreed Beverly. "We could go through the rest of the catalog card by card; find each main card that's left; look at the tracing to see if any of the entries there begin with anything from H to HI; and make new cards for the subject and added entries that turn up. But we won't find the missing H to HI main cards that way."

"But if we're going through card by card, we could look at all the added entries while we're doing it, couldn't we?" asked Jack. "That way we could spot the main entries beginning with H to HI."

"I suppose you could," mused Beverly. "I just keep wondering if there isn't a better way. You'll probably find two or three added entries for each main entry in the missing secion. You could wind up making the same main card several times if you didn't check carefully for duplications."

"Say, I just had a thought," said Jack, eagerly. "Why can't we go through the shelflist instead of the main catalog? There won't be any duplication of entries there."

"That's a great idea, friend," responded Beverly. "Just one catch: in the olden days—before I came to Central, of course—the cataloger didn't put tracings on the shelflist card. Since I've been here, we've put them on; and, of course, they're there for the printed cards and the cards we get from the Processing Center. Sorry, Janet, I realize this probably doesn't make too much sense to you. What happens is that we now buy most of our cards from other sources, instead of typing them ourselves. We used to order cards directly from the Library of Congress, but now we get them from the Processing Center. The staff there does the cataloging for all the school libraries in our county and the two adjacent ones. When we get our cards, the tracings usually appear on all of them, not just on the main card. But the earlier procedure at Central was to put tracings on the main card only when it had to be typed locally. In fact, we still do that for things we catalog originally."

"Even with your careful explanation, I'm not sure I really understand. But I'll take your word for it anyhow."

"It looks like we're back to checking card by card in the main catalog," observed Jack, gloomily. "And what about the cross-references? Until you reminded me, I had managed to avoid thinking about them."

Beverly looked distressed. "I would rather not raise that question myself. Subject cross-references can be reconstructed from the check marks we've put in the printed subject headings list. But the cross-references for names are traced on the back of the main cards. You'll have enough trouble looking at the regular tracing on all the cards, without having to turn them over to find cross-references."

"I hate to mention this," added Jack, "but haven't the regular tracings sometimes been put on the back of the main card, too?"

"Oh, gosh yes! I'd forgotten about that old procedure. You'll have to look on the verso if the tracings aren't at the bottom of the homemade cards. Still, you wouldn't have to look at the back of *every* main card unless you were trying to find name cross-references too."

"Say, you two," suggested Janet suddenly. "Why don't you just forget the whole thing? Not to inject a jarring note, but I'm really wondering if all this trouble is worth it. How bad off would people be if the cards were never replaced?"

"I don't know how bad off the users would be, but I think your husband would have to find another job. He just can't stand the thought of an incomplete card file."

"That's exactly right. So let's forget that kind of foolish suggestion and get back to the problem at hand. Now about those subject references. . . ."

•   •   •   •   •

If Janet's suggestion were taken seriously, how could Jack and Beverly find out whether the missing catalog drawer was actually proving to be a major problem for library users?

Analyze the development of the brainstorming session thus far. What alternative procedures, if any, should be considered before a final decision about the strategy is made? And how, precisely, will the subject cross-reference cards be reconstructed?

What steps could be taken in advance of the loss of a catalog tray to minimize the time and effort required to replace the cards? How likely is it that such a loss will occur in a school library? In other types of libraries? In view of the level of probability of such a loss, how much advantage will there be in trying to prepare for it?

9.
Classification Changes
Cause Split Shelving

• • • • • • • • • • • •

The Department of Religion at Yancey University (formerly Yancey College of Arts) was proud of its liberal stance. The faculty members had been deliberately selected to represent a variety of church traditions and world faiths. In fact, Yancey had been one of the first institutions in the country to endow a professorship in ecumenism. Dr. Ross Barrow, who had been appointed to fill this post some twenty years earlier, was considered by his colleagues at Yancey and by scholars throughout the western world to be one of the leading historians of ecumenical efforts.

Not surprisingly, Yancey's library reflected Barrow's expertise and research interests. Its collection of documents from the World Council of Churches alone was impressive in terms of numbers and depth. Under Barrow's careful watch, the library had acquired every known monograph and periodical on ecumenism, along with most of the official documents emanating from national interchurch and interfaith groups. The resulting materials required several ranges of stacks in the 200 Section of the library. Despite the fact that fewer monographs had been written in recent years, the reports and periodicals continued to arrive in unprecedented numbers. And just to make life more interesting for the cataloging staff, Barrow was now directing his attention to the acquisition of pre-ecumenism source materials: documents covering earlier attempts at church union, treatises on syncretism, and the like. Much of this information had to be secured in microform, which only added to the woes of the cataloging staff.

In addition to being an avid collector of ecumenical materials, Barrow paid close attention to the disposition of the items which he recommended. Each year he assigned at least one research assistant to the task of discovering whether the materials ordered during the previous academic year had yet been acquired and cataloged. Among the duties of the assistant was to find the material in the stacks and copy the call number from it. Barrow would settle for nothing less than actual inspection of the book or film. "Don't just copy the number from the catalog card," he specified. "Get it from the book. And if the book isn't there, find out where it is and arrange to see it later. I don't want a report on anything that you haven't looked at yourself."

A professor as knowledgeable and conscientious as Ross Barrow can be a library's greatest ally. He can also become a source of problems, especially for the library's cataloger of religion materials. Although Sally Carstens, in her calmer moments, greatly appreciated Dr. Barrow's interest in the library's collection of ecumenical materials, she could hardly suppress an audible gasp when she saw the three booktrucks full of scraggly, mostly unbound reports from various international missionary conferences. "What are those doing here?" she demanded of Helen Varty.

Helen, whose major responsibility in the Order Department was to handle "problem materials," just smiled malevolently and asked, "What do you think they're doing here? They're some of Barrow's newest contributions to the health and well-being of catalogers, of course. What else?"

"You are going to send them off to the bindery before they come to me, aren't you?"

"Sorry, dear. No chance. Mrs. Liner has already told me to do some quick preliminary checking and pass them on to the Cataloging Division for complete identification. Good luck!"

As Helen walked away, Sally mumbled to herself, "I must keep saying, over and over: 'Dr. Barrow is good for the University. Dr. Barrow is good for the University.' Who knows, I might even start believing it!"

Had Barrow known about this episode, he might have delayed his visit to the Cataloging Division for a week or two. In typical forthright style, however, he had decided that something must be done to solve a problem which his assistant had discovered in the library, and his action was direct —take it to the head of the division.

Other professors might simply have barged into Alice Kindal's office and started talking. Barrow was, in contrast, exceedingly courteous and thoughtful in his dealings with the library staff. Before coming to the division office he called for an appointment and stated that he had a problem in classification which he wished to discuss with Miss Kindal. At the appointed hour he arrived, identified himself to the secretary, and was shown into the office. After the usual pleasantries were exchanged, Barrow presented his case.

"My research assistant has been checking up on the things I ordered last year," he began.

"Well, if there have been any delays, I hope you'll understand," Alice interrupted. "You know, we've been short one staff member this past year and the books aren't moving as fast as we'd like."

"Oh, that's not the problem at all. I think the library's doing a pretty good job of getting the books ordered and on the shelves. My quarrel is with the classification numbers that you've been giving them. When I first came here, most of the materials on ecumenism were in the 280s. Now most of them seem to be getting placed in the 260s. This last batch that Jack—that's my assistant—searched were almost all in the 260s. I don't understand why, and I have to say, in all honesty, I don't like it, no matter what the reason."

"I'm afraid, Dr. Barrow, that I'm going to be at a disadvantage in this discussion. It's been years, literally, since I classified anything in the 200s. I don't really have any idea why the change has occurred. But if you don't mind, I'd like to call Mrs. Carstens in. She's the one who handles most of your materials and she'd be a much better person to answer your question. May I see if she's available?"

Barrow gave his permission enthusiastically, and Alice's secretary was dispatched to find Sally, who was not far away. Sally had seen Dr. Barrow go into Miss Kindal's office; she was actually staying close by in case she might be called or Miss Kindal might tell her about the interview later.

"Mrs. Carstens, I don't know whether you've met Dr. Barrow. Dr. Barrow, Sally Carstens."

"Oh, yes, of course. I've known Sally's husband for several years. He was a student in the Religion Department. How are you, Sally?"

"Just fine, Dr. Barrow. I'm enjoying my job here, even if I am learning more about ecumenical materials than I ever thought I wanted to know."

"I guess I do keep you pretty busy. But you have to admit that we're acquiring a top-notch research collection in ecumenism. The last time I was in New York for a conference, a couple of students there told me they were applying to the graduate school at Yancey mainly because of the work we're doing here in ecumenical studies. But I guess we're not here to talk about my book collecting habits. Miss Kindal, do you want to fill her in on the discussion thus far?"

"Sally, Dr. Barrow has raised a question about the classification of the ecumenical materials. You know I'm not an expert in that field, so I thought you'd better be the one to hear the problem. Have the numbers been changed from, what is it, the 280s to the 260s?"

"That's right, Miss Kindal. The seventeenth edition of the Dewey moved the number for ecumenical materials from 280.1 to 262.001. Whenever we get LC cards for books in that area, the number should now be 262.001, unless it's changed again. When this started happening, I followed our usual procedure and put the new books in the new number. We have a cross-reference in the shelflist to catch any that come through with the old number."

"Does that mean that my books are going to be in two places from now on?" asked Barrow, incredulously.

"I'm afraid so, unless Miss Kindal decides that the ones in the old number should be reclassified."

"How many books would have to be redone if we were to reclassify?" asked Alice Kindal.

"I don't really know for sure without doing a count, but from what I remember of that section, we would have to redo about three cases of books—something like one side of a three-case range."

"If my figuring is anywhere near correct," Alice interjected, "that would be close to a thousand volumes."

"I think it would be at least that many," Sally agreed.

"Speaking very frankly, Dr. Barrow," Alice continued. "I don't see how we can possibly undertake such a reclassification project right now. As I mentioned earlier, we're short one professional staff member as it is. If you want the new materials to get cataloged, we simply can't spend time on re-doing the old ones. I hate to have to be so negative, but the thought of taking on a project like that right now is almost too much to cope with."

"I don't mean to be unreasonable, ladies, but the separation of my materials is a terrible inconvenience for me and my students. I don't know why the change had to be in the first place. The 280 number was just as good as this one. Would it be any less trouble to change the new ones back to the old number?"

"I'm afraid not, Dr. Barrow," Sally countered. "It's not just the reclassification but the fact that we'd have to spend time looking up the 280 number for every new book from now on. The Library of Congress will use the 262 number, but we'd have to change that to 280. Each one would have to be done over. I think it would really waste a lot of time."

"O.K., you've got an answer for everything, it seems," responded Barrow with a smile. "While I'm asking, I might as well go the whole way. Why does this library still use the Dewey system anyway? Some of my friends at other universities tell me that the Library of Congress

Classification is what we ought to be using, especially for religion materials. And a lot of the seminaries are switching to the Library of Congress system, I'm told, because it's the only one that can handle Protestant, Catholic, and Jewish materials without crowding them all together in a few numbers. Has this library ever considered changing?"

"Yes, Dr. Barrow, we have," responded Alice a bit stiffly. "This matter has been under discussion quite intensively by the library staff and the faculty library committee. In fact, two years ago the decision was made *not* to change because the cost of reclassification would be so great. The library committee was not willing to settle for a "switch"; they wanted all the books to be reclassified. We simply didn't have that kind of money, and so they voted to stay with Dewey."

"Where was I when all this was going on?" asked Barrow.

"If I remember correctly," Sally commented, "you were on sabbatical that year. I guess you missed it."

"Well, I'm sure the decision was made conscientiously," Barrow continued. "However, I think maybe the discussion should be revived. I'm not sure that the other faculty members were fully aware of the situation. I'm going to be on the library committee next year; I'd like to look at this whole thing again, especially since I seem to have some new evidence."

After Dr. Barrow had left, Miss Kindal and Sally just sat and stared at each other for a moment.

"What happened Miss Kindal? One minute I was casually explaining the change in Dewey and the next thing I knew we were about to reopen the whole Dewey-LC business. What did I do wrong?"

"It wasn't your fault, Sally. Dr. Barrow is a good friend of the library, but he's certainly no management expert and he knows little or nothing about library classification problems. I think maybe the best thing for us to do is to be prepared for him. Why don't you let the missionary materials sit for a day or two? (I know that'll break your heart!) Do two things for me, will you? First, find out exactly how many volumes would have to be reclassified to solve the ecumenical problem. If you can, do a cost estimate on the reclassification, too. Then do a bit of historical research into the LC schedule to see how ecumenism is handled there and whether LC is really any better than Dewey. Be sure to go through all the changes and additions to the, what is it, BL to BX schedule? I think that's right. Anyway, find out if LC has made any major relocations that might give us as much trouble as the Dewey. O.K.?"

"Yes, ma'am!" Sally answered. But Miss Kindal's secretary was a bit puzzled when she overheard Sally saying to herself as she walked away:

"Dr. Barrow is good for the University. Dr. Barrow is good for the University. Must keep saying that: Dr. Barrow is good. . . ."

• • • • •

Miss Kindal's strategy is a specific one. Analyze it from the standpoint of political sensitivity. What impact will cost figures and the possible disadvantages of LC's schedule for ecumenism be likely to have upon Dr. Barrow?

Just how good is LC in the area of ecumenism? What will Sally find when she does her classification analysis?

How should the library staff react to Barrow's plan to take up the matter with the library committee? How often should such decisions about classification be reviewed, and by whom?

What should be the library's policy with regard to classification changes imposed by a central agency such as LC? If such changes are inevitable, how can the library cope intelligently with them? In what ways can a classification split, such as the one which has emerged for ecumenical materials, inconvenience or mislead a library user?

10.
The New Library
Technician Arrives

· · · · · · · · · · ·

"What's a library technician supposed to do, anyway?" asked Carolyn Peters, Seaville Public Library's cataloging assistant. "I know you told me that we'd recruited one and were sending him to STI to get his basic training, but I still don't really understand what he's going to do when he gets here."

Carolyn's question was directed to Eleanor Bartlett, Seaville's only professional cataloger. Eleanor had worked with Carolyn for more than four years, and she had always tried to foster a relaxed and open relationship with her. Even if Eleanor had not particularly liked Carolyn, it would have been to her advantage to keep the working situation pleasant, for besides the typist, Theresa Ingels, who was assigned only part-time to the Catalog Department, there were only the two of them to do the work. The serials assistant did her job mainly in the Adult Area; Carolyn and Eleanor didn't see much of her unless she had a problem. And of course there was Martin Erdman, the high school student who came in after school three days a week to do the marking and pasting work for the department; but they didn't have much chance to talk to him either.

Since Seaville had opened its Eastgate Branch Library, the workload for the cataloging staff had increased noticeably. There was even a rumor that Mrs. Carraway, the Librarian, was trying to create interest in building a branch out in the Southgate section. In view of all this activity, Mrs. Carraway's suggestion that the Catalog Department sponsor a student in the new library technician program at Seaville Technical Institute was not at all unwelcome.

Taking Carolyn's expressed concern seriously, Eleanor had responded sympathetically: "I know it's hard for you to imagine adding a new full-time member to the Catalog Department. Actually he won't be full time as long as he's at STI. But we both know there's plenty of work to be done. The filing, for example; you're always complaining about never having time to finish it. And you know when we tried to have the typist do some, it was a disaster."

"Yeah, I know. But are you sure the technician will be able to file any better?"

"I've seen the curriculum outline for the course he's taking. From what I could tell, filing is one of the things he's supposed to be learning, along with typing cards and making cross-references."

"But I thought you said he's supposed to have done some practice work during the course."

"He will be doing some. In fact, that's what he'll be doing during the first six months that he works here. He began his courses last fall; now he's ready to start what they call the 'practicum.' He'll work part-time for us for the rest of this year; then, if everything is okay, we'll put him on full time in January."

"You and Mrs. Carraway are the only ones who've met him. What's he like?"

"He seems like a very nice young man. He had to go to work right after he graduated from high school. I think he worked most of the time he was in school, too. Anyway, he's twenty-two years old now and wants to get a job that's more of a challenge. Up till now he's been working in a hardware store, and they haven't got any way for him to advance beyond what amounts to a stockboy position."

"I wouldn't think he'd make much more money working for the library than he did in the store."

"Certainly not at first, but if he does a good job here, he'll get regular raises. And he thinks he would rather be somewhere where the people are concerned about intellectual things. He said that the only things the people in the hardware store were interested in were football scores and dirty jokes."

"Is he married?"

"I don't think so. But he did say something about having a girl friend and wanting to plan a good future."

"When is he coming in to start work?"

"Next Monday afternoon. But that's just to get him oriented to the library. His classes are on Monday, Wednesday, and Friday; that way, he can be here all day Tuesday and Thursday."

"Will he be taking courses during the summer, too?"

"Yes, he says he wants to finish as soon as possible. STI is on the quarter system, and the library technician program lasts six quarters."

"All I can say is I hope he's good. I've been saving up a bunch of special jobs that I didn't have time to do. If this guy can do the routine stuff, I might even be able to catch up. Say, what's his name, anyway?"

"Nelson Hargrove. I really think you'll like him."

"I'll like him all right if he takes the filing off my hands. Anyone who can do that is a friend for life!"

The new technician was scheduled to arrive at 2 P.M. on Monday, but by 2:20 he still had not shown up. At about half past two he finally put in an appearance.

"Well, Mr. Hargrove, I thought you were going to be here at two o'clock," commented Eleanor.

"Yes ma'am, I know I was supposed to be here by then, but we didn't get out of school until late this morning and I had to get some lunch before I came."

"Of course we wouldn't want you to starve. But I'd appreciate it if you'd phone me anytime you have to come late. We plan our work rather carefully around here, and it throws us off if someone fails to show up on time."

"Yes ma'am. I'll try to remember to call next time. What's the phone number?"

"Here, I'll write it down for you. Now, for this afternoon, all I want to do is to give you a tour of the library and introduce you to some of the people you'll be working with. Then when you come in tomorrow morning—and by the way, we'll be expecting you at 8:30—we can get you started on the work you'll be doing for the Catalog Department."

"Is there any chance that I could come in at 9:00 instead of 8:30?"

"No, I'm sorry. I don't see how we can change the hours. The regular staff works from 8:30 to 4:30 with an hour for lunch. Since you'll be learning the job, we have to have someone here to supervise you. If you came at 9:00, then you'd either have to be here alone during the lunch hour or stay until 5:00. We just couldn't do that without reworking well-established schedules of people who've been here for a long time."

"O.K., but I have a class on Monday night, and it's awfully hard for me to get started so early on Tuesday."

"I'm sorry about that, Nelson, but I think you'll have to learn to adjust. Surely they expected you to be in by 8:30 at the hardware store."

"Yeah, but I didn't have a class the night before."

"Well, as I say, I don't see how we can ask other people to change their schedules for your convenience. Please just plan to make it by 8:30."

The remainder of the afternoon proceeded uneventfully. Nelson seemed to be paying reasonably close attention to what he was told during the library tour. He was polite and attentive as he was introduced to other staff members, and Eleanor relaxed a bit.

"Maybe we just got off to a bad start there," she confided to Carolyn. "But at the outset, I thought he might prove to be difficult."

"I heard part of that conversation, and that's what I thought, too. I'm still not convinced that he's going to be a reliable worker. He looks like he's more interested in meeting the young girls than in working for the library."

"Well, you can hardly blame him for that, Carolyn. After all, he is a young, redblooded male. And I don't even know for sure that he's engaged."

"I don't know what it is, but I have a bad feeling about him. I don't think he's going to work out very well."

"Don't damn him before he even has a chance! Give him time. He may do just fine."

As the next few weeks passed, Eleanor began to doubt the wisdom of her optimism. Both she and Carolyn undertook to direct Nelson's training, and they both had the same impression at the end of his first two weeks of work.

"When I tell him something, he seems to understand all right. He nods and says yes and everything, but when I check up on what he's done, it's usually wrong."

"Yes, Carolyn, I'm afraid I know exactly what you mean. I showed him how to type up some name authority cards. He said he understood—that they'd covered that in his cataloging course at STI—but when I checked what he'd finished, I found all kinds of errors: strikeovers, reversed letters, omissions, and wrong spacing."

"The same thing happened with the filing. He told me they'd done several exercises in filing in connection with his course, but you'd never know it from looking at the cards he arranged. Some of the mistakes were obviously made because of local rules he didn't know about; still, most of them were just plain carelessness."

"Well, I'm sure it's still all very new to him. Let's give him a month. Then if he isn't shaping up, I'll have to talk with Mrs. Carraway."

The pattern of distinctly erratic accuracy in Nelson's work persisted.

Eleanor tried everything she could think of to eliminate the problem: working with him, showing him his mistakes, letting Carolyn go over the same procedure with him, being understanding, being unpleasant. She stopped short only when she realized she was about to threaten him with being fired.

"Eleanor, I just can't take much more of this," Carolyn finally said. "I'm not getting anything done that I thought I would. I have to spend so much time watching what Nelson's doing that I don't even get the routine things finished on time anymore."

"Yes, I know. I realize that I've been shifting the burden onto you more and more because I seemed to have so little luck with Nelson myself. I came right to the point of telling him that we were going to have to fire him if he didn't do better, but I suddenly realized that we aren't paying him enough while he's still a student to really have anything to threaten him with. And besides, I don't have the authority to fire him unless Mrs. Carraway tells me I can."

"Are you going to talk to her about it?"

"Actually, I already have, at least in preliminary fashion. I have an appointment with her right after lunch today to talk about him again."

Helen Carraway had been extremely disturbed by the reports Eleanor had given her about Nelson's problems. The Seaville Library's agreement to participate in the library technician program had been the one factor which had made the development of the program possible. In fact, Helen had virtually assured the STI staff that she would create additional library technician positions as quickly as possible, as a means of encouraging young people from disadvantaged backgrounds and helping to keep them off the welfare roles. If the initial graduate of the program failed on the job, the whole plan could be severely threatened.

"Eleanor, I'm sure you're not making all this up, but there's a lot at stake here. I've stuck my neck out with the STI people and with our own library Board of Trustees, telling them what a great service we can render the community by hiring these young people. Not to mention the money saved by using technicians instead of more professionals. I don't mean to sound unkind, but neither you nor Carolyn has ever trained a technician before. Maybe it's just not clear to him what he's supposed to do."

"Frankly, Helen, I thought you had more faith in me than that. If you can't take my word for the state of affairs, then we might as well forget it."

"Now don't get angry, Eleanor. I know how I must sound to you, but please understand what a bind this puts me in. What I think I'll have to do is to talk with Nelson myself. Do you want to be here when I do?"

"No, I guess I really don't. I'm too involved in the whole thing to be objective anymore. Why don't you talk to him and then tell me what he says?"

"All right, if that's the way you want it."

On the following Thursday morning, there was a note on Nelson's desk to go to Mrs. Carraway's office as soon as he arrived. At about 9:10, he appeared.

"Didn't you see my note when you got here?" she asked as he came through the door. "I thought you'd come in shortly after 8:30."

"I just got here. I told Miss Bartlett that it's hard for me to get here at 8:30 when I have a late class the night before. But she doesn't seem to understand."

"Did you try to make an adjustment in your schedule?"

"Yes ma'am, but she said they couldn't do that."

"Did she tell you why?"

"Oh, she said something about the other people's schedules being already set and they couldn't change it just for me."

"Well, I'll talk with her about it later. But right now, we've got a more serious problem. Miss Bartlett tells me you're not doing very well on the job."

"Yeah, she gives me a pretty hard time, all right. I try to do the best I can, but it never seems to satisfy her. Half the time I don't know what I've done wrong. She and that assistant of hers are always finding something to blame me for."

"Aren't you aware of the fact that you're making errors?"

"Sometimes. But everybody makes mistakes. I think I'm doing it right, but they tell me it's wrong. I thought this was going to be a good job, and now I'm not so sure. That Mrs. Peters rides me all the time. I don't think she ever liked me. I think she's prejudiced against people who didn't go to college."

"Have the people in the Catalog Department ever said anything to you that would intimidate you or suggest that you were inferior as a person?"

"Oh, they don't say anything except that I'm not doing the work right, but I know they don't like me."

"Frankly, Nelson, it's hard for me to reconcile what you're saying with the reports I get from Miss Bartlett. I guess that's all for now. I'll talk with her again and let you know her response."

"O.K., but I don't think I want to stay here much longer anyhow. I've been talking to some of the other kids in the program at STI and they tell me there are good jobs to be had in some of the special libraries. And they pay higher salaries too. I've got a lead on one right now, so I may be quitting pretty soon."

• • • • •

In view of the stake that Seaville Public Library has in the technician program at STI, what should Mrs. Carraway's response be to Nelson at this point? If he leaves and takes a job in a special library, what are the consequences likely to be for the public library?

Both Eleanor and Carolyn have observed Nelson's performance on the job. Given Mrs. Carraway's reluctance to accept their assessment of his worth, how could they document their case? What advantage might there have been in Eleanor's being present during Mrs. Carraway's interview with Nelson? What disadvantage?

What is the role of the library technician or technical assistant, according to published sources? To what extent has Nelson been properly or improperly used to do filing and authority card work at Seaville Public? If he did well and stayed at the public library, what kind of future might he expect in terms of advancement or increased job responsibility?

11.
The Microfilm
Never Gets Cataloged

· · · · · · · · · · · · ·

The staff of the Eastern Theological Seminary Library had never numbered more than three professionals. Money for new positions was scarce, although the seminary administration had usually been very generous in providing student scholarships which entailed at least ten hours of work each week in the library. Accordingly, all of the professionals found that much of their time was occupied in training and supervising student assistants, most of whom would be likely to continue in the library for two to three years.

Historically, the staff had begun with only the librarian. Within a few years, a cataloger was added; and ten years after that, a circulation-reference position was created. The Librarian, Wesley Clark, continued to supervise the Order Department, in addition to his general administrative duties. Audrey Lexton, Cataloger, exercised full authority over the staff of two clerks and, normally, half a dozen students charged with cataloging, classifying, and processing the five-to-six-thousand items added to the collection each year. All work relating to the circulating and servicing of the collection itself fell under the jurisdiction of Carolyn Crowder, assisted by eight to ten student workers.

For quite understandable reasons, the Catalog Department always had a backlog of work. At the librarian's request, Audrey chose one of the students to survey the arrearage and determine the characteristics of the materials which constituted it. It was discovered that the backlogged items had two common characteristics: most were in foreign languages—primarily monograph series—and most had no Library of Congress card copy available at the time they were received. Audrey readily admitted that little follow-up work had been done on many of the items, for the daily tasks of cataloging, classifying, making authority records and cross references, typing cards, filing, pasting, stamping, and marking filled her time and that of her assistants.

Despite the existence of a backlog, the current cataloging procedures at Eastern were reasonably efficient. They simply left no margin for expansion. Anything which required special treatment had to be deferred, to prevent a delay in cataloging "standard" items. Materials with LC card copy were processed rapidly; other items might be shelved, with a location number for identification, in the Catalog Department, to await the location of LC copy or the demand of a library user. Temporary cards, under main entry, were placed in the public catalog for any items received and sent to the "deferred" shelf, so that users could know of their presence in the library and request them through the Circulation Department by specifying the location number. Audrey prided herself on the fact that even the most difficult of cataloging problems was solved whenever a user requested a book that had been deferred. Although the system was certainly not ideal, Audrey and her colleagues felt that it was a reasonable compromise under the circumstances.

One of the procedures which slowed the cataloging process was the application of a specialized theological classification system to the materials. In effect, Audrey did original classification work for all acquisitions, although the work was simplified somewhat by the fact that Library of Congress subject headings were available in advance for many items. The classification scheme, while designed especially for seminary libraries, suffered from being out-of-date by about four years. It was, however, made current to some degree by the work of the largest theological library in the country, for that library issued current accessions lists giving call numbers according to the special scheme.

Eastern had considered shifting to the Library of Congress Classification system. Wes Clark took special note of a research study, done in another seminary library, showing that the faculty had little knowledge or appreciation of the specialized features of the theological classification. In staff discussion, however, a distinct reluctance to change systems emerged, primarily because everyone wanted to avoid burdening the library user with two systems. The cost of total reclassification to LC was estimated to be something like $50,000—a figure which looked astronomical to the staff. Accordingly, reclassification was ruled out.

In her attempt to keep the basic materials moving quickly through the Catalog Department, Audrey frequently found her attention sidetracked by items in nonbook format. Some of the seminary's faculty were intensively interested in media other than books; two, in particular, concentrated attention upon art and music materials, respectively. Slides and recordings ordered for the support of these two areas proved to be such a burden to the already overworked Catalog Department that the librarian arranged with the two faculty members in question to establish an audiovisual room adjacent to their offices. Student assistants working with the faculty members were given the responsibility of supervising the use of the audiovisual area, while the library agreed to order and pay for the materials kept there.

When the faculty member involved with the preaching sections decided that tape recordings of sermons ought to be acquired, his materials, too, were sent to the audiovisual room. Although a few complaints were heard to the effect that tapes or slides seemed always to be missing, the audiovisual arrangement appeared to be a satisfactory solution to the problem, since the materials, in effect, bypassed the Catalog Department entirely. This meant, however, that there was no record in the library of the items in the audiovisual room.

Another troublesome area was that of archives and manuscripts. Church groups, individuals, and even the seminary itself wanted the library to preserve and make available the various records and documents amassed over the years. Such collections were often quite valuable for research purposes, but, as before, the cataloging staff could not undertake even a basic inventory of the materials. Wes Clark solved this problem by obtaining special funds used to employ someone during the summer to catalog the manuscripts. He was fortunate to secure the services of an experienced cataloger who also knew something of the history the church, with the result that the collection became at least usable, if not completely cataloged. The archives, however, remained boxed in a storeroom, virtually untouched.

One further type of troublesome material refused to be disposed of easily. In early years, few, if any, books were acquired in microform copy. It was sufficient to catalog the occasional item received on microfilm as if it were the printed version, attaching a note to the card indicating that the item was available only in a microversion. Microfilm reels were not classified; instead, they were assigned an accession number and stored in boxes shelved adjacent to the microform reading equipment.

More recently, however, Audrey found that a number of periodicals and other serial publications, as well as theses and dissertations, were being received on film. Examination of the film revealed, more often than not, that it contained certain defects: periodicals with missing issues, pages filmed twice or not at all, or double images impossible to read. The presence of such defects meant that before the item could be cataloged, it had to be placed on a microform reader and examined frame by frame. The amount of time consumed in this effort was, in some instances, far beyond the worth of the material. To complicate matters further, LC card copy for many of the periodicals and for all of the theses and dissertations was nonexistent. All cataloging, therefore, had to be done from scratch. Even the accession number arrangement proved to be inadequate to handle the periodicals, for many of them were still being published and could be expected to have reels added to the file later. To separate each reel in the accession sequence, simply because it arrived at a later date, was absurd from the user's standpoint.

Once more, Audrey devised a temporary solution. A section of the Catalog Department's shelving was allocated to microforms awaiting processing. Each title, whether series or monograph, was assigned a location symbol consisting of the letter "M" plus an accession number and, if necessary, a reel number, e.g., M21-3. Subsequently received reels for an uncataloged serial in microform were assigned the original accession number and the appropriate reel number in proper sequence. A temporary card was then filed, under the main entry in the public catalog, to show that the materials could be found in the Catalog Department. A legend on each of the cards read: "The title shown above is available in microform copy. If you need to see the material, please request it by title and location number (shown in the upper left-hand corner of the card) at the Circulation Desk." No attempt was made, however, to show the "holdings" information on temporary cards, although it would eventually appear on the permanent main cards.

Neither Audrey nor Wes thought the solution ideal, but it had the advantage of making the microforms available while they were awaiting the attention of a cataloging assistant. In her more candid moments, Audrey saw the arrangement as little more than a device to get her off the hook. Once a reel was dispatched to the cataloging shelves and a temporary card inserted in the public catalog, the chances of its ever being fully cataloged grew quite remote.

As faculty members and students encountered the temporary cards, they gradually learned that the materials were stored in the Catalog Department. Most of the use of the microforms came from a few faculty members; these regular borrowers began to bypass the Circulation Desk and go directly to the location in the cataloging area. Informally, a system was worked out whereby the faculty member would fill out a slip showing his name and the current date; he would paper clip the slip to any cataloging records which might be attached to the reel and leave the packet where the reel had been. When he returned the reel, he threw away his charge-out slip and reclipped the cataloging slips to the reel as he put it back in its place.

For several months, the informal circulation system for microforms worked without any difficulties. For those patrons who were not aware of the bypass, the desk attendants served as go-betweens. In such instances, the attendant filled out the slip showing name and date. When the item was returned, the attendant replaced it on the shelves and destroyed the temporary circulation record.

The system's first major challenge was leveled by Andrea Janson, Eastern's Professor of Christian Education. Dr. Janson's advanced seminar in the supervision of Christian education met on Tuesday afternoons from 3 to 6 P.M. In addition to the students from the seminary, three directors of Christian education from local churches were enrolled in the seminar. Just after the second meeting of the class, during which the seminar reports were assigned, Dr. Janson accompanied one of the outside students to the public catalog to determine whether the library could support the type of project which the student proposed to undertake.

"There are two or three dissertations available, I know," commented Dr. Janson, "and we should have the basic journals in that area. Here—let me make you a list of the main ones. You go look these up while I check in a couple of other places."

The student, Gregory Hallpen, took the sheet from his instructor and began to systematically look for each item in the catalog. By the time Dr. Janson returned from her foray into the stacks, he was more than halfway through.

"I wonder if you'd look at this a minute, Dr. Janson. Do I understand correctly that this is not available in regular form?"

"Yes, Greg. All that means is the journal is on microfilm. You have to ask for it at the Circulation Desk."

"Will they let me have it, do you think?"

"I don't see why not. You're a student in my course and like anyone else you're entitled to use the microfilm. There's a microfilm reader in the stacks on the second floor. Well, here, let's take the number to the desk and make sure they can find it for you when you want it."

As Dr. Janson approached the Circulation Desk, she recognized Phil Matthews, the student working there. Phil had attended one of her classes during the previous year. "Here's someone who'll be able to give you some help," she announced to Greg. "Phil knows the ropes now, since he's been at Eastern for a year already. Phil, this is Greg Hallpen. Greg's taking the Christian education seminar with me this semester. We've found some things that he may be able to use in doing his paper, but he's wondering how he goes about getting the microfilm. Maybe you can help him."

"Let's see what you've got there, Greg. Oh yes, that's some of the un-cataloged material back in Mrs. Lexton's area. The only time we can get that is during the day: at night they lock up the room and we can't get it until the next morning."

"That's no good for me," Greg explained. "The only time I can possibly get here is at night."

"Greg is Christian education director for a local church," Dr. Janson interjected. "He's taking this course as a post-grad."

"I really wish I could help you," Phil responded. "Maybe if you could tell me in advance when you wanted to use the film, I could arrange to get it out of the Catalog Department before they lock it up."

"I'm really not sure that I'll know very far in advance," Greg answered. "There are sometimes meetings that I have to attend in the evenings. I'll have to plan my study schedule around them and just come in whenever I have a free moment."

"This is really ridiculous!" Andrea Janson exploded. "That film was ordered specifically to support work in Christian education. The other materials are out and available for the students. Why isn't the microfilm? How long has it been in the Catalog Department anyway?"

"I'm not sure, Dr. Janson," Phil answered quietly. "Sometimes there's a date on the card in the file. That might give a clue."

As Dr. Janson moved toward the catalog to check the offending entry, it was obvious that she was angry. Her discovery in the file did not improve her attitude: "This card has a date on it that's two years old!"

"I don't know what to say except that I'm sorry," Phil repeated. "I'll call the matter to Miss Crowder's attention in the morning. Maybe something can be worked out."

"Something had better be worked out," countered Dr. Janson. "There's no excuse for a film that's been here for two years not being available to my students whenever the library's open. I'll be back tomorrow to find out what's going to be done about this."

Before Dr. Janson had an opportunity to return, the whole staff was apprised of her feelings about microfilm which hadn't been cataloged in two years' time. Wes Clark was particularly disturbed by the situation, for he valued Andrea's assistance in identifying needed materials in the Christian education field. She had been a good friend of the library, and he did not want to alienate her.

Accordingly, Wes called a professional staff conference. "Audrey, what can we do to solve this problem? It seems to me that the difficulty clearly stems from our deferred cataloging policy for microfilm."

"I suppose the solution would be simple if there were just the one periodical involved. But the title Dr. Janson found is really only one of a fairly large group. She's requested a number of these periodicals over the past couple of years. If there weren't so many, we could just catalog them and put them on the regular microfilm shelves."

"Why couldn't you leave a key to the Catalog Department with the circulation assistant at night?" asked Carolyn. "Then we could get what we needed at any time."

"We used to do that," Audrey replied. "But we had a lot of trouble. The students would forget to lock the doors again. And sometimes they'd leave the desk and go into the staff area for coffee when they were supposed to be on duty. I don't want to get started on that again."

"Well, if we can't have a key, it looks to me that you'll either have to catalog the stuff or put it somewhere so we can get to it at night," Carolyn stated flatly.

"You know we don't have time to catalog it right now," complained Audrey. "We've already got a backlog. And if we move the film to some place in the circulation area, we'll lose control over it. I think we should continue doing what we've been doing. If someone needs the film badly enough, he'll plan his work in advance or arrange his schedule so he can come in during the day. Dr. Janson will just have to understand that we can't always arrange things for the convenience of students who don't live on campus."

•　•　•　•　•

If you were Wes Clark, what would be your reply to Audrey Lexton at this point? What solution would you offer for the problem, and how would you approach Dr. Janson?

What were the causes of the crisis which has arisen over the microfilm? Analyze the validity of the procedures used by Eastern to defer the cataloging of various types of nonbook materials. What better alternatives, if any, have been devised for the handling of such materials as slides, records, manuscripts, and microforms in small libraries with limited staff budgets?

12.
An Author Finds His Book
Misclassified

· · · · · · ·

Birchland University served as the research center for the southern part of the state in which it was located. The local citizens, although proud of the school's reputation, viewed the auspicious institution with mixed emotions. The university undoubtedly had improved the area's economy by attracting grant funds from federal and state governments as well as private foundations; but the size of the campus and the steady flow of strangers into and out of the community somewhat dismayed the long-time residents of the area.

The town of Birchland was university oriented. Were it not for the student trade and for the parents and visitors who populated the many local motels, the community probably could not have existed. There was no industrial development in the region, only agriculture. Thus, it was not surprising that the businessmen of Birchland encouraged the university to schedule conferences, symposia, and various other types of meetings to attract even more visitors. Their livelihood quite literally depended upon the national and international ties of the university.

The Wyth Memorial Library, serving the Birchland University populace, had taken on the functions of a community library as well as a campus one. With its startlingly modern central building, it formed the focal point of the educational plant. As such, it was also a popular tour spot. The staff at Wyth was regularly called upon to show some visiting dignitary through the library. In order to keep from overburdening too many, they had set up a committee to plan and conduct the tours throughout the year. By the time twelve months passed, almost every professional librarian had been called upon at least once to act as host for some visitor.

Walter Smythe, Chief of the Serials Division, was serving as chairman of the tour committee for the current academic year. Thus far, he or one of the four other members had set up tours for better than thirty guests of the university, and the semester was less than two months old. Walter was beginning to understand why his predecessor as chairman had warned him: "This job is the most time demanding and thankless one a staff member can be saddled with. Don't take anything else on this year; you'll have all you can handle if you keep your committee doing its job."

Somehow these days, Walter always seemed to be falling behind in his own work. The Serials Division served as both a public and a technical services unit in that it ordered, cataloged, checked in, and saw to the binding of all of the serial publications received by Birchland. Everything from the daily newspapers to the most irregularly published monograph series found its way into and eventually out of Walter's division. In fact, it often amused him to note that he supervised more staff—thirty-three in all—than many head librarians in small colleges. At their monthly meetings the other division heads regularly gave him a hard time about "building an empire," but Walter knew that it was of utmost importance to a research library to keep its serial publications under control. Thus, when he felt himself getting farther and farther behind in his work because of the demands made by the tour committee assignment, his patience began to wear a bit thin.

"Mr. Smythe," said Kenneth Nelson, as he entered the Serials Division office, "have you had time to check on the status of that order I left on your desk last week?"

"Ken, I'm sorry to admit it, but I haven't the slightest idea what order you're talking about. I've been either giving or planning tours since last Tuesday; today is the first day I've had any time at all to clear off the things on my desk."

"Well, it's just that I'm holding the series while waiting for a decision about whether we'll get a subscription and what you want to do about analytics. I know you don't like us to let things lie around for very long, but I can't do anything more with it until I know how you want it set up."

"I'm really sorry, Ken. Can you recognize it in this pile of stuff?"

"That looks like it down toward the bottom. Yes, that's it."

"O.K., I'll check it right away and bring it to you in a few minutes."

As Ken left, Walter mumbled something unprintable to himself and started out of the office. But before he could get past the door, the telephone rang. "Yes, what is it?" he questioned gruffly as he grabbed up the receiver.

"You certainly don't sound very happy," responded a feminine voice.

"Oh, it's you, Gloria. And what can I do for my boss's beautiful secretary this marvelous morning?"

"That's better! We can't have our chief tour guide going sour on us."

"I hope that doesn't mean you've got another tour in the offing."

"How did you guess? But you won't have to plan this one. The eminent visitor is on his way over to the library right now, accompanied by the vice-president."

"You're kidding! You mean we've got to give him a tour right away?"

"Those are my orders, friend. Who gets the privilege this time?"

"How much time have we got before he gets here?"

"Maybe five minutes."

"Then I suppose I'll have to do it myself. It's nearly ten o'clock and all the sensible people are headed for coffee break by now. O.K., keep him there for a minute or two until I can break away."

"Sorry, I don't think it'll wait. I can already see the vice-president coming down the hall with a somewhat elderly gentleman in tow."

"Thanks a lot. I'll come right up. And remind me to do something nice for you someday."

Putting Ken's problem back on the stack of still untouched work, Walter headed for the director's office. As he entered, he found Gloria Unger, the director's secretary, assuring the vice-president and his guest that "Mr. Smythe will be with you right away."

"Oh, there you are Walter," said Robert Edgewood, Birchland's chief public relations officer. "We have a very distinguished scholar here who's honoring us with a visit. Dr. Barthold, may I present Walter Smythe. Mr. Smythe, this is Dr. Pierre Barthold. Dr. Barthold's field is Christian doctrine, and he teaches at a seminary in Paris. He'll be giving a lecture this evening sponsored by the graduate students in history and philosophy. He's heard about the strong collection we have in church history and asked if he could take a tour of the library."

"We've very happy to have you on campus, Dr. Barthold," responded Walter in what he hoped was an acceptably warm tone. He was still a little annoyed at having to give a tour but tried hard not to show it. "Did you have anything in particular you wanted to see?"

"No, nothing very special," answered Barthold, revealing a fairly heavy French accent. "It would be pleasant if I could spend some time looking at your books in the field of theology and church history. I have a student in Paris who hopes to come to study in America next year. He plans to apply for entrance to your university if the program and the library are suitable. I promised him that I would investigate this while I was here."

"I think, then, that we might just take a general look at the library first. After that, if you want to spend more time in the religion section, we can arrange that. Bob, what time should we plan to be through?"

"It's just after ten now. Why don't you let me meet him in the lobby at noon? We have a luncheon planned for 12:30 and that will give him time to catch his breath before it begins."

"Fine. Now, Dr. Barthold, if you'll just come with me, we'll get started."

Since Barthold was obviously near retirement age, Walter had to keep the pace slow. The professor seemed to be interested in many of the details of ordering and cataloging the collection, so much so that Walter despaired of finishing the general tour in time for Barthold to spend more than fifteen minutes in the stacks. Try as he would, however, Walter could not hurry his visitor.

It was almost 11:30 by the time Walter and his guest returned to the main entrance area of the library. Barthold was still asking questions: "You use the Library of Congress Classification?"

"Yes," Walter answered, "we do now. The director decided that the library should change to that system about ten years ago."

"Why was that? Was the Dewey Decimal system no longer satisfactory?"

"I'm not really sure what the reason was. It happened before I came. But I think that it's more economical. You see, we use printed cards prepared by the Library of Congress, and these cards carry the Library of Congress classification number more often than they do the Dewey. The more help we can get, the less it costs us to process the new materials."

"Our libraries do all their own classification and cataloging work. It would seem that your cataloging would not be so excellent if you have to rely upon the librarians in Washington. In France, we try to prepare the books so that they will best serve our own faculty and students. I would think that you might have many mistakes in your catalog if the work is done so far away."

"That doesn't really happen very much. The books we get are the same as those cataloged by the Library of Congress in many instances. And since we use their classification scheme and subject headings, we have little problem in accepting their cataloging."

"Well, let us look at this marvelous catalog for a moment then. I would like to see what the Library of Congress has done with *my* books."

Walter had not expected this turn of events. He wasn't even sure that

Birchland owned any of Barthold's books. In passing he wondered whether it would be worse not to have any or to have them cataloged incorrectly. But by then, the professor was already opening the catalog drawer and looking for his name.

"I see that you do not have my latest works," he commented rather sharply. "Ah, yes, you do have one of my early ones. This was my seminary thesis: 'La Vie en Christ.' Tell me, is this card one that was done by the Library of Congress?"

"No, sir. That one was done locally. You can tell by the typeface. Those that look as though they were done on a typewriter are ones prepared here. The Library of Congress cards are printed. See, here's one."

"Yes, yes. Then tell me, what does the classification mean for my book?"

"Well, the Library of Congress system is very complex. I would have to look up the number in the system to find out exactly what it means. But you can get some idea by looking at the first subject heading that was assigned. See, down at the bottom of the card, that first heading after number one: 'Jesus Christ—Biography.' "

"Surely you are joking."

"Not at all. You can see for yourself."

"But this is ridiculous. My book is not a biography. It is a work of devotional theology! See, look at the title: 'Life in Christ.' "

"Well, my French isn't very good, but even I can see that you're quite right. Somehow an error must have been made by the cataloger. I'm very sorry. We'll have it corrected, of course."

"I am very much surprised that such a thing could happen in a university having so high a reputation. In France, mistakes of this kind would not be allowed to occur."

"I'm really very sorry, sir. All I can say is that I will see that it's corrected."

"Yes, yes. Very well. I would like to spend a few minutes looking at the religion collection. Then I am to meet Mr. Edgewood here at 12:00, no?"

"He will meet you out in the lobby. Would you like me to come with you into the stacks?"

"No. I would rather that you stay here and see that the cataloging of my book is corrected."

"I'll do that, sir. But if there is anything more you wish before I leave you, please say so."

"No, indeed. I have seen enough. Thank you very much for the tour."

Walter watched the elderly scholar go into the stacks and wondered just how important he really was. "If he carries much weight with Bob Edgewood," he told himself, "this library may be in for a bit of trouble."

"Oh, there you are, Mr. Smythe," said Ken Nelson, rushing up. "I was just about to go to lunch. I can't find the book you said you'd take care of for me. Did you put it on my desk?"

"Frankly, young man, if you value your life you will just go quietly off to lunch and not repeat that question. I'll explain the whole thing to you later, but right now I think I have to see a cataloger about a classification number and subject heading."

Perceptively, Ken simply nodded and left. When he looked back, he could see Walter still standing at the open catalog drawer, shaking his head slowly and sadly.

• • • • •

How well did Walter handle the incident with Dr. Barthold? What should he do now? It might be argued that Ken's problem is a more crucial one than Barthold's since the serial with which Ken was working has current importance. How should Walter set priorities for action at this juncture?

The question of how to control cataloging errors is one which concerns every library. What has been written about the frequency of such mistakes? What steps do libraries take to prevent errors? How likely is it that libraries in other countries would have fewer mistakes in their catalogs?

13.
"The Checking File Disagrees with the Catalog Entry"

• • • • • • • • • • • • •

When the Carnegie Library of Valleyton was established in 1911, the inhabitants of the small community could scarcely have envisioned the population growth which was to take place over half a century later. To them, the new building was testimony to the farsightedness of the local citizens, who, despite a low per capita income, had gathered the funds necessary to maintain a public library collection and library services, thus qualifying themselves for a Carnegie building grant. They would have found it hard to imagine a day when the building would look dingy and overcrowded, with readers vying for a place to sit.

The sudden growth of Valleyton, with the influx of industrial research and development units, had taxed the old Carnegie building to its limit. Under pressure from the Library Board of Trustees and several influential businessmen, the City Council finally approved putting a bond issue to a vote. It passed by a comfortable margin, and Valleyton entered a new era of library service.

Dolores Packer found herself, as a result of the new funds, the Director of the Valleyton City Library System. There was even talk that the next step would be union with the County Library. Miss Packer knew that she would have to be ready for the inevitable expansion of services and construction of additional branch libraries, as well as for the planning of a new central facility.

In its mood of affluence, the City Council also approved the raising of staff salaries and the creation of ten additional positions in the library system. Miss Packer moved quickly to secure promising candidates for the new jobs. Within a year, she was convinced that she now had the staff necessary to undertake the kind of modernization which would make the Valleyton City Library System a significant cultural force in the community.

Although Miss Packer had begun her library work as a reader's adviser in a large municipal system, she monitored the library's technical services very carefully. Her colleagues knew her to be a shrewd manager who kept a watchful eye out for unnecessary routines which could be eliminated. She was determined not to let the procedures of the past dominate the future. In her opening remarks to the new group of employees, she announced firmly, "The one answer which I never want to hear from any of you is 'We do it this way because that's the way we've always done it.' Every routine, every procedure around here is subject to question. If the only reason for continuing a procedure is 'because we've always done it that way,' then that procedure ought to be stopped!"

With Miss Packer, these were no idle words. She prowled the library, looking for problem areas. Her staff could expect to see her appear at any time of the day or night—whenever the library doors were open, and sometimes even when they were not—never interfering, just observing and listening. Later she might comment on what she had seen, or she might send a memo suggesting a possible change. Although a few of the staff viewed her behavior as somewhat paranoid, most of them had learned to respect Miss Packer's integrity. "There's not another library director in this country who knows his library as well as Dolores Packer does," Ron Gregory was heard to say. "And I like it that way!"

Ron had been Circulation Librarian at Valleyton for three years. Although he had received a few other job offers, he liked Valleyton and was ready to stay there for at least another year or two. Among the local attractions was Martha Coolidge, to whom Ron had recently become engaged. Martha was the daughter of one of the members of the library's Board of Trustees; she was also a student in library school at the neighboring university. Ron and Martha had agreed that once she finished her degree, they would investigate the possibility of leaving Valleyton. In the meantime, Martha was working part-time in the Valleyton Library and commuting to classes thirty miles away.

During the next six months, the work entailed by the planning and construction of a new central building kept Miss Packer busier than she had ever imagined possible. Although the plans had long been drawn, changes had to be made once the funding was ascertained. In the period between the approval of the general plans and the final vote on the bond issue, costs had risen; the money would not go quite so far as initially planned. No one was better equipped than Miss Packer, however, to find ways of trimming costs without losing quality of design. But while her attention was directed to library architecture and furnishings, the day-to-day operations of the system had to be delegated to others.

Ron had often wondered why Miss Packer had never requested that the position of Assistant Director be established. "She's not the kind to try to keep all the power to herself," he had commented to Martha. "There's more than enough work now for two people. It's such an obvious answer—I can't figure out why she hasn't thought of it."

Miss Packer had thought of it. In fact, she had already presented the idea to the Library Board and had recommended that Ron be promoted to the position. Martha's father had told her about it, but she was sworn to secrecy until Miss Packer had a chance to tell Ron herself. That chance came during the next day, and Ron was ecstatic. "I'll bet your dad told you about it," he chided Martha. "And you wouldn't tell me."

"I couldn't. You know that. But it was all I could do not to let it slip out when you were talking about how Miss Packer ought to have an assistant."

Ron's jubilation because of the promotion helped to carry him through some difficult days as he began to grapple with the responsibilities of being Assistant Director. Miss Packer had delegated to him the authority to supervise the services offered in the main building. She retained control over the two branches and the bookmobile service. Ron was also asked to spend part of his time planning for the central services in the new building.

In harmony with the lessons he had learned from Miss Packer, Ron made it a habit to use an hour or so each day for observation of the various departments in the main building. During one of these impromptu visits, he was reminded of the growing pains suffered by the Periodicals Department. As Circulation Librarian, Ron had regularly been frustrated by the fact that the check-in record for the magazines was housed in a remote corner of the technical services area. Like many small libraries, Valleyton had never put cards for its periodicals into the public catalog. The current issues of the magazines themselves were displayed conveniently on slanting shelves in one corner of the main adult reading area, but the check-in file had gradually been moved away from the readers, as space problems increased.

The dissociation of the file from the actual periodicals had never been serious enough to cause complaint, so long as there was only moderate use of the collection. However, once the high school and college students began to come in to get materials for their term projects and independent research, the question of the library's holdings of particular magazines arose more frequently. The population explosion which had hit Valleyton did not bypass the public library.

What Ron's latest journey through the Periodicals Department revealed was a line of young people waiting at the service desk. Ron listened to their conversation with the attendant long enough to learn that almost every problem involved the examination of the check-in record. This meant that the attendant had to leave the desk and walk some seventy-five feet back into the technical services area, look up the title in the file, make a note of his findings, and walk back to the periodicals area. As Ron watched, this procedure took place four times in the space of thirty minutes.

It was obvious to Ron that something needed to be done to correct this ineffective arrangement. There was, he realized, no hope of moving the check-in file as long as the library remained in the old building. But he was determined that something should be done to prevent the same pattern from being carried over to the new facilities.

"I wish I could tell you that it won't," Miss Packer answered quietly, when Ron asked her about the periodicals arrangement for the new building. "The plans were drawn before you were appointed to the Assistant's position. Mrs. Belton and I talked it over for a long time, tried setting things up in a number of different ways, and finally concluded that there was no way to put the Periodicals Department close enough to the Technical Services Department so that the check-in record would be available to both. If anything, the distance may be even greater in the new setup."

Ron's next move was to look for solutions in other directions: "If I can't move the file to the patrons, maybe I can get the patrons closer to the file." He decided to call a brainstorming session to try to find the answer. Invited to the meeting were Arthur Ellender, head of the Periodicals Department; Annette Belton, head of the Technical Services Department; and Patricia Wilds, supervisor of the periodicals check-in and bindery unit.

"As you probably know," Ron began, when they had assembled in the staff conference room, "the periodicals desk attendants sometimes have to make as many as a dozen trips daily to look up something in the check-in file. This adds up to a lot of wasted time and motion, and the situation is likely to get worse once we are in the new building. We could operate this way all right when we only had fifty or so titles, but we've got nearly a thousand now, and the list is growing. I've talked to Miss Packer, and she tells me that there is no possibility of bringing the check-in file any closer to Periodicals in the new building. So we've got to find another way. I thought maybe we could bat some ideas around and see what we come up with. Any suggestions?"

"One thing we might do," volunteered Ellender, "is to set up some kind of an intercom system between the periodicals service desk and the check-in file. At least we wouldn't have to run back to the file so much."

Patricia Wilds spoke quickly to object: "I'm afraid that would make life impossible for us. We are having a hard time just keeping up with our jobs now. If one of us has to stop to answer the intercom every few minutes, we'll *never* get all the periodicals checked in. If you set it up that way, then we'll have to have another clerk to take care of the extra work."

"I wonder if it would help any if there were cards for the periodicals in the main catalog," interjected Mrs. Belton. "What do you think, Arthur? Could any of the questions you get be answered that way?"

"What would you put on the cards?"

"Well, we couldn't give you everything you'd get on the checking record, but you'd have a card to show that we have a current subscription and whether we've got any bound volumes. And there would be a location symbol for finding the bound volumes in the stacks. And any that are on film would be noted, of course."

"That would probably answer a lot of the questions. It seems as though a good many of the people just want to know whether we get a certain magazine at all. The school kids are usually looking for back volumes and need to know what's bound or on microfilm."

"Are you sure that's the main type of request?" Ron interrupted. "When I've been around the desk, the questions seemed to be mostly ones like 'Has this week's issue of *Time* come in?' "

"Sure, we get some questions like that," Ellender agreed, "but I would guess that having cards in the catalog would cut our trips to the check-in file by 60 or 70 percent."

"Mrs. Belton, what extra time and money would be involved in putting cards into the catalog for the periodicals?" Ron asked.

"Oh, it would push us a bit for awhile, but I think we could manage it without any extra staff if you'll give us a year to do it in. Or did you want it finished by next week?"

"Oh, I was going to give you a whole month," laughed Ron. "Seriously though, I guess if we've lived this way for this long, we can manage for a year longer. Are we agreed then?"

Hearing no dissent, Ron adjourned the meeting. Mrs. Belton stayed behind to talk about the technics of getting started on the task. She and Ron decided that it would be desirable to work from the check-in file and order Library of Congress cards for each title whenever possible. "Between Pat's staff and mine, I think we can start a clerk doing a little bit each day. With luck, we'll be finished in *less* than a year. But I don't want to crowd things."

About a week later, when Ron was making his rounds of the various departments, Mrs. Belton called him into her office. "I'm afraid we've run into a bit of a snag on that periodicals project," she confessed. "Pat called it to my attention shortly after our meeting, but I didn't think then that it would matter too much."

"What's the trouble?"

"Well, we knew there probably wouldn't be LC cards for all of the titles. What Pat was worried about was the difference between LC's entries and the ones we use here at Valleyton. When that file was first set up, nobody working on it knew much of anything about *cataloging*, much less about LC entries. I suspected there were some discrepancies, but I honestly didn't realize there'd be so many."

"What does this mean in terms of the project, then?"

"I'm not quite sure. If we don't follow LC's entry forms, we're going to add confusion to the catalog. But if we do, we may confuse the patrons and the periodical attendants too. Our shelving pattern is based on the form of entry used in the check-in record. And our bindery titles are done the same way."

"Is it really going to be that bad? Couldn't we just put in some cross references or something?"

"I wish it were that easy. We've got a bunch of things entered in the check-in file under *Journal* and *Bulletin* that LC puts under corporate body. Then there're some others where we've used abbreviations—acronyms mainly—and LC uses a spelled out form. I really can't get a good estimate on how bad the problem is, but I think maybe we'd better reconsider our decision. We may just be creating more trouble than we're solving."

● ● ● ●

Analyze the ways in which Ron has set about to correct the management problem encountered in the Periodicals Department's activities. He appears to be trying to emulate Miss Packer's approach. What limitations, if any, are there to such an approach?

What other solutions to the problem of the remote location of the check-in file might have been considered? What have other libraries done in similar situations?

14.
How Many Errors Does the
Library of Congress Make?

"See, I told you! Granger College is moving into the big time. Any library that buys the full LC proofsheet service is bound to be up there with the big ones."

Although Dorothy Henderson knew full well that her assistant was overestimating the significance of Granger's latest cataloging innovation, it rather pleased her to know that a subprofessional would take that much interest in the procedural changes affecting the Catalog Section. Marnie Nelson had, of course, been at Granger for seven years—certainly long enough to absorb some of the mystique associated with the Library of Congress and its cataloging systems. Even Dorothy recognized that for the old-line catalogers LC served as a sort of "fount of all wisdom" as far as bibliographic data were concerned. This attitude couldn't help but rub off on the subprofessionals.

Historically, Granger's library had relied heavily upon the cataloging services of the Library of Congress. In the 1930s, Esther Welton, first Head of the Catalog Section, had recommended and secured permission for the purchasing of LC card sets instead of typing them all locally. While this hardly seemed a daring move in modern times, it certainly had been one in Miss Welton's day. Despite the financial caution occasioned by a nationwide depression, she had demonstrated clearly that the purchase of LC cards would be no more expensive in the long run that having the sets typed and proofread locally would be. Her carefully argued management analysis of the situation had served the library as a model for further investigation. In fact, Dorothy always felt a bit smug when she heard of the apparently reactionary stance of other college library systems, for no procedure at Granger was immune to challenge or change.

The introduction of the LC proofsheet service had been accomplished in a manner befitting Granger's tradition of management analysis. Elizabeth

85

Rodgers, current Head of the Catalog Section, made it a policy to encourage her catalogers to study other systems and recommend improvements in their own. Dorothy and her three professional colleagues in the section took turns attending various library meetings; and Mrs. Rodgers herself had been the Chairman of the Resources and Technical Services Section of the regional library association. All were members of the American Library Association as well as of the state and regional groups. Dorothy, whose undergraduate major had been in economics, was also affiliated with the Special Libraries Association, so that she could keep in touch with developments in that field.

Mrs. Rodgers and her staff had talked on many occasions about the possibility of subscribing to the proofsheet service. The question had first been raised almost ten years earlier, before Dorothy had joined the staff. From her own recollection, the matter had been discussed at least four times since she arrived. In the past, however, the decision had always been negative, since rough calculations revealed that the library did not acquire enough of the titles represented by the proofsheet service to offset the cost of photoduplicating the cards locally and maintaining the proofsheet file.

Staff meetings preceding the reversal of this decision occurred fairly regularly. In order to show that the use of proofsheets would be economical in a library processing almost 40,000 volumes a year, as Granger now did, Mrs. Rodgers collected data for several weeks before the first of the sessions was called. When the professionals from the Catalog Section gathered in the conference room adjacent to her office, they found copies of the calculations which she had made.

"As you can see from the material in front of you," Mrs. Rodgers began, "I am now convinced that we can use a sufficient number of the current proofsheets to justify putting in a subscription to the entire LC output. Instead of ordering LC cards for recent imprints, we can expect to use the proofsheet as the basis of the card set, duplicating the rest of the cards locally. What we will save by discontinuing the LC card order process for these titles will give us more than enough to offset the cost of duplicating the cards and maintaining the proofsheet file. As you can see, my figures include estimates of the time required to sort and arrange the slips, but I haven't added in the cost of the catalog cases needed to house them or the time required to pull out the old proofsheets when they're no longer used."

"I guess I thought we'd just keep them indefinitely," interrupted Helen Tomlins. "How long do you think they ought to be retained?"

"It seems to me that's a decision we ought to make as a staff. So I'll just turn the question right back to you, Helen. How long will we need to keep them?"

"I guess I hadn't really thought about that part at all. Why couldn't we just keep them indefinitely?"

"One reason would be lack of space," Dorothy answered quickly. "I know the slips aren't as thick as cards, but they still fill a lot of catalog drawers in a year's time. When I went to ALA last summer, I stopped by one of the university libraries that's still using proofsheets. They kept each year's output in a separate section, and I think they told me they threw away a section when it was four years old."

"But we're buying a lot of secondhand books these days," commented Howard Tilson. "If we throw the slips away after three years, then we'll have to use *NUC* for the older stuff. Wouldn't that offset some of the advantages of having them at all?"

"As you can see from just this part of our discussion, there are a lot of factors to be considered before we make a final decision on this matter. Rather than waste time speculating," Mrs. Rodgers interposed, "I suggest that we think in terms of a one-year experiment. This won't get us completely off the hook, you understand; we'll still have to spend some long hours in planning the experiment. But in view of all the 'unknowns' here, I don't see how we can make an informed decision until we invest some time and money in trying it out. If it doesn't work, then we'll be that much wiser, and the loss shouldn't be all that great."

Dorothy felt a little uneasy about the decision to experiment. "It's not that I think it's such a bad idea," she commented to Jo Ann Taylor, as they walked back to their desks. "I just keep thinking that with all the experience other libraries have had with proofsheets, we ought to be able to profit from their mistakes."

"Theoretically, I agree with you," responded Jo Ann. "But when it comes right down to it, each library has its own traditions and staff eccentricities and procedural oddities. I suppose I'm cynical, but I honestly can't see that the experiences of other libraries will help us much. You know as well as I do that half the places using proofsheets never even made an advance study of their advantages and disadvantages. And I'd be willing to lay money on the fact that even less have evaluated the situation afterward."

"I know. You're probably right. I just get a little disgusted with the fact that we have to keep going over the same ground. Somebody ought to be able to come up with some guidelines so libraries won't have to repeat their mistakes forever."

"Fine! When we finish our experiment, you can volunteer to write some."

"O.K., I get the point. I'll shut up and get back to work."

Despite her capitulation to Jo Ann's logic, Dorothy was still not fully convinced that an experiment was necessary. She recognized it, however, as a pragmatic solution, if not the best one; and she participated without complaint in the studies that followed.

Several initial decisions were made concerning the utilization of the proofsheets. Although most of the preliminary negotiations were held only with the professional cataloging staff, Granger College's Librarian, Carl Jimson, joined them on occasion to discuss their progress. In addition, Jack Tarlton, Head of the Order Section, attended most of the meetings and participated in the decisions which had potential effects on his section's work.

A catalog case for the proofsheets was placed in the work area, situated between the Catalog Section and the Order Section, so that the staff in both units would have easy access to it. Since the experiment was designed to last for only a year, no plans were made for retention of the slips; that decision would be contingent upon the success or failure of the year's trial. The proofsheets were ordered cut and punched. One of the clerks in the Catalog Section was assigned to sort them, removing those representing titles in non-Roman alphabets and those for music scores, since Granger bought foreign materials primarily in the Western European languages and it had no program in music.

Once the slips were sorted, the clerk arranged them in alphabetical sequence by main entry. Dorothy and Howard had been in favor of sequencing them by title instead of main entry, but Jack Tarlton had objected on the grounds that it would mean retraining his searchers. Jack had been considering the possibility of refiling all the order records by title, but he didn't want to initiate such a revolutionary procedure without further study. He reasoned, convincingly, that it would be too confusing to introduce another wide-reaching change at the same time that the proofsheet experiment was being conducted.

The Order Section searchers were instructed to check the proofsheet file to try to find card copy for any current item that was about to be ordered. "Current" was defined as published during the calendar year immediately preceding the year of the experiment or during the year of the experiment itself. If no proofsheet was found by the order staff, but an LC card number appeared in the material, then no LC cards were ordered. In such cases, the cataloging staff rechecked the proofsheet file after the material arrived. Those current items for which LC copy could still not be located were then routed to a "Hold" shelf for one month, after which the proofsheets were checked once more. If copy still had not appeared, LC cards were ordered immediately. After the cards came, the proofsheet file was again checked; for those current items, a careful tabulation was made in terms of the final availability or lack of availability of the proofsheet, together with the elapsed time from the initiation of the order to the final cataloging of the material.

At the end of the first three months of the experiment, a preliminary review was conducted. As everyone expected, few conclusions could be drawn so early in the year. Mrs. Rodgers was pleased to note, nonetheless, that proofsheets had been found for better than a third of the current items and that the percentage was rising steadily. She had also prepared some figures showing the average time required to order and receive LC cards for materials not defined as current, but for which LC copy had been found in the *National Union Catalog*. The elapsed time from order date to date of release from the Catalog Section could be expected to be something like three months, without the proofsheet; but her preliminary data showed that with a proofsheet, the time might be reduced to two months, and perhaps less.

"How much strain is this putting on our card reproduction unit?" Howard wanted to know.

"You're right, of course, Howard, in your concern there," responded Mrs. Rodgers. "We knew that having the proofsheets duplicated would increase the load on that unit, though they've been using the same procedure for the cards we do from scratch for some time now. I'm afraid it's too early to detect signs of strain there. Since the same people do our work and the work for the library users and so on, the question of priorities may come up. I have Mr. Jimson's approval for giving the proofsheet duplication work top priority in any event."

"Does that mean that faculty and student copying jobs will have to wait while the cards are done?" asked Dorothy.

"Yes, I suppose it might. Or it might mean that photoduplication would have to add another person. That's part of what the experiment is designed to show."

"I've noticed one problem, Mrs. Rodgers," commented Jo Ann. "But no one else has mentioned it. Have any of you felt that the number of errors on the cards was increasing since we started using the proofsheets?''

"What kind of errors, Jo Ann?" asked Mrs. Rodgers quickly.

"Mostly typographic ones, I think. Misspellings, reversed digits in numbers, things like that."

"Now that you mention it," interjected Howard, "I think I have found more errors in the proofsheets than I noticed when we were using the printed cards. But I don't really see the proofsheets all that often, since most of the work I do is on books that don't have LC copy."

"I guess the reason I see them more is that I revise the work of the people who do standard adaptive cataloging," responded Jo Ann. "I seem to be spending more time making sure that corrections have been made neatly and accurately than I ever did before. And since the slips are not as thick as the cards, we have to be more careful about erasing a hole in them."

"All right, now," said Mrs. Rodgers. "The question is whether there are more errors on the proofsheets than on the printed cards. I suppose, logically, this could be the case. The whole purpose of proofsheets is to give the printer a chance to check the copy and make sure it's right."

"But isn't it still important to find out how much time this is adding to our routines?" asked Helen.

"It would certainly seem so," responded Mrs. Rodgers. "So how do you think we should go about it?"

• • • • •

What procedures would you suggest at this point? How long should the problem be studied before conclusions can be validly drawn about the error rate on the proofsheets? What is the current LC process for producing proofsheets?

Analyze the steps which the Granger Catalog Section has taken thus far in its attempt to decide about the value of using proofsheets. How much validity is there in Dorothy's argument that an experiment ought to be unnecessary in view of the fact that other libraries have had years of experience with proofsheets? How could this experience be systematically tapped?

15

A Special Classification Scheme
for a Special Library

· · · · · · · · · · · · ·

Although the sign on the door read "Information Services," Pauline Templeton still referred to her domain in the First National Bank of Charterville as the library. "I suppose I'll always think of it as the library," she told her roommate, "Even though my new duties are considerably different."

"I'm still not at all sure I understand this new job of yours," commented Anna. "What exactly are you doing that's different from what you did before?"

"It's not so much that I'm doing different things, I guess. It's more that my priorities have changed. Under the old job description, I was pretty much the 'Keeper of the Books'; but now I'm expected to concentrate more on getting information for the staff. All the files of reports and technical data are gradually being transferred to my section. And I'll be getting two more professional librarians—no, 'information specialists'! I've got to start using the right terminology. Anyhow, I'm getting more help to do the job."

"So what are you going to do with all this new stuff they're dumping on you?"

"Anna, you don't have the right attitude about this. They're not 'dumping' it on me. I'm really pleased about the change. Without those files, I haven't been able to answer more than half the questions that come to the library. Now I can begin to do a really good job of providing information— and that's what I've wanted ever since I came to First National. This way, there'll be *one* place for all the staff to call. And all the material will be at my fingertips."

"Sorry, friend. I didn't mean to malign your glorious new job. I just thought you had plenty to do without the added responsibility. But if you like the idea, great!"

"I don't mean to suggest it won't involve more work. But I'll get more satisfaction out of it this way."

"Won't you have some trouble getting those files away from the people who have them now?"

"A few of them aren't too happy about the idea. But Mr. Caldwell has the power to centralize all the materials needed to provide information service. So they don't have much choice. My main problem is what to do with the report literature. It's never been organized very well; if I'm going to be able to use it efficiently, it's going to have to be cataloged in some way or other. But, hey, I'd better get to work. I've got to see Mr. Caldwell at 8:30."

John Caldwell had been an officer of the First National Bank for six years and an employee for twenty. When he accepted the post as Vice-President for Information Services he stipulated that he must be accorded the power to create a centralized system. He had made a few enemies in the process, particularly among the staff of the Advertising Division, because they were used to having certain reports and looseleaf services close at hand.

As Pauline arrived that morning, she heard the end of an exchange between Caldwell and another man, who turned out to be the head of the Advertising Division. Pauline recognized him, as he emerged from Caldwell's office, saying: "All I can do at this point is hold your feet to the fire, John. If that so-called information service of yours slows up our operations in any way, I'm going to the president about it. I'm predicting that this whole thing will be back to normal and the files returned to our office within six months."

"If I were a betting man," called Caldwell after him, "I'd take you up on that. But you just wait and see."

As the advertising manager left, he nodded curtly to Pauline but made no further comment. Pauline stuck her head into John's office cautiously. "Maybe I ought to come back some other time," she suggested.

"Oh, don't let Bill worry you. He's always making dire predictions and threatening to take things to the president. But I know the president is just as anxious for this to work as we are. What Bill doesn't know is that his budget for materials would have been cut anyway. Having the stuff scattered through the whole bank has caused a lot of duplication and wasted time. The president is on an economy kick, and he's not about to let things go on the way they were."

"I guess I'd feel a little better about the whole thing if I hadn't taken a good look at the materials we collected from Advertising. And that's only part of what we'll eventually have to cope with. Honestly, Mr. Caldwell, I don't see how they *ever* found anything. I can't figure that the reports were in any kind of order, except maybe roughly by place of origin."

"I hope you realize, Pauline, that I'm depending on you to put those materials into some kind of usable shape. I'm no librarian. I don't have the slightest idea what to do with them."

"That's what I wanted to see you about. I've looked at the files pretty carefully. The reports are very specialized, in most cases, and I have doubts that we can get Library of Congress cards for them. We've been using the LC Classification for the books in the library, but I really don't think LC will be suitable for these other things."

"Well as I said, ma'am, that's *your* province. Don't expect me to talk intelligently about what classification scheme to use. I wouldn't know a classification system from a card file."

"All I really want is your permission to devise a new scheme for arranging these materials. I've looked at the systems described in the literature and gotten some ideas. I think I can invent a scheme that'll fit our collection better than anything currently available."

"Great! As long as you know what you're doing, go to it. The main thing is to be able to give people like Bill an answer when they call. I don't care how you do it, just do it!"

"Fine. Then I'll get to work."

During the next six months, Pauline labored almost feverishly to get the new materials arranged in manageable fashion. Borrowing from existing systems and inventing some of her own, she gradually constructed a classification scheme for use in filing the report literature. Although the system was basically subject oriented, it heavily reflected the interests of the various departments in First National. In the subarrangement, she tried to preserve the geographic approach which a number of the departments had apparently been using.

Although the new scheme worked quite well for locating information about certain regions, it did not index specific data within the reports. Once her first professional assistant was employed, Pauline shifted attention from the file arrangement problem to that of information indexing. Jerry Morton, the new employee, was inexperienced; Pauline found that, under supervision, he could take care of most of the library routines and answer many of the run-of-the-mill questions coming in by phone. He could not be expected, however, to help her much in the creation of the indexing system.

As time permitted, Pauline scheduled interviews with the staff in the various departments of the bank. From them, she obtained a profile of their information needs and the type of approach they would be most likely to take to the materials. Within another three months, she had the full, though still rough, draft of an indexing system which could, she felt, be successfully applied to the report literature in the bank's information service. In essence, the scheme was a classified one, with an alphabetical index of terms. She hoped, with Caldwell's permission, to attempt to automate the system.

"As I see it," she told him in one of their early morning meetings, "an assistant can select terms from the index list. Then the terms will be keyed into the computer, along with the number of the document as assigned under our present classification system. The computer will then automatically assign the numbers associated with the indexing terms and store the document numbers in conjunction with the numbers of the relevant terms."

"Hold up there a minute! My knowledge of computers is strictly from the calculation end. What you're saying makes a certain amount of sense to me, but as usual I don't have any idea whether it will really work. If you'll draw up a proposal, I'll see whether we can get the computer time needed to try it out."

"Well, we can do it manually with a classed catalog for awhile, but the whole thing will get out of hand before long. The size of the file alone will be tremendous in a few years. It would be more economical to put it on computer before it runs us out of the library."

"Fine. I agree. So write up the proposal."

To Pauline's great pleasure, the computerized version of the indexing system attracted much interest from the bank's president. Although she did not talk with him about it directly, Caldwell reported enthusiastically that the president had liked the idea immediately and authorized an appropriation to implement the system. "And I think some of the money will come out of Bill's budget in advertising," he added gleefully.

A second professional assistant was added to Pauline's staff shortly thereafter. At her request, Jerry Morton was promoted to the post of librarian, to free Pauline to spend full time on the indexing project. Then, upon Caldwell's recommendation, Pauline was accorded the title, Director of Information Systems.

During the ensuing months, Pauline's system became largely operational. She mentioned her work to several other librarians, and her reputation gradually spread. Within a year, she was invited to speak to the local

Special Libraries group about her work, as well as to the regional conference of the banking association. Her work was also cited by the bank's president in his annual report, and he mentioned First National's "automated information system" during a television interview, giving Pauline credit—by name—for having created it.

"You're getting to be so famous, the next thing I know you'll be moving out on me," announced Anna one evening.

"I hope you know that fame is not the moving force in my life. But I have been wanting to mention something to you. Yesterday I got a call from a bank in New York. They've heard of the work I've done here, and they want me to fly up for an interview."

"I guess I'd better start looking for another roommate."

"It may not come to anything at all. But I'll have to admit it sounds very interesting."

"You want me to start packing your things?"

"Oh come off it, Anna. I haven't left yet."

But Anna's confidence proved to be well placed. Within three weeks, Pauline had visited the New York bank and agreed to accept a position as director of an information system three times the size of First National's. John Caldwell expressed his regret at her decision, but he recognized that Charterville didn't have the money or challenge to hold Pauline there.

"I wish you all the luck in the world," he told her. "You've done a really fine job here, and I'm sure New York will benefit from our loss. One thing I'd like to ask, though. Do you think that Jerry Morton could take over your job here?"

"Jerry's certainly bright enough, and he knows our our systems pretty well. Yes, I'd back him for that promotion."

"Good. I think I can get it set up right away so he can start working with you before you leave."

As Jerry and Pauline went over the routines and various responsibilities he would inherit, Jerry seemed to grow more and more depressed. Pauline began to wonder whether the increased demands of her job would prove too burdensome for Jerry. But whenever she tried to talk with him about it, he just passed it off as unimportant.

"I'm worried about Jerry," Pauline commented to John Caldwell during her last week at First National. "He seems to be—well—almost unhappy about the new job. I'm getting a little uneasy about him."

"Don't let it bother you. Jerry's probably just tired. After all, we don't have a replacement for him yet, and he's been trying to do two jobs at once."

"You're probably right. It might be wise to keep an eye on him though. I don't want my system to get messed up before my chair even gets cold."

Caldwell promised to watch over things very carefully. Within a week after Pauline's departure, however, Jerry asked for an appointment.

"Mr. Caldwell, I'm not sure I'm the right person for this job. Miss Templeton was a genius; there's no question about it. The system she invented is really great, and I don't want you to think I don't appreciate what she's done for First National."

"Then what's the trouble, Jerry?"

"I've tried as best I know how, to figure out what she was doing and how she updated the classification scheme she was using. But for the life of me, I can't find any memos even, to show how she did it."

"Didn't you ask her about that when you were learning the job?"

"Yes. And she told me not to worry about it. She said she'd make a few notes before she left. If she did, I can't find them."

"Surely it can't be such a hard job to figure it out from the computer program and the outline of the classification. I think you're overreacting. If Pauline could make it work, I don't see why you can't just keep it going."

"It's not that simple, sir. The program is there and the classification scheme is typed up, but she's made all kinds of handwritten additions to it. And I frankly don't fully understand what she meant by some of the terms she used. It'll take me the better part of two months, I think, to figure out what was going on. And I'm not sure that any updating I do will make good sense."

"Jerry, if you can't do it, I don't know what we can do. You're the only one who's worked with the system enough to understand it at all. And if the documentation on it isn't complete, you're the one best equipped to produce it."

"Well, I don't know, sir. I must say I'm not too happy with the prospects. It would be a whole lot easier if we were working with a standard system instead of one devised locally. I really wonder whether it's worth all the effort to keep it up. I was thinking that maybe a keyword index would do the job just as well."

• • • • •

If you were in John Caldwell's place, what would you do now? Given Jerry's reluctance to inherit Pauline's system, how wise is it to try to maintain that system?

If you had Jerry's job, how might you go about finding out the information needed to keep Pauline's information classification system up to date? What justification would there be, if any, for abandoning her scheme and moving to another approach, e.g., keyword indexing?

What are the dangers associated with the creation of a local classification system? At what point, if any, are the advantages likely to out-weigh the disadvantages?

16.
Why Catalog the Entire Serial Just for One Issue?

• • • • • • • • • • •

"Betty, may I talk to you a minute?"

"Sure, Mariann. Just let me make a note on this invoice and I'll be right with you."

Betty Newton, Chief Acquisitions Librarian, checked and initialled the last of a group of bills, shoved the pile aside, and directed her attention toward Mariann Zenger, Ashley University's principal serials cataloger. "Now, what can I do for you?"

"Take a look at this order slip."

"O.K. What am I looking for?"

"Here's what came with it: volume 20, number 1, for winter of this year. Do you see any indication that we're supposed to get any more issues?"

"You're asking whether we have a subscription?"

"Mainly, whether you're *placing* a subscription. I've already looked in the serials file and there's no slip for it. I assume that means we either haven't ordered it or the order's in process."

"Then you want to know whether any more of it is on order?"

"Yes, please."

"All right. Stay here a minute and let me go look."

Betty took the order slip and moved quickly to a file marked "Continuations." Finding nothing there, she leafed through a few slips awaiting filing. Finally, she asked the Acquisitions Department's chief typist whether she might be in the process of doing the order card. Shaking her head, Betty returned to Mariann. "We don't seem to have any record for it. Do you think we should?"

"I don't really know. It's just that I've never had one like this before. All the material that comes to me is either on subscription or is coming as a gift or exchange. Why did we buy just one issue of the *Southern Banking Review?*"

"You're right. It is sort of strange. What do you think we ought to do?"

"Dr. Ormand in Economics ordered it. Does he come in very often?"

"Sure, we see him all the time. Eco. is putting in a doctoral program, you know, and he's the head of the departmental library committee."

"Nobody ever tells me anything. When did Eco. get a Ph.D. put through?"

"Actually, it's not approved yet, but Ormand was told to go ahead and try to strengthen the collection. Everyone says it's just a matter of time; the money's already there, thanks to our friendly local business community."

"If that's the case, I'd think Ormand would be putting in a subscription to *Southern Banking Review* and maybe even ordering a back file. I wonder why he just asked for one issue. Well, there's not much percentage in speculating. Will you ask him about it?"

"Be happy to. He's a nice guy. He probably meant to order the whole thing, anyhow."

"Thanks, Betty. Let me know what happens, will you?"

"Sure. Just as soon as I see him."

As might be expected, Dr. Ormand failed to make one of his almost daily visits to the Acquisitions Department that afternoon. But when he stopped by her desk the next morning, Betty showed him the order slip and asked whether he had meant to put in a subscription."

"To tell the truth, Mrs. Newton, I don't really remember. We've been ordering so much these last few weeks that all the titles are beginning to look alike. Still, I know something about the *Southern Banking Review;* it's a pretty good journal. Sure, go ahead and put in a subscription."

"What about getting the back run?"

"No, I don't think we really need that right now. We can pick it up later on if we want it."

A few minutes later, Betty encountered Mariann at the card catalog. "I just got the word from Ormand. He says that he's favor of getting a subscription, so I'm putting it through that way. Can I get the slip and the first issue back from you?"

"It's on the top of my desk. Just pick it up as you go by. And thanks."

When Mariann returned from lunch, she was somewhat startled to find a foot-high pile of periodical issues in the center of her desk. "What's all this?" she mused. "I wonder where this came from."

A preliminary glance at the slips in each issue showed them to be a contribution from the Gifts Section. All of the items were journals in economics, and no one of them showed that a subscription had been entered.

Mariann was puzzled. Seeing Harold Greene, Gifts and Exchange assistant, sitting at his desk, she picked up the issues and headed his way.

"Hi, Mariann. What's on your mind?"

"Harold, it seems I have a problem. Do you know anything about this stack of new periodicals?"

"Let me look at them. Oh, those! Yeah, those are the ones Ormand asked me to get for the Eco. Department. What's wrong? Did I goof them up or something?"

"I really don't know. Yesterday I got one from Acquisitions with no sign of a subscription having been placed. Now these. What did Ormand say when he asked you to get them?"

"He said to request sample copies and let him see them. After they came in he looked them over and told me which ones he wanted cataloged, and he took the rest away with him."

"So you just sent them on to me?"

"Only the ones to be cataloged."

"Great. I guess it didn't occur to you to give them to Betty to have a subscription entered. What am I supposed to do with just one issue?"

"Look, I don't know anything about this except what I was told. Ormand asked me to order sample copies, and he told me which he wanted cataloged. He didn't say anything about any subscriptions."

"And I suppose you didn't ask him, either!"

"Why should I?"

"Well it seems to me that anybody with a grain of sense would know that you don't catalog one issue of a periodical by itself."

"Now look. If you're going to stand there and blame me for doing what I was told, I'm going to leave. You can do whatever you damn well please with the stuff. Just leave me out of it!"

With that, Harold jumped up from his desk and strode out toward the public catalog. Mariann was furious, but she at least had the good sense to let her temper cool a bit before she took the matter to Betty. As calmly as she could, she recounted her conversation with Harold; but by the time she had finished the story, she was angry again.

"Betty, I've got better things to do with my time than catalog a bunch of sample issues."

"I understand, Mariann, but Harold was right when he said he was just doing what he was told. He's not a professional librarian, and we've given him specific instructions not to question the faculty's judgment. You should have brought the matter to me before you gave Harold such a hard time. It's not really his fault."

"I guess you're right and I'm sorry. But you'd think that even Harold would have the sense to ask whether they wanted a subscription. So what do we do now?"

"We talk to Ormand again, poor man. He's going to get pretty tired of all these problems, I'm afraid. It's a good thing he's a patient man. Leave the stuff with me, and I'll ask him about it next time he passes through."

Dr. Ormand obligingly wandered in that afternoon, and Betty directed his attention to the pile of periodicals which Mariann had left with her. "Dr. Ormand, we seem to have a small problem here. Our Gifts and Exchange assistant says that you told him to have these issues cataloged. But you didn't say anything about placing a subscription."

"That's right, Mrs. Newton, I only want these. We don't need subscriptions."

"I'm afraid I don't understand. Are you saying that you want us to catalog a single issue of a periodical?"

"Sure, why not?"

"What good would a single issue do you or your students?"

"Mrs. Newton, there's an awful lot of trash in the economics and banking field. Some of it shouldn't be in the library at all, but material like this is valuable under certain circumstances. We want our students to be able to come to the library and see examples of the periodicals they might use, even though we don't have the money to subscribe to all of them. Besides, most of these wouldn't be used more than once or twice a year, if that."

"If you don't mind, Dr. Ormand, I'd like you to talk to our Serials Cataloger, Miss Zenger. She can tell you what such a policy would mean to the library. I think there may be some factors that you're not aware of."

"Well, I don't have an awful lot of time right now. Could we do it in the morning? Say at 9:30?"

"I'm sure that will be fine. I'll tell Miss Zenger to meet us here at 9:30."

When Betty reported the gist of the conversation to Mariann, she almost caused an explosion.

"He didn't really say that. He couldn't have said that. You must be kidding."

"I know it sounds crazy to you. But that's exactly what he said. They want a collection of sample issues to show the graduate students what's available in the field. And they don't want to put in a subscription or get back volumes."

"All I can say is it's a good thing the afternoon's almost over. I just can't cope with such foolishness anymore today. I'll see you in the morning. Maybe I'll take a tranquilizer or something to calm me down. This day has been simply ridiculous!"

Mariann, for whatever reason, seemed much calmer the next morning. When Dr. Ormand arrived, she greeted him pleasantly. "I understand, Dr. Ormand, that there is some confusion about the library policies relating to the handling of new periodicals."

"Frankly, Miss Zenger, there's no confusion in my mind. We have ordered some sample issues and we'd like to have them cataloged. I don't see what the policies of the library have to do with this at all."

"Perhaps I phrased it badly. But it seems to me that you don't fully understand what the library must do to catalog one issue of a periodical. The system that we follow requires us to catalog even a single issue as if we were dealing with the whole set of volumes. The cards are prepared on the assumption that we might fill in our holdings at some later date. We have to do a full bibliographic search to establish the form of the entry, find out if there have been any title changes or major changes in format or coverage. It's not a simple process, and it costs us a lot of money. Sometimes I spend as much as four or five hours on just one journal!"

"That's indeed interesting. I had no idea you did all that. But the fact remains that we have no plan to buy anything more than these issues. I really can't see why you can't just give them a number—or whatever it is that you do—and put a card in the catalog under the title. Nobody cares how many other titles it may have had in the past. And, as I said, we certainly don't plan to buy any future issues."

Mariann had prepared herself for an argument, but she had not expected Ormand to be so adamant. Faced with what she viewed as a stubborn refusal to give up, she decided to withdraw to regroup her forces and call up reinforcements. "We seem to be at a stalemate here," she said. "I think maybe I'd better talk with the head of the Catalog Department at this point. Perhaps I can talk to you again later."

"All right," Ormand agreed somewhat reluctantly. "But I'm not sure if there's anything left to say. It may just be a matter of whether or not the library is going to do what the faculty asks."

Both Betty and Mariann winced a bit at the last remark. Neither was looking for a confrontation, although Ormand seemed to be moving in that direction. Mariann broke away quickly when she saw Winston Holton, Head of the Catalog Department, enter the room.

"Mr. Holton, I seem to have gotten myself into a bit of trouble. I thought I could handle it without bothering you, but I guess I was wrong."

"O.K., Mariann. What's the problem?"

As rapidly as she could, Mariann recounted the discussions which she had had with Harold, Betty, and Dr. Ormand during the past two days. Holton began to look a trifle worried.

"Is Dr. Ormand still around?" he asked Mariann.

"Let's see; yes, I believe he's still talking to Betty. Do you want me to ask him to come over?"

"No. I think I'll just go talk to him for a minute. Why don't you go on with your work? I'll handle it from this point on."

Mariann reluctantly moved back to her desk. She was sure that she was right in not cataloging single issues of periodicals; nevertheless, the look on Holton's face told her that she had gone too far without consulting him. Dejectedly, she picked up the item on top of her desk, only to discover that it was another non-subscription, single-issue item. "Here we go again," she told herself.

• • • • •

Analyze the behavior of each of the principals in this situation. To what degree did each discharge his responsibilities properly or improperly? How could the unpleasantness associated with several of the discussions been avoided?

What arguments can Holton present, beyond those offered by Mariann, against the cataloging of a single issue of a periodical which will not be placed on subscription? What compromises could be offered to satisfy Ormand's purposes without committing the library to the expense of cataloging a lone issue? What problems, if any, would be encountered if the library accepted Ormand's suggestion to put a number on the issue and one card, under title, in the catalog?

If the stalemate continues—that is, if Ormand will not compromise and Holton refuses to catalog the issues—how is it likely to be resolved? Who holds the power in this clash of viewpoints?

17.
"A Misfiled Card
Is a Lost Card"

· · · · · · · · · ·

"I don't care how nice a guy he is—he's a management nut!" With those words Miriam turned her back on Phil and nearly ran into the Head Cataloger of Anderson University, Rolene Burnet.

Miriam Corren was the newest reference assistant in the Anderson Library. And, as Phil Walton had discovered, Miriam had strong ideas about almost everyone and everything. Most of these ideas were voiced during the daily morning coffee break. It was at the end of one such interlude that Miriam barely missed colliding with Mrs. Burnet.

Phil had worked in the Reference Department with Miriam long enough to be able to listen to her outbursts and not get too deeply involved. He had worked his way up to Assistant Head of the Department; he knew some of the frustrations that Miriam must be enduring. Still, Miriam was inclined to be quick tempered, and her reactions were not always based on full knowledge of the situation. This was what Phil was trying to point out when Miriam had finished berating the new assistant to the library director. "If you'd get to know him, you'd find that he's really a nice guy, and he's trying to do a good job."

Miriam's objection to the new assistant, Sheridan Allen, centered upon the fact that Mr. Allen had been employed specifically to design better procedures and gather data for a full-scale systems analysis. Staff gossip had it that he would be a "hatchet man," looking for inefficiency and recommending to the director the firing of nonproductive personnel.

Phil had heard all the gossip, but he also knew that Allen had been a management engineer for a tool manufacturing company before he went to library school. Phil figured that anyone who would take an extra year to learn the library business—and probably take a cut in salary—deserved to be given the chance to prove his worth. "Lord knows," Phil had commented when the Allen appointment was announced, "this library could use some improvement in efficiency." He was not particularly amused when Miriam, who had overheard the remark, suggested that the efficiency might begin with the Assistant Head of Reference "who regularly takes twenty minutes for a fifteen-minute coffee break."

Despite Miriam's comments and dire predictions of corporate disaster in the library, brought on by Allen's "harebrained schemes," Allen proved to be a "nice guy" and generally won the support of the administrative staff. Even some of the lower echelon could be heard to comment favorably on a few of his labor-saving suggestions.

Miriam noted sarcastically that Phil had been brainwashed. "You just wait till he turns his beady little stop-watch eyes in the direction of the Reference Department. Then you'll find that being a nice guy won't help a bit." But Allen was spending most of his time in the Catalog Department and consulted very infrequently with the reference staff.

There were various rumors emanating from the Catalog Department about adjustments being made in some of the routines. Miriam reported to Phil that one of the changes was in the filing procedure. A tabulation was being kept of the number of errors made by each filer, as noted by the filing revisers, but no one seemed to know what was to come of the study. A couple of weeks later, Phil picked up the information that many of the filers would no longer be "revised" (he had always wondered why "checking up" on someone's work was called "revising" in libraries). Since the Catalog Department staff always seemed to be going through crises regarding the filing of cards, Phil decided that Allen had once again "picked a winner."

Some months later, Phil had to admit that he had been just a bit worried, initially, that the elimination of filing revision might increase the errors. Allen had assured the head of reference, in an administrative staff meeting, that the statistics showed that well-trained filers made, on the average, less than one error per hundred cards filed. Further, Allen had maintained, when the revisers were themselves revised, they were found to miss between 10 and 20 percent of the filers' errors. Once this was reported to Phil, he decided that his fears had been groundless.

Approximately six months passed after the revision of experienced filers had been abandoned before any major problem arose. In fact, Phil had almost completely forgotten about the change, until he was uncomfortably reminded of it by Miriam's loudly-voiced complaint.

"Hey look," she demanded. "Here's this list that I was supposed to check for the French Department of items they want ordered. I've just checked the first six books, and found five filing errors. What's going on around here?"

Although Miriam was outspoken, she was—as Phil had always been ready to admit publicly—the most reliable staff member they had, at least in terms of her attention to bibliographic detail. If she said that she had found five filing errors, Phil had no question about the accuracy of the statement. "What did you do about them?" he asked.

"I haven't done anything yet, because I'm too angry to talk to anyone but you." Phil breathed a little easier after that, for Miriam had not always shown such restraint.

"You know, this could just be a fluke," Phil replied. "Over the years any catalog is bound to have filing errors. The ones you found probably were made decades ago and you just happened to see them now."

"Good try, boss," responded Miriam. "Even *I* thought of that. But these are new imprints, and the cards that were misfiled were all recent ones. I know because I went back and checked."

"O.K. You win. I'll have to talk with Jean to find out how we should handle this. It sure looks like our management expert has done us in this time." With this, Phil trotted off to find Jean Hulbert, Head of the Reference Department.

Jean listened to Phil's account of Miriam's problems, went with Miriam to look at some of the offending cards, and arranged to call a meeting of her staff the next morning. When all of the reference personnel were assembled, she asked if anyone else had noticed an increase in the number of filing errors. Two of the library assistants—ones who worked primarily on interlibrary loan requests—reported that they had found more errors in recent months, but they had just assumed that it was to be expected in a large file. Jean wanted to know where they had gotten that idea, and one replied, "Well, that's what one of the catalogers told me when I mentioned it."

After Jean had adjourned the meeting, she talked with Phil again. "I wish I could be sure that this is really a trend and not just coincidence. One of my deep prejudices is against misfiled cards. On my first job I had to file a lot, and the reviser nearly drove me crazy by repeating, every time I made a mistake, 'A misfiled card is a lost card.' I hated that reviser until I started working in reference; then I learned what she meant."

Jean's decision was to call Mr. Allen and ask for an appointment to discuss "a problem which has arisen in connection with the filing in the card catalog." Allen volunteered to come to Jean's office immediately. Phil and Miriam were summoned to participate.

After Sheridan Allen had heard the evidence which Miriam presented, along with the comments from the interlibrary loan assistants, he expressed his regret at what had happened. "I really don't think the lack of filing revision had anything to do with this, though. All new filers are revised until they achieve a 99 percent level of accuracy. After that, they are turned loose. But they are spot-checked at irregular intervals. They don't know when this will happen until right before they begin to file."

"I realize that you are using all the right precautions," said Jean. "But I used to file, and I know that my level of accuracy varied considerably from day to day. My state of mind had as much to do with it as anything. And sometimes, I would be interrupted by a friend who wanted to talk while I filed. On those days, my reviser was nearly ready to fire me."

"Yes, we are well aware of individual differences and changes in mood. When a filer's accuracy is calculated, it isn't just for one day's run; it's over a period of a couple of weeks, with at least two hours of filing a day." Allen then described exactly what the calculations involved and volunteered to go back to his office for more detailed information if Jean would like.

"I know your system is saving the Catalog Department a lot of money," Jean admitted, "but I still worry. I just keep thinking that 'a misfiled card really is a lost card' as far as the reference staff is concerned."

Phil winced when he saw Miriam's triumphant and somewhat malevolent smile. Without saying a word, she was clearly conveying the message: "I told you so." And Phil remembered that indeed she had. "How do you decide between inexpensive procedures and a quality product?" he wondered. "Or is that really the issue?"

• • • • •

If you were the Assistant to the Library Director and you were charged with causing an increase in filing errors as a result of your management decision, how would you proceed to defend that decision now?

Was the management expert wrong in his decision? What fallacies, if any, were present in his reasoning concerning the need for continued filing revision of experienced workers?

At no point has the Catalog Department staff been brought into the discussion, except in conjunction with the earlier question raised by the interlibrary loan assistant. Should the reference staff have gone directly to the head cataloger (or to the filing reviser) rather than to the assistant to the director?

Is a misfiled card *really* a lost card? Why?

18.
The Best Books Take Longer to Get Cataloged

· · · · · · · · · · · ·

Robert Johnson cleared his desk of the last of the day's cataloging snags and cleared his mind of the problems of being Head Cataloger at the Centertown Public Library. The weekend beckoned cheerfully to him, and he had promised himself that the next two days would be completely relaxed. "All I want to do is to lie in the sun, eat, sleep, and read," he had announced on Friday to Miriam, his wife.

"Well, if you're going to be so lazy, the least you can do is to bring home something good for Bobby and me to read. Seems to me that there ought to be some fringe benefits from being married to a librarian."

Remembering Miriam's admonition, Bob decided to stop by the Children's Room to pick out something for Bobby and then get a book for Miriam from the Current Literature Shelf. There was no trouble in selecting an item for Bobby—the boy was all wrapped up in science fiction and space travel. Mrs. Anderson, the Children's Librarian, had selected things for Bobby before and was able to find a book which she knew Bobby wanted to read. It had been in circulation and had just been returned.

Getting something for Miriam proved to be more troublesome, for the Current Literature Shelf was populated with titles which Miriam had already read or which would not, he was certain, agree with her idea of enjoyable reading for a lazy weekend. Bob was about to give up in despair, when he remembered that one of those annoying cataloging snags was actually a best-selling biography of a leading French politician. Miriam had majored in history, with emphasis on French history; the book would certainly please her, and its reviews had been very good.

Returning to his desk, Bob quickly removed all the cards and slips from the book, which had been placed on the typist's shelves for completion of the catalog cards. Feeling rather pleased with himself, he headed for the loading dock exit, waved a happy goodby to Bill Martin, the library's maintenance man, and drove cheerfully home to begin his glorious weekend.

"I sure was right about those fringe benefits," crowed Miriam, when she saw what Bob had brought. "I've been wanting to read that book for months. The wretched publisher won't put it out in paperback, and it sells for $10 or something like that. But you may be sorry you brought it. I'm likely to stay up all night reading it!"

Bob could hardly imagine staying up all night to read a biography—and of a Frenchman at that—but he was glad that Miriam was pleased. Bobby, too, was delighted with the book selected for him, and the weekened promised to be a success.

The weather didn't cooperate much. Saturday was a dreary, showery day. Still, the Johnsons were resilient, and they easily amused themselves indoors with their respective reading matter. Late in the afternoon, however, a call came from Miriam's father. Miriam's mother had suddenly been taken quite ill, and the doctor wanted her in the hospital. Miriam told her father that they would meet him at the hospital as quickly as possible. The relaxed weekend was unquestionably over.

To everyone's relief, Miriam's mother was not seriously ill. The doctor assured them that she would be able to leave the hospital in a few days, but he wanted her to stay for observation. On Sunday her mother was feeling much better and highly restless. "I wish I had something good to read. I've been through all these magazines and I'm tired of watching television. Why don't you bring me a good book?"

Miriam remembered her highly-prized biography and decided to be generous. "I know Mother will like it," she told Bob. "I think I inherited my interest in French history from her anyway. You don't mind if I let her read it, do you?"

"Be my guest," Bob replied.

"O.K.," she said. "In that case I'll run over to the hospital with it now, before visiting hours are over."

"Good. Maybe that will give me a chance to get back to my book. This weekend hasn't gone according to plan at all!"

Bob had little occasion to reflect on the incident until Thursday of the next week. He was busily engaged in plotting work schedules and training sessions for a couple of newly employed clerks when Ralph Saunders from the Reference Department came up. "What can I do for you, Ralph?" Bob asked.

"I've got an impatient patron out front who says it's been over a month since he was told a book he wanted had arrived. It still hasn't been cataloged—at least there's no card for it—and he's really angry. He says someone (I haven't the slightest idea who) told him he could have it in two weeks, and it's been a month. Do you think you could track it down? The order file shows that it came in a month ago. It must be somewhere in cataloging."

"Can you stall the guy for awhile—like a day or two?" Bob inquired.

"Maybe, but I'll have to promise him that I'll call him by tomorrow afternoon at the latest."

"Good enough. I'll certainly be able to locate it by then. Leave the information with me, and with luck I'll have it for you before the day's out."

As soon as Bob saw the author and title of the book, he realized that luck was certainly not with him. "I don't know why I didn't ask him what it was," he chided himself. "But if I had, I don't know what I would have told him. How do you tell a colleague that the reason his irate patron can't find the book he wants is because you have taken it home to your wife?!"

Within minutes, Bob was calling Miriam. "Hi, honey, what's up?" she asked, as she recognized his voice.

"Oh it's that miserable book I brought to you. A man is here waiting for it. Somebody promised it to him a couple of weeks ago, and now he's angry because we can't produce it. Could you get it back from your mother and bring it down to the library this afternoon?"

"I really don't see how I can, honey. Mother's gone to the doctor for a checkup. The only reason he let her go home was that she promised she'd come into the office today so he could make sure she's all right. I know I won't be able to reach her for at least another hour."

"I guess that'll have to do. I told Ralph that we'd try to locate the book today, but if I can get it by tomorrow, that should be time enough."

"I'll call her as soon as I think she might be home. Don't worry, you'll get the silly book back. But I guess I'll never get to finish it."

"If you get it back by tonight, I'll buy you a copy. See you later."

Bob managed to avoid Ralph for the rest of the day. But at home that night, Miriam's news was not encouraging. "You're not going to like this, dear. Mother finished the book while she was in the hospital. Being the generous soul that she is, she lent it to the woman sharing the room with her. And now that woman's left the hospital and we haven't been able to reach her. Mother thinks she was going to stay with her daughter for awhile, and we don't know her daughter's name."

"Oh, great! What do I tell Ralph?"

"I guess you'll just have to tell him the truth."

"Yeah, sure, just like that. He doesn't like me all that much anyway. This'll give him all the ammunition he needs to cut me down sometime when he wants to make the Catalog Department look bad. There's got to be some other way."

By breakfast time, Bob had come up with an ingenious solution. "I'll call the office, tell them I've got an errand to do before I come in, and then I'll go by the bookstore—be there when it opens at 9:00—and buy a copy of the book to replace the one you lent your mother. How's that?" asked Bob, triumphantly.

"That's great," Miriam answered, with something less than complete enthusiasm. "I just hope they aren't sold out. The whole thing sounds a little sneaky to me, but I suppose it will solve the problem. Have you got enough money with you?"

"They'll charge it to our account. It'll work out, you'll see."

Bob was at the door when Baker's Bookstore opened that Friday morning. "Hi, Mr. Johnson. We haven't seen you for a month or two. You used to be one of our best customers." The greeting was extended by the owner, Jim Baker, whom Bob had known for several years.

"I'll be your best customer again if you can help me out now," responded Bob. "Can you sell me a copy of Rouget's biography of Piagette, in a hurry?"

"Wish I could. We're all out at the moment. I'm expecting a new shipment any day now, but you know how it is: it could come this morning or next week, for all I can tell."

"Jim, this is terribly important. Do you have any idea where I could buy a copy? I've got to have it this morning."

"Well, I don't usually like to send business to my competitors, but I think that Warren might have it in stock at his store out on the West Loop. I'll even let you use my phone to call him, if you like."

"You're a true friend. Many thanks," said Bob gratefully.

Warren's store did have a copy of the book, and the clerk agreed to hold it for Bob. It took more than twenty minutes to drive out to the Loop, and Bob had to write a check to cover the price; but when he finally got to the library, a little after ten o'clock, he had the book in hand.

While the rest of the staff was on the morning coffee break, Bob got a plastic book jacket from the Order Department, attached it to the book, put the source information on the title page, and handwrote the accession number at the bottom of the title page. Then he put the cards and workslip into it and put the volume on the typist's desk. When she came back from coffee break, Bob asked her to rush the book through, which she promptly did.

Half an hour later, the book was back on Bob's desk, ready for Ralph's customer. Triumphantly, Bob took it out to Ralph.

"Where was it all that time?" Ralph asked, a bit irritatedly.

"Oh, there was a hangup about the form of the name of the biographee. The Library of Congress couldn't make up its mind about his middle name. I'm sorry it took so long, but evidently no one marked it 'rush,' and we just put it through the normal routines. It was waiting for the typist to finish with it."

"O.K., and thanks. It would be nice, though, if these bestsellers could be processed more quickly. It's bad enough to have to wait for the jobber to get around to sending them. If the cataloging gets fouled up, too, it's really a mess. And those of us on the 'firing line' wind up taking the blame."

"Yeah, I guess you do, at that. I'll see what I can do to try to speed things up," responded Bob, a bit guiltily, though Ralph only viewed it as an unusually conciliatory attitude.

It was Friday afternoon again, and Bob prepared for his weekend with considerably less enthusiasm than had marked the previous Friday. As the rest of the cataloging staff got ready for the mass 4:30 P.M. exodus, Bob saw Geraldine Kelley, his chief assistant, pick up a volume from the booktruck next to the typist's desk. As she started to walk out with it, Bob called her back.

"What are you doing with that book?" he demanded.

"I was just taking it home over the weekend for my husband to read," she answered defensively.

"Those books aren't processed yet. The staff isn't supposed to take home anything that isn't ready for the shelves," countered Bob.

"But Mr. Johnson," protested Geraldine, "we've always taken new books home while they were still in process. Nobody can check them out, so we're not depriving anybody. I always bring them back by Monday. What harm does it do? They'd just be sitting here till Monday, doing no one any good."

"You may have 'always done it,' but that doesn't mean it was a good thing. From now on, nobody in the Catalog Department will take home any book which hasn't been fully processed and properly checked out at Circulation. Is that clear?"

"Yes, sir. I'm sorry, but I didn't think I was doing anything wrong," responded Geraldine, almost in tears. She replaced the volume on the book-truck, turned, and walked quickly out the back door without further comment.

Bob felt like a heel. "I don't care, though," he counselled himself. "I've learned my lesson, and things are going to be different around here from now on."

• • • • •

Review Bob's actions throughout this "crisis" situation. Did he make any mistakes in judgment? What might he have done differently, and what might the outcome have been if he had changed some of his decisions?

Two extremes in policy relating to the circulation of uncataloged books have now been observed at the library. What other policies could be instituted which might be more reasonable solutions to the problem than the rather restrictive one which Bob has now imposed?

To what extent might the problem have been forestalled by instituting "priorities" in the cataloging of newly-acquired materials? What types of cataloging priorities, if any, might be established for a public library like this one?

19

"Why Is Everything I Want Always at the Bindery?"

. . . .

Mary Carter had one favorite sentence which she inserted into the conversation whenever someone complained about a library routine that caused difficulty for a user: "The trouble with this university is that it's too big to respond to the little people." And although it usually annoyed Mary's co-workers when she voiced her oft-heard platitude, many of them were forced to agree with her.

State University was indeed large: 20,000 students, give or take a thousand. Nobody ever spoke in terms of individuals; only large numbers seemed to be of any consequence. The library had a huge central building and numerous satellites scattered in remote corners of the campus. Anne Warrnet, head of the library's Bindery Section, found herself unable to remember precisely how many different locations were serviced, but she knew there were more than thirty-five.

Other than the director or associate director of the library, Anne was the only person who might be expected to remember where all the various departmental and special collections were housed, for she was the one who deployed clerks and student assistants throughout the campus to collect and bring in the periodicals and serials in need of binding. Despite the apparent decentralization of the collections, the Technical Services Division maintained tight control over all acquisitions and cataloging functions, including the physical processing of library materials. Thus, Anne and her workers were expected to do the actual gathering of bindable units; they could not delegate the task to a departmental librarian.

The Bindery Section was no small operation. While Anne was the only professional in the unit, she supervised a corps of library assistants, clerks, and student workers. During the height of the school year there were usually some fifteen people involved in binding procedures. That number might increase to twenty or more during a particularly affluent summer.

The sequence of operations followed in binding periodicals and other serial publications was one which had not changed significantly since Anne had joined the library staff five years earlier. However, she had only been made head of the unit during the previous year, and she felt that she was still learning routines. Once she understood them all, Anne hoped to be in a better position to suggest alterations.

The basic procedure was not at all difficult to remember. There were, of course, dozens of exceptions related to such difficulties as the lack of a title page or index, the replacement of missing or damaged issues, and changes in title or format. It was possible, nonetheless, to describe the fundamental routines in a few introductory paragraphs to the section's procedure manual:

The basic steps in gathering materials for binding are as follows:

1. Pull a group of bindery cards from the Bindery File.

2. Since all of State's serials are classified, retain the bindery cards in the classification order maintained in the file. Work with no more than twenty cards at a time and take them to the stacks (or departmental library).

3. Find the current issues of each title represented by the cards in hand. Work systematically from one card to the next, completing the work on one before going on to another.

4. Look at the bindery card for the call number, the author and/or title, and the binding instructions. Then look at the issues on the shelf to determine whether a volume is ready to be bound. No current issues should be removed for binding unless at least one issue of the next volume (or binding unit) is on the shelf. (In other words, do not take away the latest current issue even if it completes a binding unit.)

5. When a bindable unit is found, put a strong rubber band around all the issues; place the bindery card just inside the cover of the top issue. It is not necessary at this point to determine whether the volume has any missing issues, but be sure that no issues which belong to that binding unit are left on the shelf.

6. Put the unit (or units) of that title on a booktruck, and continue the procedure by taking the next bindery card, etc. (see step 4).

7. When all bindery cards have been checked against the shelves, take the truck back to the Bindery Section. Cards for which no bindable unit could be pulled should be given to the section head, who will determine what further steps must be taken.

Anne's job consisted of looking at the bindery card to ascertain whether the shelf had been previously checked without a binding unit having been pulled. A pencilled notation was placed on the back of the card whenever this occurred. However, once a bindable unit had been pulled, the pencilled date representing an unsuccessful previous check was erased. If Anne found no pencilled date, she examined the title for any peculiarities that might suggest a further check; if none were found, she pencilled on the current date and sent the card back to the Bindery File. Those cards that showed a previous date were held for further checking to determine whether something had gone wrong with the subscription or some frequency change had been introduced by the publisher of the serial.

The volumes which had been banded and returned to the section were then checked carefully for completeness. Two of Anne's more experienced assistants worked with these items. When they had finished with a truckload, the units were dispersed in several directions: to the shelflister, if the unit was complete and involved no change from the previous handling; to a "Hold" shelf, if the unit was incomplete in some respect (missing issue, mutilated issue, missing title page or index); or to the section head, if the unit had some special problem associated with it (separate supplements, a title change, a major format change, etc.).

Those units which were cleared for shelflisting were then entered as bound volumes on the shelflist card. The full call number was pencilled inside the volume on the title page, and the unit was forwarded to the bindery typist. The typist used the bindery card and the pencilled call number as the basis for preparing a multipart form supplied by the commercial binders with whom the library had a contract. One section had been added to that form: a slip which could serve as a notice to the Circulation Department that the volume had been processed for the bindery. Once the typing of the multiform had been completed, it was proofread by one of the assistants; and, if all was correct, the various parts of the form were separated and sent to the appropriate files. At that point, the circulation record was released.

The Bindery Section maintained a rather elaborate group of files for items in various states of completion. Volumes which were being held for some reason were represented in a file in the section, but no multiform slips were prepared for them until they were either released for binding or were "boxed" for the shelf and entered on the shelflist. In the latter case, the Bindery Section forwarded the box and its contents to the Processing Section for marking, etc., and assumed that the return of the issues to the shelves would obviate the need for a circulation record.

If all of the binding procedures were going smoothly, a volume could be pulled from the current shelves, checked, shelflisted, and processed for shipment to the bindery within seventy-two hours. But if any delays occurred, or if the process began toward the end of the week, the time could be increased to as much as seven days. Further, if the binding unit proved to be incomplete or otherwise troublesome, the holding period could become a month, three months, or, in a few cases, more than six months.

If State University had been a small institution, with a staff numbering only a few people and a binding workload of perhaps a thousand titles each year, the Bindery Section's procedures might have occasioned no trouble for the Circulation Section. Anne was a bright and imaginative young woman, but even she failed to comprehend the size of the operation which she supervised. From time to time, a small binding arrearage developed. It was almost always confined, however, to those materials which were being rebound, very rarely to the ones being bound for the first time. So long as the periodicals and serials were moving through the section on a regular basis Anne was satisfied and felt that things were under control.

Randolf Harrison, Chief of the Circulation Section, did not share Anne's satisfaction. If he came to work on any morning of the week and did not find a stack of call slips on his desk, he assumed that all the students had gone home or that no one had come to work at the circulation desk on the previous evening. He could predict, usually quite accurately, that the majority of the call slips would represent periodicals and serials which were not on the shelf and were not checked out. In order to discover what had happened to these materials, some unfortunate soul had to be sent to the Serials Section to determine whether the missing item had been received. Once its existence and presence had been established through the checking record, the search was transferred to the Bindery Section, where the request for a check of the files was usually greeted with a groan and a grudging acceptance of the call slip.

Randy had, at one time or another, used every one of his regular assistants to perform this often unrewarding search process. It had become such an odious task, however, that he finally assumed it himself, partly to avoid the long conferences which the assistants inevitably engaged in upon their return from—as they called it—the Lion's Den. Each staff member seemed compelled to enumerate his harrowing adventures in Serials and Bindery, thus prolonging the search time and keeping Randy from his own duties. His other rationale for doing the job himself was to find out just what it entailed and to begin to tabulate the time and effort involved in locating these items.

After six months, Randy was, he believed, armed with sufficient statistics to make a compelling case for changing the bindery procedure. He submitted his evidence to John Crispen, Associate Director of the Library, because it was John's responsibility to supervise the day-to-day operations of the system. Randy had calculated that on the average, the Circulation Section received two queries per day from library users in the main building, relating to periodicals or serials which were "in process" in the Bindery Section but had not yet been represented in the circulation file. The time lag between receipt of the search request and receipt of the circulation slip from Bindery was discovered to be 7.5 days, counting all days on which the main building was open. The mean time required to determine where the unlocated item might be, including elapsed time while the Bindery Section staff looked through its files, was calculated to be 213 minutes. In computing the 213-minute figure, Randy had been generous: only hours during which the bindery staff was on duty were considered. If circulation staff time were extracted from the figure, the number of minutes could be reduced to 178. This meant that, on the average, slightly more than one hour per day was being spent by the circulation staff in trying to verify that apparently missing periodicals and serials were actually in the Bindery Section. In other terms, something like eight work weeks per year were being expended by the Circulation Section in this effort, not counting the time spent by the library patron or the assistant who had to discuss the matter with the patron and check the circulation file initially—a procedure which usually involved going through the day's checkout slips to make sure the item had not been charged out during the last few hours.

The Associate Director was impressed with Randy's summary. As a first step, he photocopied the data and sent it to Alvin Candler, Chief of the Technical Services Division. Crispen himself was serving temporarily as Chief of the Public Services Division, which made communication in that direction somewhat simpler. Randy had told him that the Chief of the Reference Section had already received a copy.

Before Crispen had a chance to call a meeting of the staff members involved in the matter, he received a typed reply from Candler.

Dear Mr. Crispen:

After reviewing the information submitted to you by Mr. Harrison, I feel obliged to comment on some of its implications. I have talked with Miss Warrnet, Chief of the Bindery Section, and have determined to my satisfaction that she is working effectively, that her staff is performing well, and that no significant backlog exists in the Section.

The thrust of Mr. Harrison's study seems to point toward some change in the procedures followed by the Bindery Section. These procedures have been developed over a long period of time, and I cannot see any point at which they can be adjusted without creating more problems than are solved.

Although we can discuss the matter at great length, spending valuable time to no great advantage so far as I can tell, the likelihood of finding a new system which would reduce the time of the Circulation staff, and not increase the time expended by the Bindery staff in direct proportion, is not great. I am inclined, therefore, to do nothing further about the matter.

Sincerely yours,
Alvin Candler
Chief of the Technical Services Division

At staff coffee that morning, John Crispen overheard some of the circulation staff griping about how much time they were spending trying to locate materials that were not checked out. One assistant commented cheerfully, "I always tell them it must be at the bindery. That usually shuts them up, and sometimes they don't even ask me to do anything else about it."

Mary Carter also overheard the conversation. "Oh, great," she moaned. "No wonder all my friends keep asking me why everything they want is always at the bindery! It's the same old story: the university is just too big to bother with the little people."

• • • • •

The bindery problem seems to be reaching an impasse. What steps should John Crispen take at this point?

Randy Harrison appears to have done a good research job relative to the search for missing periodicals and serials. Could Alvin Candler have produced any facts and figures which might have supported his desire to maintain the status quo?

What should Anne Warrnet's role in the matter be? If you were Anne, and were asked to suggest possible alterations in the bindery routines in order to prepare the circulation record more promptly, how would you proceed?

If Crispen decides to hold no further official discussions on the matter, what should Randy Harrison do?

20.
A Library User Is Confused by Reclassification

· · · · · · · · · · ·

Not all of the staff members had been happy about it when the chief librarian at Wilmont University finally decided that the Library of Congress Classification system should be adopted in place of the Dewey Decimal system. Wilmont's collection numbered about 800,000 volumes, which meant that complete reclassification was out of the question unless supplementary funds and staff could be secured. With money and time heavily in demand to purchase and process new materials supporting several recently established master's and doctoral programs, there was little hope that any of the older materials could be reclassified, except selectively, over at least the next five years.

Guidelines had, of course, been issued for the switch to LC. Beginning on January 2, every new book transmitted to the Cataloging Department was to receive an LC call number—or so the rumors had it. Actually, the directive specifically exempted the half dozen or so special collections maintained by the library, as well as the books in the reference section. In fact, there were numerous exceptions: audiovisuals, serials, added copies, added volumes of sets, government documents, and theses, among others. Anything in these categories was to retain whatever type of location symbol had been employed prior to the change to LC.

Dr. Allen, Chief Librarian, had been careful to present the whole matter of changing classifications to the library's Advisory Committee. This committee was composed of five faculty members and three students, in addition to the chief librarian. With the exception of the librarian, each was appointed by the university president for a three-year term; and the members were normally chosen to represent as wide a spectrum of academic interests as possible. At each May meeting of the committee, at least one new faculty member and one new student representative joined the deliberations.

The Advisory Committee, although originally formed "to provide guidance to the librarian in setting policy for library services to students and faculty at Wilmont University," had over the years been more and more used for policy endorsement rather than guidance. Some of the more aggressive committee members occasionally expressed dismay that their work reflected a rubber-stamp mentality, but their sporadic efforts to revitalize the committee had always been received with apathy by their colleagues.

The Advisory Committee ordinarily met monthly during the academic year and at least once during the summer. Wilmont's change to LC had been proposed to the committee at the May meeting preceding the January during which the switch was to be implemented. In general, Committee members seemed pleased about the adoption of the LC system. Dr. Rollen, Assistant Professor of Sociology and new both to the university and to the committee, impressed the librarian with his forthright comments at the October meeting:

"I don't see," Rollen interrupted, after some fifteen minutes of explanation from Dr. Allen, "why we have to worry about matters like this. All of us are convinced you know your business. As far as I'm concerned, if the LC Classification will save money and help your staff turn out books faster, then it ought to be adopted. We're not here to get involved in the internal workings of the library; that's what you're hired to take care of!"

Seeing agreement on the faces of the rest of the committee members, Allen, who served as chairman of the group, terminated the discussion. No one even thought it necessary to take a vote, and the secretary was instructed to record "the sense of the meeting" as favoring the change to LC.

Allen officially announced the new classification policy to the faculty through a letter distributed by campus mail early in December:

LIBRARY MEMORANDUM, NUMBER 5

To: All Faculty Members
From: Martin S. Allen, Chief Librarian

Beginning on January 2, all *new* books coming into the Wilmont Library will be assigned call numbers according to the Library of Congress Classification system. Until now, Wilmont has used the Dewey Decimal Classification system; however, a cost study has revealed that to continue to follow the Dewey scheme in a library such as the one at Wilmont will be disproportionately expensive.

A shortage of staff time and of money will prevent the

reclassification of most of the older books. Thus, works already classified by Dewey will, under normal circumstances, *not* be changed to the Library of Congress system. Additions to multi-volume sets, new copies of works already classed in Dewey, and new volumes of currently received serials will continue to be given Dewey numbers. *New* serials, *new* sets, and *new* editions of older works will, however, be classed according to the Library of Congress scheme.

All special collections and materials not now classed in Dewey will remain in whatever system is currently being used to arrange them. This means, for example, that U.S. government documents will continue to be shelved according to the Superintendent of Documents Classification, as has always been the case.

Copies of the *Outline of the Library of Congress Classification* will be available, free of charge, at the Circulation Desk in the main library building. The staff there will be happy to assist you in learning about the new system. We urge you to take advantage of our help in this regard. Further, we hope that you will aid us by getting word of the policy change to the students.

Should you have any questions about this decision or its implications for your work, please write or telephone me, care of the Librarian's Office.

The students, in turn, were notified about the change by means of an article in their campus newspaper, *The Climber,* for December 15:

LIBRARY TO BEGIN NEW SYSTEM ON JAN. 1

Dr. Martin B. Allen, Chief Librarian, has announced that a new classification system will be introduced to Wilmont on January 1 of next year. All new books will be given numbers from the Library of Congress system instead of Dewey Decimal numbers.

The Library of Congress system is, according to Allen, more modern than Dewey and cheaper to apply to Wilmont's books, which are expected to number over a million in another five years.

The new books will be put in a separate section close to the circulation desk, Allen reported. Students will be able to spot the new numbers easily, he said, because they begin with one or two letters of the alphabet, followed by numbers between 1 and 9999.

Posters showing a summary of the new system are to be displayed in the library to help students understand the change. Allen has invited anyone needing help with the new system to call him or drop by his office in the library.

The circulation staff cleared a floor of the stacks by shifting the Dewey sections to make room for the LC-classed books near the main desk. Copies of the *Outine of the Library of Congress Classification* were purchased in quantity for free distribution to anyone who asked for one. The technical services staff assistants prepared charts showing the broad subject areas in LC and their equivalent Dewey numbers, to be posted adjacent to stack entrances, exits, stairways, and elevators.

Despite the decision not to reclassify any special collections, the reference staff found, within the first year's experience with LC, that a divided collection caused problems for both the staff and the library patrons. One professional cataloger served as advisor to the reference reclassification project, with student assistants doing most of the clerical work. By the end of the calendar year, the entire reference collection had been weeded and reclassified. Meanwhile, the stack level which had been cleared to accommodate the rapidly-growing LC section had been filled, and the levels below and above were being readied for the overflow.

To the dismay of some of the staff members who had offered dire predictions about a student uproar concerning the change, the shift to LC seemed to go relatively unnoticed by students and faculty alike. Circulation statistics continued to rise at the normal rate. The only hostility encountered came from the wife of a professor emeritus, who complained, "I can't find the new poetry books in the stacks anymore. They're all mixed up with the novels and the short stories."

In the midst of this apparently tranquil scene, during May of LC's second year of use at Wilmont, a crisis emerged. Dr. Rollen arrived late, and in obvious annoyance, to the regularly-scheduled meeting of the Advisory Committee. In typical fashion, he began talking the moment he entered the room, without even waiting for the chairman to acknowledge his arrival.

The words came forth so fast that Allen was hard pressed to catch all their implications. The story which emerged was, as best he could tell, something akin to the following:

James Wilson, Rollen's first master's thesis advisee in sociology, had just finished his final oral examination for the degree. During the course of the exam, Dr. Anderson, one of Rollen's colleagues in the department and a member of Wilson's master's committee, pointed out that the candidate seemed to have ignored the material to be found in some of the "classic treatises" on public welfare. The comment caught both Rollen and his student off guard—Rollen, because he should have noted the omission himself, even though he did not think highly of the works to which Anderson referred, and Wilson because he was simply unaware of the works in question.

Wilson's ignorance of the sources was not serious enough to cause him to fail the examination, but it had embarrassed Rollen. Wilson's oral was the first which Rollen had chaired at Wilmont, and the incident marred it. After the examination had been concluded, Rollen took Wilson aside to find out why he had missed seeing the treatises.

"Honestly, Dr. Rollen," Wilson protested, "I didn't think the material in public welfare was very important to my topic."

"Sure, we both know it was peripheral, but you still should have checked the older sources," Rollen countered. "Why didn't you?"

"What I did was get a general call number from the library catalog. Then I just browsed around in the stacks, looking at recent titles. I really didn't see many books there that looked very old."

Further questioning revealed that Wilson had looked only in the LC-classed section of the stacks. Had he browsed in the Dewey area as well, he probably would have found the works to which Anderson referred, for they were available there in mutiple copies and editions.

Needless to say, Rollen was angry about the whole affair. He directed his wrath, however, not against Anderson or Wilson but against Allen, charging that the split of the library collection between LC and Dewey was at the heart of the trouble.

"I think," concluded Rollen testily, "this Advisory Committee ought to instruct you as chief librarian to make certain that all books currently arranged by Dewey are immediately reclassified into the Library of Congress system."

Allen privately dismissed this statement as prompted by Rollen's embarrassment and anger. As chairman of the committee, however, he felt obliged to recognize all viewpoints and allow them to be discussed. "I realize," he said to Rollen, "that the split seems to have caused your student some trouble; still—"

"It sure as hell did!" exploded Rollen. "But it wouldn't have happened if the library had been doing its job right. Just so this won't get shoved under the rug like half the other things coming before this so-called Advisory Committee, I'm going to put this in the form of a motion: I move that the library be directed to reclassify all materials still in the Dewey Decimal system, said reclassification to be completed by no later than December 31 of next year."

To Allen's chagrin, one of the student members of the committee seconded the motion without hesitation. In the rather heated discussion which ensued, Allen tried to point out rationally the severe economic and staff problems which such a directive would occasion. But Rollen would not be deterred.

"It's your business to solve the administrative problems," Rollen stated flatly. "Do it any way you like, but do it!"

Because Allen served ex officio as chairman of the committee, he normally did not vote on proposed motions. This time, however, he hoped that if the motion were not defeated, he would at least be able to cast a tie-breaking vote against it. But the motion passed, five to three: Rollen, the three student members, and one other faculty member had voted "yes."

The remainder of the meeting was anticlimactic, at best. As Allen disposed of some perfunctory matters relating to the annual library lecture series and an increase in the Art Department's library allocation, he found himself reflecting on the irony of the situation. "How often," he thought, "I've wished that this committee would take its charge seriously and give me some real guidance. Then, when they finally do get around to doing something, it has to be this. If I can't convince them to rescind their decision, I wonder if they'll help me find the funds to carry it out."

• • • • •

What should Allen do at this point, given the mandate from his Advisory Committee?

Analyze the incident which brought about the crisis. What measures, short of full reclassification, might have prevented it from occurring? Why were the efforts of the library staff to minimize the problems of a divided collection not effective in this case?

What advantages and disadvantages have other libraries reported in changing from Dewey to LC? To what extent are the arguments which Allen presented to the Wilmont students and faculty to justify the switch to LC supported by the experiences of other university libraries?

21.
A Cooperative Processing Center
Develops a Backlog

. . . .

For five years, the Eastern Valley Library Processing Center had been operating as a cooperative agency to acquire, catalog, and process most of the books being added to the collections of the sixteen public library systems within a 200-mile radius. The center, established through funds available from the federal government, was able to report for the first time, at the end of the preceding fiscal year, that it no longer needed federal subsidy. The fees paid by the constituent libraries now covered the cost of maintaining the center.

Ralph Alexander was the first and only librarian of the Processing Center. He had been the Head of Technical Services in the Marketon Public Library and a prime mover in the establishment of the center. It was only natural that he should be offered the position of chief administrator of the center, and he was pleased to accept. The venture, as he saw it, presented a challenge and an opportunity to render a significant service to the area. Ralph was the right person for the job. He was forty-seven years old, with a background in cataloging and administrative experience in a public library system, and a personality which combined firmness and precision with a fair and open mind.

Although few people fully realized it, were it not for Ralph Alexander there would have been no Processing Center. During its first five years of life, he did, at one time or another, every necessary professional and clerical job, keeping procedures running smoothly all the while. Gradually, he acquired the services of subprofessional and clerical assistants, developing a staff numbering nine workers in addition to himself. Once that was accomplished, he shifted his attention from the daily routines to planning the center's future. Ralph was shrewd enough to realize that the center would have to achieve greater efficiency, probably with about the same number of staff members, in order to continue to provide the quality of service to which its sixteen customers were accustomed.

Ralph also realized that he was working too many hours a day, without adequate time for vacations. He caught himself becoming short tempered by the end of each week, and he knew that part of the problem was the fact that he could not look forward to a free weekend. Only on the weekends, unfortunately, could he find the peace and quiet he needed to do some serious planning. His wife and two sons were also showing signs of exasperation because of Ralph's heavy schedule. Finally, he promised them, and himself, that he would ease up—once the new equipment had been installed at the center and certain revised routines implemented.

By the end of May, in the center's sixth year of operation, Ralph had drafted most of the revisions in procedure. He had not as yet been able to record all of them in a manual, but he had drawn up the necessary flow charts and was in the process of receiving bids on the new equipment.

After considering a number of different machines, Ralph had decided to purchase an electrostatic copying device and an offset duplicator. These would, he believed, offer maximum flexibility for duplicating catalog cards and other items which the center provided for its customers, while not committing the center to the purchase of unreasonably expensive machinery which would become quickly obsolete.

On June 15, the bids were opened and contracts let for delivery of the new equipment by the end of July. Ralph breathed a sigh of relief, began to make firm plans for a long camping trip with Jean and the boys, and told his staff that he was going to be incommunicado for the first two weeks of July. But on June 27, Ralph Alexander suffered a major heart attack. Two days later he was dead.

When the Processing Center's staff returned after the July Fourth holiday weekend, general dismay and gloom were evident. Out of loyalty to Ralph and the work he had begun, they continued to go through the motions, but they showed no enthusiasm for their tasks. Ellen Jelson, who had been the general staff manager of the center under Ralph's direction for the past two years, assumed responsibility for keeping the operations in motion. Despite her best efforts, staff morale noticeably sagged, with a resultant decrease in productivity. Ellen consoled herself with the fact that there was always a drop in number of books processed during the summer, when various staff members were away on vacation, and orders from the member libraries diminished for the same reason. She told herself that things would be back to normal by fall, if the center could get a new director.

To the center's Advisory Committee fell the responsibility of replacing

Ralph Alexander. This committee, composed of one representative from each of the member libraries, together with the librarian of the center, had been created primarily to reach decisions about the procedures to be adopted by the center. Most of the committee members were catalogers from the staffs of the various libraries, although the Chairman, Richard Moshen, was the Director of the Marketon Public Library.

Unfortunately, Moshen was away on vacation during most of July and August. Interviews for a new librarian at the center finally got underway in early September, but the most likely of the candidates indicated that he would not be able to assume his duties until January 1.

George Wilson, Advisory Committee member charged with bringing recommendations for securing a new librarian and operating the center in the interim, talked at length with Ellen Jelson. As a result, Ellen agreed to continue coordinating the activities of the center until the arrival of the new director.

When Walter Metson began work on January 2, he found seven staff members busily engaged in their various tasks. His initial conference with Ellen Jelson did not, however, confirm his first impression that everything was under control. Ellen reported that one clerk had resigned at the end of December to take a job with a local insurance company, and that the best reviser had left the city in November because her husband had been transferred. The loss of these two workers had, she noted, resulted in the development of a backlog of about 300 volumes.

"I thought maybe if we began using the new equipment it might help," she told Walter. "But we couldn't find anyone who knew enough about it to even unpack it. Some of the changes in routine that Mr. Alexander recommended can't go into effect until we have the offset press. So, between losing two staff members and not being able to get the new equipment into operation, we've just tried to hang on as best we could until you got here."

Walter quickly recognized that as a staff manager Ellen was quite competent. But she obviously did not fully understand the new system which Alexander had planned, and was not even completely aware of what it entailed. The new equipment stood against one wall, as yet untouched. A combination of depression about Alexander's death, general confusion, and lack of firm direction had left the staff demoralized and the center in a precarious position.

With a healthy degree of self-confidence born out of his long experience in public library cataloging, Walter began to try to recoup the losses.

After carefully studying the flow charts which consituted almost the total written legacy from Ralph Alexander, Walter arranged for the new equipment to be uncrated and put into operation. Then, with the help of his Advisory Committee, he began to solicit applications for the two vacant staff positions. Meanwhile, he and Ellen agreed that Sarah Wimberly should be promoted to the position of chief reviser.

One week later, while Walter was up to his elbows in printer's ink, working to get the offset press operating properly, he was called to the telephone.

"Mr. Metson? This is Geraldine Ellis. I'm librarian at the Eastmark Public Library. I don't believe we've met yet, but I've got a problem, so I decided to call you."

"I'm glad you did, Mrs. Ellis. I've seen your name on my list of librarians, but I haven't really had a chance to visit with all of you yet. What can I do for you?"

"Well, we've had some books on order from the center for over six months now. It's never taken that long before to get them here. I want to know what's wrong."

"Although I can't say definitely, I expect the problems caused by Mr. Alexander's sudden death are at the bottom of it. But maybe I'd better let you talk with Mrs. Jelson. She's the one who knows where everything is."

"Quite frankly, Mr. Metson, I've been talking to Ellen Jelson about this for the better part of three weeks, and I haven't gotten a straight answer yet. I'm tired of her stalling. That's why I asked for you."

"I'm sorry if there's been some mixup on this. I'll try to straighten it out, though. Could you send me a list of the titles that haven't come through?"

"I'll be more than happy to, if it will get some action," agreed Mrs. Ellis.

When the list arrived two days later, Walter undertook to check it himself, after the rest of the staff had left for the day. So far as he could discover, the orders had never been placed at all. He could find no record of them in any of the files, though card copy was on hand for most of the titles since the same books had been ordered for other libraries serviced by the center.

The only reasonable procedure, Walter concluded, was to talk with Ellen and try to find out what had happened. But the next morning, before he had a chance to call her into his office, he received another troublesome telephone call, this time from Richard Moshen, Director of the Marketon Library and Chairman of the center's Advisory Committee.

"Metson, I'm calling for my Head of Technical Services," Moshen began quickly. "She tells me she's been trying to get a sensible explanation out of your Mrs. Jelson for over a week now. All she gets is doubletalk."

"Am I correct in guessing that you've ordered some books from us that haven't arrived?"

"That's right. We sent the order through last July and still no books."

"It would help us if you would send a list of those items not received; then—."

"Look, Metson, I don't have time to run around making lists of books that were properly ordered. I don't know what's going on over at that center of yours, but if we don't get at least some of those books within the next two weeks, we may just have to think about going back to doing our own processing."

"Really, Mr. Moshen, I hope you won't make such a far-reaching decision so hastily. After all, you've been one of the main supporters of the center."

"That's quite true. But my technical services people aren't all that happy about the quality of work the center turns out, and I can't see that we're saving much money on the deal. If you can't deliver the books quickly, we might as well do it ourselves. We haven't even been able to cut the number of people in cataloging at Marketon, and that was supposed to be one of the main benefits of having a Processing Center."

"I appreciate your position, Mr. Moshen, but please don't make a decision at this point. Let me try to find out what's happened, and I'll call you back."

By the time Walter hung up the phone, he was visibly shaken. Even though he had only been on the job for six weeks, he was well aware that the loss of Marketon's business could place the center in a precarious financial position as well as deprive the Advisory Committee of its leadership. With this prospect facing him, Walter immediately called Ellen into his office to provide an explanation of what was happening.

Though generally a well-controlled, seemingly unemotional woman, Ellen startled Walter by breaking into tears when he put the question to her.

"I just don't know what you expect of me," Ellen cried. "We were all so upset when Mr. Alexander died; we just couldn't seem to keep things going right. When I tried to get some of the girls to work faster, they resented it. Jean—you know, the one who quit in December—told me one day that she wasn't hired to work for me and she was tired of having me boss her around all the time."

"But what about the orders that were never received by the libraries?" asked Walter, in a belated attempt to divert attention to the intellectual aspects of the situation. "Did you ever find out what happened to them? Were they ever even ordered at all?"

"I wish I knew," said Ellen, the tears starting again. "One of the girls thinks that Jean threw them away, probably for spite—or maybe she just didn't want to have to bother with them. I couldn't get any proof, so I told Mrs. Ellis and the others that I was 'working on it.'"

Since the discussion was obviously painful for Ellen and nearly out of control in any case, Walter suggested that they wait and talk about it again later. Once she had left, he felt the edges of panic creeping over him. "They never taught me in library school how to handle weeping women," he muttered. But underneath the awkwardness of the moment, Walter was convinced that the future of the center might well be determined by how he handled this problem.

· · · · ·

What immediate action should Walter Metson take? How should he proceed on a long-term basis?

Walter has obviously acquired a Processing Center endowed with serious problems. What factors were chiefly responsible for the present state of affairs? In what ways, if any, was Ralph Alexander to blame for Metson's problems?

Richard Moshen of the Marketon Library has leveled some serious charges against the center. What steps should Walter take to determine whether the quality of the center's work is adequate?

Library literature is replete with arguments and examples showing, ostensibly, that centralized processing ought to be less expensive than local processing. What reliable evidence could be drawn from that literature to counter the Marketon claim that they can process materials more cheaply locally? What reasons could be advanced to explain why the development of the Processing Center has not enabled the Marketon Library to reduce the number of cataloging staff members employed?

22.
The Serials Catalog
Becomes Machine-Readable

· · · · · · · · · · · · · · · · ·

Elaine Parker had always felt somewhat defensive whenever she attended professional library meetings because she was connected with one of the largest university libraries which had made practically no attempt to automate. Western University had for many years, of course, utilized punched-card equipment in its Accounting Department and had even been proud of its pioneer applications of EDP. The library was, in fact, forced to adopt unit record techniques in order to continue as part of the university financial system. When the university installed its third generation computer, however, the library ignored the development and continued producing the still acceptable keypunched records.

Inevitably, at the various conferences and institutes which Elaine attended, someone would ask, "What is Western doing these days in automation?" And Elaine usually answered evasively, "Well, we're talking about it, but we haven't quite decided what we want to do. We feel it's better to take our time in planning and make fewer mistakes later." Unfortunately, Elaine was privately convinced that no one at Western was even doing much talking, much less any planning.

Just when Elaine had almost given up hope of ever seeing any automation project undertaken by the Western Library, the director announced, at his monthly meeting of department heads, that Western was ready to begin its automation program by converting the Serials Catalog to machine-readable form. Elaine received this announcement with some ambivalence, for she was the head of the Serials Department and would inevitably be involved in any project affecting the Serials Catalog. She was somewhat annoyed that she had not been consulted in this decision, though she consoled herself with the thought that her numerous memos to the director must have had some effect. "At least," she told herself, "I'll finally get a chance to put all my conference-going to some practical use. It might be sort of fun to try something new."

After a few months, Elaine's initial enthusiasm for the innovative possibilities of the project was significantly lessened. Although she remembered conference attendees talking about the problems of bureaucracy in university administration and blunders on the part of the computer center, she had always gotten the impression that the values of automation were greater than any negative effect generated by the problems. Now she was not so sure that all obstacles could be, as one institute speaker had phrased it, "overcome by skill, tenacity, and good personal relations with the computer people."

To her dismay, Elaine found the project to have more negative aspects than she had imagined. The basic design of SERCAT, as it was called, was formulated not by the library staff, but by the personnel of the university's Information Services Center. The Library Director, Dr. George Monahan, assured Elaine and the other library staff members involved with SERCAT that no procedure would be put into operation without their approval. As Elaine discovered, however, this assurance was almost meaningless, for it was practically impossible to raise compelling objections to a procedure when you had not been present at the session during which it was proposed and established.

Elaine viewed, for example, the use of fixed fields in the coding of the serials record as wasteful of space on the magnetic tape. The ISC staff, on the other hand, presented only the option of selecting between two fixed-field designs, not even acknowledging the possibility of using variable fields. "Why haven't you considered a variable-field format?" she asked Ann Elden, their ISC consultant.

"Oh, we talked about it a little," Miss Elden had replied rather casually, "but we decided that fixed-field coding would be more efficient for searching."

Elaine started to protest, but Miss Elden had made the statement with such assurance and finality that further discussion seemed futile. On reflection, however, Elaine wished she had demanded more justification.

To compound the problem, Ann Elden proved to be the individualistic type. She was young, moderately well experienced in computer programming, but almost totally ignorant about library systems. Miss Elden was also extremely conscious of the fact that she was competing for status with her colleagues, and she saw the library assignment as her chance to achieve recognition. It was perhaps for this reason that Miss Elden elected to design SERCAT without reference to published literature in the field and without any attempt to view the operation of serials programs in other libraries.

Elaine once asked her why she had made no move to visit libraries with operational automation programs.

"We wouldn't be able to use their programs anyhow," Miss Elden had replied. "Every computer configuration is different. If we tried to use their system on our equipment, it would just blow up. We'd waste a lot of time and still not get anything that would work for us."

Again, Elaine could not argue the point convincingly, for she remembered that many of the computer experts had said the same thing at conferences. Despite this, she instinctively felt that mistakes could be avoided if Miss Elden would at least talk with others who had tackled the serials area.

When the completed design for the serials format was finally submitted, Elaine's worries were partially allayed. Ann Elden had obviously studied the existing serials record style very carefully and had talked enough with Elaine and with the Assistant Director for Technical Services to produce a format not obviously out of line with the Library of Congress MARC for serials. Even though Elaine would have felt more secure if she had been a party to all of the discussions held prior to the determination of the format, she could not honestly say she was unhappy with the results.

Elaine expected that she would have ample time to study the new system before making any attempt to implement it. She received the final report on Monday afternoon; on Wednesday morning, Blanche Woder, Assistant Director for Technical Services, asked her to come into the office.

"Dr. Monahan has been stuying Miss Elden's report," Mrs. Woder began, "and he sees no reason why we shouldn't begin the keypunch operation on the serials records right away. Unless you have some objection, we'll start next Monday morning."

Elaine, caught quite offguard, reacted negatively: "No, I don't think we should start so soon. I've only had a day to study the report, and I'm not sure the format is right. Aren't we going to experiment with a few records before we start a keypunch operation on the whole file?"

"I thought it was clear in Miss Elden's report. She worked with a test file, and her studies show the format to be all right. Why should we wait? Aren't you the one who's been pushing us to get started automating?"

"Of course I've wanted us to get started, but we shouldn't make a lot of foolish mistakes just because we're in too big a hurry."

"Well, the decision was Dr. Monahan's. I guess you'll have to talk to him if you want to postpone the starting date. But I think I ought to warn you that he's pretty anxious to get going, and so is Miss Elden. Unless you can come up with a convincing reason for postponement, I don't think he'll agree."

Elaine was annoyed with herself for not having given Mrs. Woder any significant reasons for delaying the keypunching, but she had never felt comfortable with the assistant director. Mrs. Woder, who had been hired some five years after Elaine had come to Western, was appointed to the position which Elaine had turned down. Since Blanche Woder knew that Elaine had been the first choice for the assistant director's job, the relationship between the two had never been a close one, though it certainly was not hostile. Elaine felt, however, that she was no longer directly involved in the decision-making process, for Mrs. Woder and Dr. Monahan concluded many of the negotiations without doing anything more than having Mrs. Woder ask Elaine for her opinions. There were very few situations, Elaine discovered, which required that she sit down with Mrs. Woder and Dr. Monahan to discuss a problem.

The reason for Elaine's desire to postpone the keypunching operation was one which she was embarrassed to explain to Mrs. Woder. The fact was that the serials holdings records were known to be inaccurate, although the precise nature of the errors and their extent had not been specified. Over the years, with numbers of different clerks working on the files, mistakes had been made and were later compounded by inept attempts at correction without complete verification against the volumes on the shelves. Elaine, having discovered some of the inaccuracies herself, repeatedly asked for more assistance in the Serials Department, though she had not been explicit in requesting it for the purpose of correcting errors. Neither Dr. Monahan nor Mrs. Woder had been told directly that the holdings records were not reliable.

It was clear enough that Elaine would have to take her problem to Dr. Monahan. She called his office to request an appointment and was told to come right away if she liked.

"You haven't been in to see me for a long time, Elaine," said Dr. Monahan in greeting. "I have the feeling that it's not the desire to renew an old acquaintance that brings you here now, though. What can I do for you?"

"I guess I've come to ask you to postpone the start of the keypunch operation for the serials."

"Somehow that surprises me a great deal. I thought you were one of our most eager automaters."

"Well, I am most of the time, but I think it's a mistake to begin keypunching until we go through the holdings records and get them cleaned up."

"What do you mean 'cleaned up'? Aren't they in good shape now?"

"I suppose I should have told you this earlier, but they haven't been in good shape for a long time. I was counting on the automation program to give me the time and money to go through them and get them straightened out. It didn't occur to me that you'd want to start keypunching so soon."

"What exactly is wrong with the records?"

"Oh, a lot of little things. The list of bound volumes in the serials record sometimes doesn't agree with what is on the shelflist card. Some of the volumes listed as incomplete are actually complete now, and vice versa. And some of the serials holdings cards have an abbreviated version of the catalog entry on them. Things like that."

"Have you any idea how many of the records are actually wrong?"

"No, not really. I haven't even had time to keep up with the current problems, much less go back and make estimates on the errors inherited from the past."

"This does begin to sound rather serious, Elaine. I think I'd better get some others in on this before we go any further."

Before Elaine quite realized what was happening, Dr. Monahan had called his secretary on the intercom and asked her to see whether Mrs. Woder and Miss Elden could come to the office right away. As luck would have it, they were both available and appeared in less than ten minutes.

Elaine sat without comment as Dr. Monahan outlined the problem to the newcomers. He had scarcely finished his opening statement when Miss Elden made one of her own:

"Frankly, Dr. Monahan, if you are serious about getting this project operational, you'd better not postpone the keypunching. ISC has a lot of requests for programmers and systems analysts. If you authorize a delay, I must put you on notice that I will withdraw from the project."

"We certainly don't want that, Miss Elden," responded Dr. Monahan. "Still, it would be foolish for us to have all the records keypunched only to find out they're wrong."

"I've never pretended I knew anything about the library business, so I won't tell you how to run it. But I just can't continue if the project stalls at this point. We may be able to find you someone else to work on it later, but I can't promise anything."

"How do you feel about this, Mrs. Woder?" asked Dr. Monahan.

"This whole thing comes as something of a surprise to me," Mrs. Woder replied. "I know there've been a few errors that the reference staff has discovered, but I had no reason to believe the records as a whole were as unreliable as Miss Parker suggests. I really don't know what to recommend."

With obvious reluctance, Dr. Monahan pronounced his decision: "I wish we had more time to find out just how bad the records really are. But I think a delay at this point will just sacrifice the project's momentum. It's my decision that we go ahead with the keypunching, but that we give Elaine here some extra help so she can work ahead of the keypunchers. That way maybe we can get a reasonably correct record into the computer."

• • • • •

If you were Elaine, how would you react to Dr. Monahan's decision? What would you do at this point?

Analyze Elaine's actions regarding the serials automation project. In what ways, if any, could she have prevented the development of the crisis that now faces SERCAT?

To what degree was Ann Elden responsible for creating the problem, if at all? What would she have found, had she studied the literature on serials records automation in advance of designing the system for Western?

23.
Local Revision
of LC Subject Headings

. . . .

"This list is impossible! I can never find anything in it that isn't at least ten years behind the times." The speaker was Louise Ranger, newest appointee to the staff of the Subject Cataloging Division of Altmeister University Library. Louise had come to Altmeister straight from library school, with two advanced degrees in hand: a master's degree in library service and a second master's in sociology. Her colleagues in Subject Cataloging found her to be an interesting young woman, but somewhat more impressed with her own importance than seemed to be warranted.

"You'd think she was the only person here with two master's degrees, the way she acts," commented Grace Howard. Grace was a long-time subject cataloger, specializing in Romance languages and literature; her comment was addressed to Alfred Miller, whose speciality was the life sciences.

"Really, Al, doesn't she know that other people get annoyed with LC subject list just like she does?"

"She'd realize it if she ever stopped to think about it," answered Al. "You've forgotten how it is to be young and idealistic and impatient, that's all, Grace. She'll come off it eventually. Just give her time. Every young colt around here gets broken to the bit; you know that."

"I suppose I do. I'd be more sympathetic, though, if she didn't keep talking about 'when I was in graduate school'! Everybody around here has attended graduate school for at least a year, in addition to doing a library school stint. Just because some of us didn't get another degree doesn't mean that we don't know anything."

"Now, take it easy, Grace. You know the old psychology; she's probably being aggressive because she feels young and inferior. Everything is new to her and she's low on the totem pole here. Maybe if somebody gave her something important to do she'd calm down a bit."

"Are you sure you aren't a psychoanalyst instead of a zoologist? Every

139

time I work up a nice hate, you spoil it all by making my enemy look human and frail. You know I'm a sucker for that approach. Poor little Louise,
alone and unprotected! O.K., so what do we do to help?"

"I don't know exactly. Maybe we could start by inviting her to join us
for lunch. I've noticed she usually goes off by herself. And she's really not
such a bad kid. She's been around a lot and has some fascinating stories to
tell about her trips to the Far East."

Feeling conciliatory after Al's comments, Grace decided to go ahead
and ask Louise to lunch with them that noon. Louise responded with such
obvious pleasure that Grace had to admit to Al that his diagnosis was probably correct.

Al invited another of the subject catalogers to join them: Harold Sut-
ton, who had a doctorate in linguistics and had been at Almeister for nearly
ten years. The luncheon conversation proved to be light and relaxing, though
Al noticed that Louise tended to hold the spotlight. After some chatter about
trips overseas and life in the Altmeister community, Louise turned the discussion in a new direction.

"Not to change the subject, but I would like you people to help me
out. I've really been on the point of turning in my resignation. Until today I
haven't even felt as though anyone in this place cared whether I was alive or
dead. But even having some show of friendship doesn't fully solve my problem."

"What's the trouble?" asked Al.

"I'm not exactly sure. Maybe that's why I haven't quit yet. Mainly it
has to do with the way the work is done, I guess. When I was in library
school, they talked a lot about the inadequacies of contemporary classification systems and subject headings. I got the idea that libraries with subject
specialists would be experimenting with new systems, not just perpetuating
old ones. That's why I wanted to come to Altmeister. I thought I'd have a
chance to be creative and develop a really good subject retrieval system for
sociology."

"And no one seems to care whether you have any special knowledge in
sociology or not," added Hal.

"That's right."

"I don't know if it will help any," continued Hal, "but I had the same
problem when I first came—and that was nine years ago last month. What
happens eventually is that you get used to the structure of the LC systems
and stop bothering to try to rework them. Lots of times you can use your

subject knowledge to better advantage in helping the reference staff than you ever will in the cataloging end. And I find I often get asked about whether to buy certain things for the collection."

"I'm just not sure that'll satisfy me," contended Louise. "Those LC headings, for example, are badly out of date and sometimes misleading. And the cross-reference structure looks really crazy in places. There's an awful lot that could be done to improve the situation if we just didn't have to wait for LC to get around to it."

"Well then, how would you go about updating LC?" asked Grace, with a tinge of sarcasm in her voice. She caught a disapproving look from Al, but Louise didn't seem to notice the tone.

"What I'd like to do is to go through the LC list and pull out the headings related to sociology. Then I'd—"

"But wait a minute," Grace broke in. "How would you know which ones were terms in sociology?"

"I guess I couldn't be 100 percent sure, but with my background in the field, I think I could spot maybe 85 or 90 percent of them. And I could take the major headings and pick up the others from the 'see also' references. Besides, a lot of headings refer to LC classification numbers. I could take those that had 'H' class symbols after them."

"Well, maybe, but I'm not sure," pondered Grace.

"I don't see any reason why it wouldn't work," commented Al. "What I want to know is what you would do then."

"By constructing a 'tree' of the references, all the way down to the most specific term, I could get an idea of what LC thought the structure of sociology was. You know, the National Library of Medicine people did something like that when they made up the Medical Subject Headings. I think they called it a 'tree structure.' Anyway, by looking at the hierarchy of terms, I could see which terms are incorrectly related and where inconsistent terminology is used, and things like that."

"That seems to make some sense. Then what?" asked Hal.

"Well, then I'd make a critique of the structure and suggest revisions of terms and cross-references."

"But what makes you think that you're qualified to second guess LC? After all, LC has a better staff of subject experts working on the list than Altmeister can ever hope to get," Grace interjected.

Again Louise ignored the barb and continued calmly: "I know LC is supposed to have a lot of subject specialists. But my cataloging teacher said that LC sometimes has trouble getting staff members who are really qualified in the areas that have vacancies. Besides, changing LC's catalog would be terrifically expensive; but that doesn't mean we couldn't try some new systems here. Who knows, maybe LC would like what we've done and use it as a base for their own revisions."

"I don't know about *that,*" said Hal. "My question would be whether any one person can successfully design or revise a list of headings. What if the terms you want to use are out of date, too? After all, you've been out of school—as far as your sociology work is concerned—for how long?"

"Yes, I see your point. I've been out for three years, and things do change rapidly. Actually, though, I didn't mean that I'd just adopt my own suggestions. What I had in mind was bringing in some of the faculty from the Department of Sociology here, and getting them to help me."

"That's a new twist," acknowledged Al. "I wonder if they'd even be interested in library subject headings."

"My theory is that you never know until you try," commented Louise. "I don't see that it could do any harm, and it might help."

After the group returned to work, Grace stopped by Al's desk to continue the discussion. "I don't see how she can be so sure of herself," she fumed. "Maybe if she had a doctor's degree in sociology, but not on the basis of a master's!"

"You'll hate me for this, but I really think her idea's not too bad. I told her to talk with Mrs. Olson about it and see what response she got."

"Al, you're a traitor. I think the whole thing's absurd, and here you go encouraging her. Well, maybe our boss will have sense enough to shoot her down, even if you don't."

Andrea Olson, Head of Subject Cataloging, had begun work at Altmeister as a student assistant while she was an undergraduate majoring in history. After graduation she had stayed on in the library, taking a leave two years later to go to library school. Some seven years after that, she had enrolled for graduate work in the Altmeister History Department and had finally received her Ph.D. just the previous semester.

Mrs. Olson, whose husband was a faculty member in Altmeister's Department of Philosophy, had proved to be a competent subject cataloger. As head of the subject cataloging unit, she managed the operation skillfully, although she had never particularly enjoyed dealing with knotty personnel problems. Her staff characterized her as "easygoing," but they respected her subject competence and organizational ability. The fact that she had a Ph.D. was the one thing that had most impressed Louise.

On Al's recommendation, Louise decided to write up her proposal for revision of the subject headings in sociology and submit it to Mrs. Olson. After Andrea had read the document, she called Louise into her office.

"Your suggestions for doing something about the subject headings in sociology are very interesting, Louise. I'm inclined to let you try your plan, but I'm not sure how much time this would take away from your other duties. We can't afford to let the books pile up while you work on something that may or may not pay off in the future."

"I don't really have any idea how long it would take to do this. I suppose it's the kind of thing I could pick up and put down as I have the time. If I were really noble, I guess I'd do it on my own time, so it wouldn't interfere with my regular work."

"I didn't mean to suggest that you not take *any* job time to do the study. But you know how pushed we are, and I've just learned that our English literature cataloger will be leaving us in a month."

"Do you think I could take off an hour a day to work on this?"

"Why don't you try that and see how it goes? If you need to adjust the schedule later, we can talk about it again."

When Grace learned that Mrs. Olson had approved time off for Louise to work on her project, she reacted quite negatively. Once again, she spouted off to Al.

"If I'd had any idea the boss lady would approve that harebrained scheme, I've have entered a formal protest."

"Hey! Why are you so angry about it? Just because you didn't think of it first?"

"You know that's not true, Alfred Miller. I just think the whole idea's ridiculous."

"What's wrong with it?"

"Everything! In the first place, it will take hours and hours to find all the so-called sociology headings in the list. She's got to check the main list and all the supplements. And when she's finished, what has she got? A mess of terms with all kinds of 'see also' references that won't combine into a neat array. Didn't you see that article a couple of years ago?"

"What article?"

"I can't remember where I saw it. It must have been in one of the journals that gets routed to us. Anyhow, some guy who teaches in library school did practically the same thing. I can't remember what field he used. But he showed how tangled up the references were, and said it was a waste of time to try to go at it that way. I think he recommended starting over again, from scratch. Anyway, he discarded the procedure as faulty."

"But that doesn't necessarily prove it won't work in some other field. And besides, if it makes Louise happy to try something like this, why not let her?"

"It can't come to anything, no matter how successful it is. You know that Altmeister will never change any LC headings until LC does it first. And I can guarantee that the people at LC aren't going to pay any attention to the fantasies of a young, self-styled sociologist who doesn't have anything to her credit but a master's degree."

"There's probably not much point in arguing with you when you're in this kind of mood. But I don't think you have any right to say what LC will or will not do. They might be very much interested in what Louise comes up with."

"You've got your opinion and I've got mine. But one thing's for sure. If I start seeing books pile up on Louise's desk while she's off working on that idiot project of hers, there's going to be trouble."

· · · · ·

If you were Louise and sensed the hostility which Grace is developing toward you, how would you handle the situation?

Discuss the pros and cons of taking "time off" from regular duties to pursue a project such as the one Louise has devised. Suppose that Grace's predictions come true; to what degree would a failure affect the chances of other subject catalogers getting similar concessions from Mrs. Olson?

Grace has challenged Louise's scheme as being absurd and has given reasons why she feels that way. How valid are Grace's objections? Is there a published study which concludes that such a procedure is ineffective? What other published literature could be cited to support either Grace or Louise in this context?

24.
Proposals for a
Regional Union Catalog

· · · · · · · · · · · · · ·

For almost ten years the State Librarian, Warren Granger, had been waiting for a propitious moment to begin requesting funds from the state legislature for the development of a regional union catalog. As Warren envisioned it, the union catalog would be the first step toward a regional information network. It would at least bring bibliographic information under some kind of control; and with the catalog as a base, plans for statewide cooperation could be developed.

Technically, the regional catalog would encompass only one state. The State Library staff, however, viewed this, too, as only an initial condition. Two of the bordering states were interested in tying in with the network, but their state librarians had assured Warren that they were not sufficiently advanced in their planning to implement a union catalog any time soon. If Warren were to initiate a catalog, the other states would probably be gradually drawn into it.

Some "seed money" from the federal government finally enabled Warren to explore the idea of a union catalog on a deeper basis. The funds were sufficiently ample to allow him to organize several multi-county library meetings in which school, public, college, university, and special librarians discussed what the bibliographic network might do for them and what their responsibilities to it would be.

From these meetings, it was clear that the majority of librarians were pleased about the idea of a regional union catalog. Some were quite enthusiastic and ready to begin work; a few were amenable to the concept but pessimistic as to its chances of success. Warren had expected this range of response and was not discouraged by what he encountered. In a systematic attempt to determine the attitudes of those librarians who did not attend the county meetings, he mailed a questionnaire to everyone known to be in charge of a library located in the state. Although he undoubtedly missed a few, he felt that he had at least given wide publicity to the network concept and had provided almost everyone with a line of communication for the expression of opinion.

The responses to the questionnaire proved to be distributed in almost precisely the same pattern as the one which emerged from the county meetings. And even though the percentage of returns was slightly less than 65, Warren felt that he had a strong mandate to explore the concept further.

The next step was to call together the librarians of the state's largest libraries, in an attempt to discover what problems might be encountered in designing a union catalog in book form. No one seemed to want anything less than a book catalog, for a card file at one location—even a central one—was viewed as inflexible and old-fashioned. The prime question seemed to be whether the catalog should be computer-produced or should be reproduced from cards by photo-offset techniques.

Warren's meeting with the heads of the large libraries proved to be somewhat less of a success than he had hoped. Each representative seemed to be committed to the idea of a union catalog, but few demonstrated any basic knowledge of what would be involved in its creation. Warren had asked the head of his own processing unit to sit in on the meeting as an observer. Janet Quinnel, who had worked for seven years in the State Library and ten years before that in the Western College Catalog Department, listened to the statements of the attending librarians with considerable interest; but Warren caught glimpses of her face during parts of the discussion and saw looks of amazement and sometimes amusement there.

"If you are going to get anywhere with this matter of a union catalog, Mr. Granger," Janet had told him later, "you'll need to call a different kind of meeting."

"What do you mean?" he asked. "I know we didn't get beyond a general discussion of the idea, but a few more sessions together should change that."

"I wish I were that optimistic. The problem won't ever be solved by more meetings of these people, as far as I can see. Honestly, Mr. Granger, those librarians don't know anything about what's involved in a union catalog. We'd be lucky if they recognized a main entry card! They're just too far away from the actual cataloging problems to do anything more than ruin the plan."

Warren was thus left with a tactical dilemma: should he risk alienating the library directors by bypassing them in favor of their head catalogers;

should he call a meeting of the directors and ask them to bring the catalogers also; or should he continue with the established pattern and simply
force the directors to get the needed information from their cataloging staff?
The first alternative seemed politically unwise, while the third plan would
surely involve garbled information and undersirable delays occasioned by the
need to get more data from the home library. Accordingly, Warren asked all
the directors to bring someone from the cataloging staff to the next meeting.

Surprisingly, almost half of the library directors sent their head catalogers instead of coming themselves; the remainder brought someone from
cataloging with them. But if Warren had hoped for a truly productive discussion, he was again disappointed. The catalogers raised several objections to
the basic reporting plan which Warren had drafted with Janet's help. The
major roadblock appeared to be local procedures which, if changed, might
mean additional costs for many libraries.

"We order our cards from LC," noted Mrs. Acker from Cedar College.
"Right now all we get is eight cards per set. If we have to do another one
for the union catalog, in many cases we'll have to photocopy it or type one
up or something like that."

"Your library is big enough now that you ought to be duplicating your
own cards, not buying them from LC," countered John Emery, from the
State University. "Don't you get the LC proofsheets?"

"We've talked about it, but we haven't decided yet just what we'll do.
Our Librarian is new on the job, and he wants to study the whole situation
before he makes any changes of that proportion."

"At Calder, we're doing our own card duplication," interjected Allene
Picton, Librarian. "If we have to send a card to the union catalog, that
means we'll run off another copy when we do our own set."

"That'll still cost you some money, though," objected Emery. "You'll
have not only the cost of the extra card, but the work of separating it, pack-
aging it with the others, and sending it off to the union catalog."

"We do our own cards at Bosnell, too," spoke up Edna Jacons, Assistant Librarian for Technical Services. "We're already working with the LC
depository set and sending reports to the *National Union Catalog* and *New
Serials Titles.* I must admit I dread the thought of having to get involved in
another union catalog. Still, I guess it'll be worth it in the long run."

"Are we going to have to put the cards in alphabetical order before we
send them to the union catalog?" asked Mrs. Acker.

"It's going to be a big enough job to get them collected and to record all the locations in one place. The local libraries could at least do the preliminary arrangement, couldn't they?" Emery responded.

"Well, I was just wondering. We don't have a very big staff at Cedar. The collection's grown a lot faster than we anticipated. Each new step is going to cost us time, as well as money."

"Be grateful that you're not being asked to send it to the catalog in machine-readable form!" countered Emery.

"If you did that," answered Mrs. Acker, "you'd just have to count us out."

"Come on, now," Warren interposed in a conciliatory tone. "We all know that we want to make this as painless a process as possible for everyone involved. Why don't I compile your suggestions and criticisms at this point and draft a revised procedural statement? You can look it over, and then we can meet again and hash out the details. O.K.?"

The group seemed agreeable to this procedure.

"Just one more question," said Emery. "Where is this union catalog going to be quartered? Who's going to do all the work of compiling this data?"

"We're working on that," answered Warren. "I hope to have an announcement to make to you about it by the time we have our next meeting."

After the group had left, Warren compared notes with Janet to assess their situation.

"Sure. Some of the libraries are going to have to put out some extra effort," Janet commented. "But if they really want a union catalog, they've got to be ready to pay for it. Some of them will have to be willing to compromise. You notice, though, that nobody was talking seriously about pulling out. Even our conservative friend, Mrs. Acker, is trying to go along with the group—unless, of course, you go to a machine-readable input!"

Warren was encouraged by Janet's summary of the situation. He shared her confidence that the procedures could be worked out so as to minimize the costs to participating libraries.

The succeeding step, which Warren had not considered a particularly difficult one, proved to be much more time-consuming than anticipated. He had assumed that one of the libraries would provide space in which to house a staff employed to develop the union catalog. Ideally, he would have liked to offer the State Library's facilities; however, he and Janet had both been forced to recognize the unfortunate reality of the situation. Their building was already overcrowded, and they simply had no work space in which to install a new department, especially one which would be dealing with an operation as large and complex as the development of a union catalog.

Warren decided to try and persuade the State University Library to accept the task. Since the new library building there had been completed only eighteen months earlier, it seemed that space should certainly not be a major problem. "And we are, as you realize, preparing to seek funds to support the program," Warren told Dr. Johnson, Director of the Library. "All staff and materials costs would be subsidized; the university would simply absorb the overhead. And, with luck, we might be able to help in that direction, too."

Adam Johnson had long been a supporter of the network concept. Occasionally, when Warren waxed particularly enthusiastic about the values of cooperative library service, Dr. Johnson had to exert considerable willpower to avoid reminding him that the State University Library had been advocating such cooperation even before Warren was born. Johnson viewed himself as the most recent in a long line of library directors committed to integrated regional library service.

"I expected you'd be on my doorstep begging for a place to put your union catalog," Johnson kidded Warren. "I just wondered how long it would be before you got here."

"Then you're all ready to say yes?"

"Unfortunately, it's not quite that simple. We could probably find a place for the union catalog for a year or two, if we're forced to. Actually, though, our Catalog Department is already beginning to get a bit crowded, and we haven't even been in this building for two years."

"I guess having a place for a year or two is better than nothing," Warren countered. "But it's going to take some time to get the funds lined up and work out all the details of the procedures with the participating libraries. We might not even get things off the ground before next year."

"You know we're ready to help in any way we can. But if things continue going the way they have been, there may not be any space available by next year! Well, don't let me discourage you too much. I'm sure there'll be other libraries you can use, even if we can't oblige you. How about Bosnell University? Jim Williams and I have always worked together to try to avoid duplication of effort. His staff has a good bibliographic collection, and the university is not looking for more students. Their space situation might be a whole lot better than ours."

"Thanks," said Warren, with a bit of weariness creeping into his voice.

"If you weren't able to do anything, I had thought of talking to Williams anyhow. I guess that's my next stop."

Warren tried not to adopt a defeatist attitude, but when Jim Williams began to explain about the crowded conditions in the library building, Warren knew what was coming.

"I'm not saying that we couldn't do it if we had to," explained Williams. "But I'd think that Johnson over at State U. would be in a better position to take on a job like this."

"Actually, he referred me to you," Warren interjected.

"I'm a little surprised at Adam. I don't know how many times we've talked about lack of space—at least we did before he got his new building finished. Maybe he's forgotten how the other half lives! Anyhow, as I say, we can probably come up with a little space if you're desperate for a place to set up shop. But I don't think you'd be happy with it for very long. How about the Calder College Library? They've got a new building and I hear there's a lot of empty space in it. You might be doing them a favor to use some of it."

Sometime later, after Warren had returned to the State Library, he recounted his experiences to Janet.

"Have you done anything about Calder?" she asked.

"No, not yet. Why?"

"Well, I don't mean to add more problems, but I certainly wouldn't want to be stuck over there, miles away from any major collection. Have you ever seen Calder's reference and bibliography section?"

"Oh, I've been there a couple of times—once for the dedication of the new building. Things looked pretty good to me."

"I don't mean to sound like a snob, but their collection isn't half as good as ours. And ours is poorer than the ones at State U. and Bosnell."

"But Janet, all we need is space."

"Come now, boss, you don't really mean that. You know as well as I do that once all those cataloging records start coming in, with all the contradictions and problems to resolve, it's going to take a really good collection of bibliographies to do the job right."

"I guess you're right," admitted Warren reluctantly. "But it looks as though we either cram ourselves into a library that will always have designs on our space, or we settle for one that has lots of space but no supporting materials. So which do we choose?"

. . . . .

The dilemma facing Warren appears to be rather acute. What other solutions to the problem of locating the union catalog headquarters might he project? What does library literature say about the location of such a program?

Criticize the steps which Warren has taken thus far. What alternatives did he have at various points, and what might have happened if he had proceeded in a different fashion?

Is the union catalog the most desirable first step in developing a network, or might other projects be undertaken more profitably first?

25.
A Young Cataloger
Attends a MARC Institute

· · · · · · · · · · · · · · · ·

His friends in the Catalog Department kidded him, saying that he only wanted to go to the MARC Institute because his name was Mark—Mark Henderson. But Mark sometimes thought he detected a tinge of unpleasantness in the teasing, for there were catalogers at the Eastvale Public Library who had been employed for over ten years but had never attended a conference at library expense.

As it turned out, Mark became the first member of the library staff—which numbered some thirty professionals, counting branch supervisors—to have his entire way paid to a meeting, at least as far as anyone could remember. The only exception was, as might be expected, the director of Eastvale, who managed to get to all the major conferences; but everyone assumed that he was on a generous expense account. The rest of the staff might hope to be given time off and perhaps transportation reimbursement, but only if they were on the program or held an office in the association sponsoring the conference.

One of Mark's friends in the Central Reference Department at Eastvale had often been heard to complain about the fact that so few staff members ever got involved in the workings of national, regional, or state library associations. Bryan had been particularly interested in the activities of the American Library Association while he and Mark were in library school, but Bryan had been somewhat disillusioned by his first job experience. "How can I get elected to an office in ALA if I never go to the meetings?" Bryan asked dejectedly of the group of young professionals who gathered each morning for coffee. "But then, I can't get money to go to meetings if I don't get elected to an office. I suppose I ought to be noble enough to go anyway, without being paid or even getting the time off. But I sure can't see spending my vacation at ALA every year!"

Both Mark and Bryan had been impressed during their library school days with the strong professional concern of one of their professors. Mark particularly remembered the professor saying, "You can't expect your head librarian to hand out travel money lightly. You'll probably have to pay your own way to conferences for awhile. Still, don't forget to *ask* for money. Even the poorest libraries can sometimes come up with funds for someone to go to a special institute. It could just be that no one ever asked for it, so no one ever got it before."

Remembering this advice, Mark decided to approach the Eastvale Director of Libraries, Frank Wernan. To his surprise and great pleasure, Mr. Wernan agreed that Eastvale ought to have someone at the MARC Institute. "You realize, I think, that I'll have to talk with Miss Kellson first. But if she is agreeable to letting you have the time off, I don't see why we can't authorize the funds to pay your way."

Mark had actually already mentioned the possibility to Agnes Kellson, Head of the Catalog Department. She was quite willing to let Mark go, but she had little hope that Wernan would approve the expenditure. When Mark reported his success, however, Miss Kellson received the news without enthusiasm. "Congratulations," she commented perfunctorily. "You seem to have managed to do something no one else around here has accomplished."

Wernan's final approval came in the form of a memo two days later, and Mark began to plan his trip. He carefully filled out the registration form and negotiated with his travel agent about airline schedules. Until about a week before departure time, Mark was excited about the opportunity. Then he began to wonder whether he would know, or even recognize the name of anyone else at the conference. Although Mark was not a particularly shy person, he realized that he could feel rather uncomfortable with a group of total strangers. His colleagues at Eastvale offered no sympathy or help, for few of them had acquired friends who would be likely to attend a MARC Institute.

Despite his last minute fears, Mark found his trip to be easy. It turned out to be fairly simple to strike up a conversation with the other people attending the conference, for each person was given a name tag which included his library affiliation. Mark truly enjoyed the trip, found most of the talks stimulating, and developed quite an interest in the possibilities of using MARC tapes in a library system like Eastvale.

Mark's library school experiences had at least partially prepared him to appreciate the idea of machine-readable cataloging records, but he had never fully understood the flexibility of MARC until he listened to the reports presented at the institute. He discovered, for example, that the full tagging and field delineation of the MARC records made it possible to sort and rearrange them in an almost infinite variety of ways. When he learned of the applications that produced special bibliographies and current awareness lists, Mark became convinced that Eastvale should subscribe to the tapes and maybe even undertake to process them for the entire state.

Although Mark's return home involved a few delays in making airline connections, his excitement about MARC was not noticeably dimmed. Even the unethusiastic welcome from his colleagues affected him only slightly, though he would have been pleased if they had shown a bit more interest in hearing about his experiences.

Since Mark felt some responsibility as the first staff member to be fully subsidized at a conference, he decided that he at least ought to offer to prepare a report on his trip. His director seemed not to have thought of such a possibility, but he welcomed it and suggested that Mark's report be delivered orally to the professional staff. In consequence, a staff meeting was announced for the following Monday afternoon, for the express purpose of hearing about the proceedings of the MARC Institute.

Despite a busy weekend, Mark spent almost five hours preparing for his Monday seminar. He timed his speech carefully and even tape-recorded some of it to find out how he sounded. On Monday morning, he secured permission to have several exhibits photoduplicated for distribution to the staff that afternoon.

The meeting went well; the staff was attentive and asked many questions. Even Bryan was impressed with Mark's ability to conduct such an interesting session—a reaction which may have given Mark the needed courage to approach Mr. Wernan that afternoon after the meeting had ended.

Mark went to the director's office with a plan firmly in mind. Mr. Wernan greeted him warmly: "That was a fine job you did today, Henderson. I think the staff really enjoyed it and learned a lot too. We ought to do this kind of thing more often."

"I'm glad you liked it, Mr. Wernan. Going to the institute was really a great experience for me. But I was wondering whether Eastvale might become a MARC subscriber."

"Well, now I don't know about that. What would be the point of it?"

"Doesn't the city have a third generation computer?"

"Yes, that's right."

"Then we could buy the MARC tapes, use the city's computer, and probably get some low-cost or free programming help. With a little experimentation, we could begin to turn out an SDI service for our staff and maybe even for some of our patrons.

"Whoa there. What makes you think we could afford all that?"

"Well the tapes won't cost more than $1,000 a year, and if we can get free programming time from the city, we could use our staff here to work on it. I'd even be willing to do it on my own time, just to have the experience."

"I don't know, Henderson. This is all pretty speculative. Still, I guess it's worth thinking about. Tell you what—let me mull it over for awhile, and we'll talk about it again later. I'm sort of rushed at the moment, but I'll get back to you."

Although Mark had hoped for a more positive response, Wernan's comments did not particularly dismay him. He did begin to wonder, however, whether he should have taken his idea to Miss Kellson first; but he had concluded in his own mind that the purchase and use of MARC tapes would extend far beyond her jurisdiction.

The following Monday at coffee break, Mark mentioned what he had done. He was entirely unprepared, however, for the response he received from Bryan: "You don't really think Wernan was serious when he said he'd think about it, do you? He probably just said that to get rid of you. The way I see it, Wernan doesn't buy ideas he hasn't thought of himself—which is why nobody has ever heard of anything innovative happening here."

"Do you think it would have been better if I'd gone to my boss first?" Mark asked.

"I don't think it would have made any difference at all, except that it might have kept Miss Kellson from getting angry because you went to see Wernan without telling her. I just think you're being naive. There's nobody in authority here at Eastvale who wants to rock the boat. As long as we keep getting our money from the city fathers and nobody complains too much, Wernan and company think we're doing great."

Mark still wasn't willing to believe that Mr. Wernan would dismiss the idea of subscribing to the MARC tapes so lightly. However, by Friday, Wernan still had not said anything further about the matter, and Mark began to get restless. Finally, on the following Monday morning, he stopped by Wernan's office to try to make an appointment.

"Oh, Mr. Wernan's out of town until Friday," the director's secretary reported.

"Can I see him on Friday then?" asked Mark.

"I don't see anything on his calendar for Friday morning. How about eleven o'clock?"

"Fine. I'll be here."

When Mark arrived for the appointment, Wernan greeted him a bit coolly: "What's on your mind, Henderson?"

"I just wondered whether you'd had a chance to think about what we talked about a couple of weeks ago; you know, the MARC tapes."

"Oh that. I guess I had sort of forgotten about it. I've been away all week, and what with one thing and another, things have been pretty hectic around here. Still, I don't want to mislead you into thinking that I might eventually approve the idea, when that's not really the case. The fact of the matter is, we don't have money to spend on experiments right now. Maybe in a couple of years. Besides, by that time maybe some other public libraries will have done the experimenting and we can profit from their mistakes."

"You don't think we could even consider it, then?"

"No, I'm afraid not. I'm sorry to sound so negative, but it's really out of the question. I don't mean to be rude, but I've got a doctor's appointment in a few minutes. My secretary didn't know about it when she set up this time for you. If you don't mind, I'd like to leave now, but we can talk about it again later if you like."

Mark was so stunned by Wernan's attitude that he could manage only, "No, I guess that won't be necessary. Thank you anyway." As he made his way back to the Catalog Department, Mark remembered Bryan's caustic assessment of "Wernan and Company."

"How could it happen," Mark asked himself, "that such an exciting idea could be dismissed so casually? What do I do now?"

• • • • •

What should Mark do now? Analyze his tactics up to this point. What mistakes, if any, has he made?

If Mark had taken Bryan's comments seriously, what might he have done differently in terms of his approach to Wernan?

What factors ought to be considered before making a decision to subscribe to MARC tapes at Westvale? What experiences have public libraries reported when utilizing the MARC tapes? If Eastvale wanted to compile a realistic estimate of the costs involved, including those associated with programming support, what kind of information would have to be gathered locally?

26

"This Is the Card Catalog. . . ."

• • • • • • • • • • • • • • • • • • •

"Just one more week of freedom before the horde descends on us again," commented Alison Tate to no one in particular.

"What did you say, Alison?" asked Pamela Greene, who had just settled herself at a nearby table in the staff lounge.

"Oh, I was just telling myself to enjoy life while I can. Next week the students will be back. Then there will be masses of humanity wanting to know where the pencil sharpener is and how to get to the john."

"Come on now, I thought the life of the university reference librarian was just one long glamorous encounter with interesting people. We catalogers are supposed to be the misanthropic ones!"

"Yeah, that's the line I picked up in library school, too. But after six years at the reference desk, I sometimes think there couldn't possibly be a question a student could ask that I haven't already answered at least ten times. If I hear someone ask once more, 'Where is the *Readers' Guide?*,' I think I'll scream."

"No you won't; you'll smile sweetly like you always do and take him over to the bibliography section. And with your best professional attitude, you'll ask, 'What is it you're looking for in the *Readers' Guide?*' And before you're through you'll have introduced the unsuspecting student to half a dozen indexes he didn't know existed."

"You're probably right. I think what I'm dreading most is those wretched orientation sessions with the freshmen. Every year we go through the motions, but I'm absolutely certain the effort is wasted on 90 percent of them."

"I wish you hadn't said that. You probably don't know, but I've been recruited to do the part on the catalog this year. Your boss decided to diversify—or maybe just pass the buck. But anyhow, I wound up volunteering to explain the values of the card file. Being young and innocent, I didn't know enough to say no. Besides, they keep telling us the main thing wrong with catalogers is that they don't know their users."

"Good luck, kid. By the end of next week you may know more about your users than you ever wanted to. Some people don't know when they're well off!"

At that moment the two were joined by several other staff members also lunching in the lounge. The conversation turned to different matters, but Pam still felt a bit edgy about the cynicism in Allison's remarks. She began to wonder whether she might regret having taken on the orientation assignment so casually.

Grace Henson, Chief Reference Librarian at Calson University, had over the years organized more than fifty orientation sessions—two or three a year for better than twenty years. Although the program was a fixture at Calson, Grace tried to vary the procedures to produce something appropriate for each generation of freshmen. One day she hoped to be able to introduce the library by means of programmed learning sequences, perhaps using an on-line computer system. She had studied the techniques, but until now there had been little willingness on the part of the university administration to invest any funds in developing appropriate materials. Discussions preliminary to the allocation of funds were going on, and with luck Grace might be permitted to experiment with programmed techniques the following fall. But she estimated that, at best, it would be two years before they could do away with the present orientation program entirely.

For this year, anyway, the program had to remain the same as always: freshmen, in groups of about twenty or twenty-five at most, would be scheduled to tour the main library building. They would be introduced to the circulation procedures, the card catalog, the reference services, and various special collections such as manuscripts, documents, and rare books. The major difference this year would be that people from the various sections and departments were going to describe their own areas, rather than the reference staff doing it all. Grace wasn't sure how this would work, but it might have the advantage of relieving the tedium of hearing only one person; and it would certainly save wear and tear on the reference staff.

Pam Greene thought she had volunteered for the job of introducing the card catalog. Actually Grace had asked the Chief Catalog Librarian, Warren Carlson, for permission to recruit her for the orientation program. "Pam is young and pretty," Grace commented to Warren one day.

"Yes, ma'am, I've noticed that," responded Warren with a gleam in his eye. "Our male student assistants have noticed it too. They fall all over themselves to do things for her. And she's not only pretty, she's interested in other people, too. Add to that the fact that she's as bright as they come and you've got a real winner. And you want her to help with the orientation program for the freshmen."

"You're some kind of a mind reader! How did you know that's what I was going to ask?"

"I've got spies everywhere. We know what's going to happen before it's even plotted."

"O.K., so it doesn't really matter how you know. Can I have Pam?"

"Sure, if she's willing. I never commit any of my staff to something they don't want to do. Why don't you ask her?"

"All right, I will!"

Grace Henson approached Pam somewhat indirectly. Finding a few of the cataloging staff together at staff coffee break, Grace joined them and outlined her problem. "What I need is one of you to do the part on the card catalog. Any takers?" she asked.

Pam obligingly voiced her willingness to participate, thinking all the time that she was volunteering. But Warren Carlson overheard the conversation and smiled to himself. "That Grace is a shrewd operator," he thought. "I wonder how often she's conned me into doing something when I thought it was my own idea."

The planning of the part of the orientation which would take place in the catalog area was left largely up to Pam. Grace told her what she had in mind in terms of the length of the presentation and the topics to be covered: "You probably don't want to take over ten minutes. The tour has eight stops; figuring ten minutes per stop and five minutes travel time between, the whole thing will take about an hour and forty-five minutes. If your presentation gets too long, then the rest of the people will have to try to cut theirs short."

"Are we going to have a meeting of everybody doing the tour, so we'll know how to coordinate our efforts?" asked Pam.

"I've thought about it, but some of the ones who're participating are still away on vacation. They'll be back in time for orientation but not any sooner. Besides, some of them, like Bert Jessup in Manuscripts, give tours of one kind or another all the time."

"Well, I guess I was thinking that it might help me to know what the others were doing. But anyhow, you said you had some suggestions about what I ought to try to cover?"

"Yes. The main thing is for the students to know something about how the catalog is arranged and how to use it to find the materials they need. In the past, we've usually told them about the fact that this library has a divided catalog, and that the serials holdings will be in the computer printout, and about the things like documents and manuscripts that they won't find here. And of course we try to make them understand that they should ask the reference staff for help if they have any problems."

Pam was not completely satisfied with Grace Henson's suggestions. One of the main problems that most students seemed to have in using the catalog was understanding the concept of a "main card" and the fact that subject headings did not necessarily show all the materials in the library relating to a specific topic. She also thought they ought to learn about the LC subject headings list so that they would use the subject part of the divided catalog more effectively.

For several days Pam practiced her speech carefully and timed it down to the half-minute. She watched herself in the mirror, and finally she tape-recorded the talk to get a sense of the sound. Each example that she intended to use had been chosen deliberately to illustrate a point as precisely as possible. She even tried to inject a little humor into the selection of subjects to be mentioned. On the night before the beginning of the tours, Pam felt well prepared but apprehensive. "I might as well be giving a performance on the stage," she thought. "I don't think I'd be any more nervous than I am right now. All I hope is that the freshmen will be more scared than I am."

When the first group arrived, Pam discovered that they were certainly not scared—at least they gave no evidence of it. The catalog stop was the third on the tour, and Pam had imagined that the students would be at least reasonably alert at that point. But as they straggled up to the catalog, they looked more bored than anything else.

"As you can see," Pam began. "this is the card catalog. It's probably a lot larger than anything you've ever used in your high school library or even in a public library unless you come from someplace like New York. And this catalog is arranged somewhat differently from most of the ones you may have used. It's divided into two main sections: one part has the cards representing the authors and titles of the books in the library, and the other has the cards for the subjects of the books. If you'll follow me, I'll show you exactly what the difference is."

With the first group, as with later ones—and there were to be more than forty groups during the four-day period—the students tended to drift about the catalog area rather than follow her promptly to the section she wanted to show them. As she introduced them to the concept of main card and told them about the subject headings list and the serials printout, most of them listened quietly, though one or two always moved away and held their own conversation just out of earshot.

Pam had tried to time her presentation to allow a few minutes—at least two or three—for questions from the group. Most of the freshmen were content to let the speech end without question, but a few seemed to be determined to try to embarrass her. One boy in the first group wanted to know, "Where do they keep the sex books? Do they lock 'em up?" The question brought a few giggles from the others on the tour, but Pam fielded it nicely.

"We only lock up the ones that people steal. If they're 'protected,' " Pam said pointedly, "an asterisk will appear at the beginning of the call number. And that just serves to emphasize what I said earlier about being careful to make a note of everything in the call number, not just part of it."

Although some of the questions emanating from later groups revealed a certain amount of sophistication on the part of a small number of the freshmen, most of them came, listened politely, and left without comment. A good many appeared to be almost in a daze, moving and responding more from instinct than from will. By the time the tenth group had come and gone, Pam understood how they must feel. "I can't even remember what I've told which group anymore. The whole thing is beginning to blur, and this is just the end of the first day!" she told Alison, who was on duty at the reference desk. "If I see another main card or subject heading I think I'll scream."

"Ah, yes," responded Alison, with a wicked smile. "Our champion of interpersonal involvement is finding out why working with the public isn't quite as glamorous as it's cracked up to be. How many groups did you do before they asked you about the sex books?"

"One! But at least I was prepared for it when it came around again. The thing that really bothered me, though, was that so many of the kids looked really beat down, like they'd been up all night for a week."

"They probably have. Didn't you see their schedule?"

"No. Why?"

"By the time they get to us, they've already been talked at by a dozen or more university officials and officers of student associations. And then they stay up half the night talking. It's no wonder they're practically asleep on their feet by the time they get here."

"That sounds like cruel and unusual punishment."

"It is. But next year, they say it's all going to be different. Of course, they've been saying that for as long as I can remember, so I'll believe it when I see it."

For the next three days, Pam tried every device she could think of to catch the imagination of the students on tour. She recast her presentation in terms of what she thought their experiences might be. Instead of telling them, "This is the card catalog," she began with: "Let's imagine that you have just been assigned a term paper on Ibsen for your English course."

Pam decided that her new pitch was more interesting, but she still felt discouraged. At the end of a grueling week, she could evade her feelings no longer. "Mrs. Henson, I think this whole tour business is wrong," she announced at her first opportunity. "These kids are worn out and they couldn't care less about the card catalog at this point."

"I know that, Pamela. I guess we've all known it for years. And we really do hope to improve the situation next fall. This is probably the last orientation session that will be done this way. But we're not sure yet what the new format will be. By the way, I've heard a number of compliments from the students and the staff about how well you did in presenting the card catalog. You shouldn't feel too discouraged. As these sessions go, your part was outstandingly well received."

"I'm grateful for that, of course. But I still think there must be a better way."

"Of course there is. What I want to know now is whether you'll work with us to design a section of the new orientation program. We need a good, service-minded cataloger to do the parts related to the catalog. And we'd like to put in a section on the classification scheme."

"At this stage, I'm so exhausted that I can't even imagine what I could do."

"That's all right. I know how you feel. But think about it, and we'll talk it over again sometime next week."

• • • • •

If you were in Pam's place, would you accept Grace Henson's invitation? If you were given the task of designing a new kind of introduction to the card catalog, how would you go about it? Whose help, if anyone's would you solicit in carrying out this task?

Since programmed learning techniques have been suggested as a possible orientation device, what information is available on these procedures, especially as related to the teaching of skills in the use of the card catalog? What prepackaged materials, if any, are marketed currently to meet this need? To what extent could a programmed learning approach be expected to solve the various problems which Pam encountered in trying to orient the freshmen?

If programmed learning is not feasible or is considered inappropriate to the teaching of the use of the catalog, what other devices might be considered?

27.
An Automated Library
Runs Short of Funds

• • • • • • • • • • • • •

Ashton University had been created—right in the middle of the desert—as a privately-supported institution to incorporate the valuable educational innovations of the twentieth century. "We will not be bound by the traditions and mistakes of the past," its president announced at the groundbreaking ceremony. "It is our aim to take full advantage of the psychological and technological advances of our century in order to create a setting which will promote learning at every turn. If the computer can help us further this goal, then Ashton will have the best computer ever designed by the mind of man. But it will always be the mind of man that we seek to serve, never the computer."

Twelve years after the groundbreaking, and ten years after the opening day, Ashton had only partially lived up to the expectations of its first administrative officer. The predicted enrollment of 15,000 students had yet to be attained, although there were regularly about 8,000 to 9,000 students on campus or registered for some kind of continuing education. Of these, only about 4,500 were resident students, for Ashton had encouraged commuters and part-time attendance.

Ashton's first president had, however, found better opportunities for the exercise of his talents elsewhere. After five years of coping with campus planning, academic standards, complex equipment, and money raising, he submitted his resignation and moved on to assume the chancellorship of a hundred-year-old state university. Although some of Ashton's faculty viewed this as a traitorous move, many were pleased to see the university acquire the services of Paul Yarden, a veteran college administrator who combined a belief in high academic standards with a very practical talent for attracting wealthy donors.

In keeping with the philosophy of the first president, Ashton had employed as chief librarian a young man of high enthusiasm but somewhat limited experience. He had envisioned the Ashton Library as a completely automated information storage and retrieval system. During the affluent years of Ashton's development, the library had been encouraged to lease its own computer and acquire by rental or purchase the necessary peripheral equipment. Thus, its first librarian set about to produce all library records by means of computer manipulation and control.

As the money began to be less plentiful, some of the library's automated procedures suffered. And when threats were finally made against the retention of its separate computer facilities, the head librarian quickly moved to seek another position. He left, in fact, one week before the first president departed the campus.

Ashton's second librarian—now called Director of Library and Information Services—brought to the university more experience and wisdom with regard to general library administration and management techniques. Wallace Carlton had, in his interviews with President Yarden and other campus officials, made it clear that he was not wedded to the idea of a completely automated library.

Although Wallace had been aware, during his visit to the campus as a candidate for the directorship, that the library was somewhat behind in processing current materials, he later discovered that the situation was actually much worse than he had been led to believe. Alan Cross, his predecessor, had, during his five-year tenure, developed a computer-based book catalog as the only public listing of the library's holdings. In the fourth year of Cross's stay, the library had been deprived of its separate printing capabilities—as an economy measure, Cross was told. What Wallace had not realized at first was that no eye-legible version of the catalog had been produced since the initial one, that is, since the first book catalog had been issued at the end of the library's third year of operation.

Wallace was justifiably unhappy with himself for not having discovered how far behind the catalog was. He had—logically, he thought—assumed that there were printed supplements to the catalog which he simply had not encountered during his brief stay on campus. There were, in fact, no such supplements, although the data for bringing the catalog up-to-date had been carefully prepared and stored on magnetic tape.

Shortly after he became aware of the state of the catalog, Wallace called in Richard Kelvin, Coordinator of Technical Services, for a strategy conference. Kelvin had been hired primarily as a computer and systems man, with some experience in computerized indexing techniques. Wallace had sensed, from talking with some of the catalogers, that their respect for Kelvin's bibliographic expertise was extremely low.

"Dick, I guess it's no secret to you that we are in pretty bad shape as far as our catalog is concerned. I can honestly say I was stunned when I found out that no revised catalog and no supplements have come out since the first run. That was almost two years ago, and we don't have an up-to-date list. For a growing institution, that's almost criminal."

"I'm not sure you fully understand the situation, Mr. Carlton. We don't have any cataloging backlog; the technical services work is right up-to-date. It's just that the university won't approve our spending the money to do a new edition of the printout, or even to do any supplements. The magnetic tapes are all there, ready to go, and the programs are all written. I keep talking to people about it, but they never give me the go-ahead."

"I don't mean to sound naive, but why haven't you considered reverting to a manual catalog? It seems incredible to me that a university library could go about its business with a catalog that's two years behind the times. Hasn't there been any complaint from the public services people?"

"Sure, they've given me hell about it, just like they did Mr. Cross. If you want to know what I think, Cross left because of staff pressure as much as anything else. Look Mr. Carlton, I was hired to do a special kind of job. I never tried to pass myself off as a librarian, and I don't know anything much about library cataloging. Cross put me on the staff to get that computerized catalog started. And he gave me the title of Coordinator mainly so he could justify the salary he was paying me. I can see the handwriting on the wall as well as anybody else. Maybe it'll help you to know that I'm just about to complete negotiations for another job. If you want a traditional cataloging system, you're going to need someone else anyhow."

"I appreciate your laying it on the line, Dick. In many ways I'll be sorry to see you leave. I was thinking perhaps of working out a transfer for you—and I can probably still do it if this other job of yours doesn't come through. I would like to know, though, whether you think there's anyone in technical services who could run the division."

"Paula Kircher has been in on the systems design from the beginning. She's been my salvation because she knows the library end of it and has been willing to learn about computers. If I were in your shoes, I'd promote her. You won't get anyone better from outside."

"Thanks. That's what I wanted to know. From what I hear from the catalogers, at least, they think Paula is competent and they respect her. She sounds like a good choice."

Within two months, Kelvin had resigned to accept his new job and Mrs. Kircher had been promoted to the position of Coordinator. Paula and Wallace Carlton had almost daily meetings for the next few weeks, trying to devise a system for catching up.

"My husband's beginning to complain that you see more of me than he does," Paula announced one morning.

"You tell him I've got more important things to do than cope with jealous husbands. If he wants to come help us out of this mess, he can spend all day with you if he likes," snapped Wallace.

"Thanks a lot! In view of Jerry's total ignorance about library cataloging and his hate for computers, I think I'll just try to lure him away for a romantic weekend instead."

"Look, Paula, we've been talking so much about this catalog business that I'm getting fuzzy on what we've accomplished thus far. Why don't you just review the situation and bring me up-to-date?"

"O.K., this is the way I see it. Our first problem was the fact that there'd been no printed version of the public catalog except the first one, and it was two years out-of-date. But the catalog data had been produced and stored on magnetic tape in anticipation of the issuing of a cumulative list—or at least a cumulative supplement. Said supplement was axed by the university because we didn't have enough money in the budget. You've begged and pleaded and threatened, but Yarden still won't let you have the money."

"Lord knows I've tried, Paula."

"Sure, we know you did. But we're still stuck without a catalog that the staff and patrons can use. And to make things worse, we got generous and distributed copies of the first catalog to practically everybody on campus. Now they want to know why it's so badly out-of-date and when they'll get a new one. Even if we eventually get permission to run a supplement, it's a cinch we won't be able to distribute 500 copies like we did for the first one."

"You're so right! So, now where are we?"

"Well, we've got several options at the moment. We can probably finagle the money to do a simple multicopy printout of the titles that have been processed since the last computer run. The cheapest version would be just an author list. And by the way, one of our catalogers asked me why we didn't make it a title list, if we had to settle for just one entry point. She thinks the title list would satisfy the people who want to know whether a particular book is in the library and it would also give a sort of primitive subject approach through the first title word—you know, a kind of elementary keyword approach."

"I guess I can see her point. But I still don't really understand why we can't just get busy and produce a *card* catalog like any normal library. We don't have to go back and redo the entries that went into the original printout, but we could start with the material that's come in since then."

"My only objection to that is time and cost. In the first place, we've never written a program to produce catalog cards from the tapes we have right now. That would entail a high development cost that we really can't afford."

"Couldn't we put it into the experimental category and get one of the master's or doctoral candidates in the Computer Science Department to take it on as a project?"

"Two years ago we might have been able to con them into something like that, but these days they're way beyond being interested in working with a simple little problem like formatting data to be printed out on card stock."

"If it's so simple, how come it costs so much?"

"The concept is simple; the actual writing of the program and getting it debugged is tedious and takes a lot of computer time. That's where the cost comes in."

"Tell me again. Don't you have *any* readable version of the recent catalog data?"

"Yes, there's one, but it's bulky and very awkward to use. We have packs of punched cards for all of the titles cataloged. Each deck is banded together and filed by the call number of the title represented, to form a kind of temporary shelflist. That's what the circulation people use when they get in a bind."

"And you said something once about the acquisitions people having a file, too."

"What they did was to retain a copy of the multiform order packet that the computer generates through its purchase program. Every title that's been received but is not represented in the first printed catalog has a slip under main entry in that file. Actually, that's not quite accurate: they have a slip under whatever the main entry was expected to be when the material was first ordered. But that's the file that the reference people and interlibrary loan people use most often."

"And you don't think we could just take those slips and photograph them to make a catalog for the staff to use?"

"The slips are pretty badly marked up. You can read most of them easily enough, but they serve staff purposes reasonably well right where they are. I don't see much percentage in photographing them unless we are planning to make them available to the public. I'd be awfully embarrassed to do that."

"But these slips do have the call numbers on them?"

"Yes, and in some cases—I wish I could say all—the main entry has been corrected when it was found to be wrong."

"Do you think we really ought to be continuing the current procedures? Doesn't this simply add to the problem and put us farther behind?"

"That's the factor that worries me most. If we are eventually going to establish a card catalog, we might as well begin now."

"How many new titles are we expecting to add this year, anyway?"

"The way we're going, I'd guess something over 30,000. The total collection was slightly over 200,000 last year, but in the first years of operation, we processed books like crazy. When the university opened, we had more than 50,000 volumes already on the shelves. We slowed down a bit after that, but we've done nearly 30,000 each year. I don't think we'll ever get much above that until we enlarge our staff."

"In view of of our financial condition, I doubt that we'll have money to order much more than we're getting right now. By the way, how are we doing on our serials printout?"

"You do have a way of asking embarrassing questions! Now that's *another* story. But I'm not sure you're strong enough to hear it."

• • • • •

Considering Ashton's current financial pinch and the prospects likely for the future, which of the alternatives proposed by Paula appears to be most useful? What are the priorities in this situation? Whose needs should be considered first?

What other alternatives might be proposed for Ashton? Since money for experimentation might be available if some interest could be generated on the part of students in the Computer Science Department, what kinds of "experimental" projects could be devised to help the Library?

How likely is it that money will be available for maintaining a card catalog, if it is not allocated to make possible the printing of a supplemental book catalog in multiple copies? What does the published literature reveal about the relative cost of book catalogs versus card catalogs?

28.
An Information Retrieval Problem?

"Got any good students this year? Ones with a science background?" asked Mildred Everts, as she encountered Doris Hardy in the corridor outside the office of the Comstock University Library School.

"The usual crop," answered Dr. Hardy. "But the new ones haven't been here long enough for us to find out how good they are. There are a few with science backgrounds, though. Why?"

"Oh, one of my friends who works out at Palmer Research Lab says they need someone to help them set up an information system for their library."

"I thought Palmer already had a librarian."

"That's what I thought, too, but I guess we were both wrong. The library was set up by one of their research staff; they've never had a professional librarian. There's somebody working out there now—I don't think she's a librarian though."

"I take it they want to hire one of our students."

"That's what Bill said. He thinks it ought to be somebody with a science background. And he said something about their being able to help set up an automated system."

"We might have one or two students sophisticated enough to undertake that kind of job. Anyway, I'm curious about the situation. What's your friend's name? Would it be all right for me to talk to him about it?"

"Sure, why not? Just call the Palmer Lab and ask for William Andrews. I don't know the extension number, but the operator will get him for you. Tell him I told you to call. I may even get a chance to talk to him in the next couple of days, and I'll tell him who you are."

"Maybe I ought to wait till the first of next week, then, so you'll have time to lay some groundwork for me."

"O.K. I should be seeing him on Friday. He comes over to the bio-

171

chem seminars every month, and he usually stops by the Med School Library while he's here. I'll tell him that the Library School's illustrious professor of cataloging is interested in his problem. That ought to impress him."

"If it doesn't scare him away! Anyhow, thanks Millie. I'll give Mr. Andrews a call next Monday."

When Dr. Hardy placed her call to the Palmer Lab, she wasn't quite sure what reception to expect. The operator promptly connected her with an office where a pleasant masculine voice answered, "Hello, Andrews speaking."

"Yes, Mr. Andrews. This is Doris Hardy. I'm not sure whether Mildred Everts has had a chance to speak to you yet, but I'm—"

"Oh yes, you're the one who teaches in the Library School over at Comstock. Glad you called. Millie told me you were interested in our problems out here."

"I am interested, but from what she could tell me, I can't be quite sure what you need. Before I can suggest a student—or anyone else—qualified to help you, I ought to find out more about your situation."

"It would be a lot easier to show you than to tell you about it over the phone. Is there any chance you could come out here anytime soon?"

"How would it be if I brought along a student who might be qualified for the job? Things might move faster that way."

"Sure, that'd be fine. When do you think you might be able to come?"

"Since I don't teach on Tuesday and Thursday afternoons and the student I have in mind is free then, would either of those days be possible?"

"Let's see . . . I've got an experiment cooking right now, but it ought to be past the critical stage by next Thursday. Would that be too soon?"

"No, I don't think so. How about two o'clock?"

"Good. Do you know how to get here?"

"I can find the building all right, but how will I find you?"

"Just check in with the receptionist. She'll call me to come down. We operate under pretty tight security here."

"That makes sense. I guess it really wouldn't be such a good idea to let spies from the competition wander around unidentified. All right then, I'll check with my student, and unless I call you again, we'll plan to see you at two on Thursday."

Doris Hardy knew of two students whose background and maturity might qualify them to assist in the Palmer situation; and one of them, Wendy

Person, was in her afternoon class in Advanced Cataloging and Classification. As Dr. Hardy entered the room, she stopped to ask Wendy to remain a few minutes after class.

Wendy Person had enrolled in library school primarily to obtain the credentials necessary to become Comstock's chemistry librarian. A twenty-eight year old, Wendy already held a master's degree in chemistry and had worked three years as a subprofessional assistant in the chemistry library on campus. Dr. Hardy knew that she had been involved in the implementation of a computer-based current awareness system for the chemistry faculty and had been the supervisor for the desk attendants in the chemistry library.

In order to complete the library school program as quickly as possible, Wendy had resigned from her position in chemistry to attend school full time. Her funds were, however, running low and she had mentioned to Dr. Hardy that she would like to find a job requiring no more than about ten hours per week. Because of Wendy's chemistry background, Dr. Hardy immediately thought of her for the Palmer situation.

When Wendy came up to the desk after class, Dr. Hardy reviewed quickly the conversations she had had with Mildred Everts and William Andrews. "I was wondering," she concluded, "whether you'd like to go out with me Thursday and look things over. Don't feel you have to, but I knew you were interested in augmenting your income, and this might be a way to do it."

"Thanks, Dr. Hardy. I am interested, and Thursday is a good time for me. Shall I meet you out at the Lab?"

"Why don't you just ride along with me. I'll be coming back to campus afterward, and that'll give us some time to talk about our impressions of the set up."

Wendy and Dr. Hardy arranged to meet at the library school to drive out to the Lab. The ride took about fifteen minutes. As the main building of the Palmer Research Laboratories came into view, they were impressed by the modern architectural design. The elegance of the exterior proved to be repeated in the reception area. An attractive young woman at the desk took their names. She had obviously been alerted to their coming, for she immediately produced identification badges for each of them. While they signed the register, the receptionist called Bill Andrews.

The two were greeted shortly thereafter by a genial man of medium build, probably somewhere between forty-five and fifty years of age. He extended his hand to each of them in turn and motioned to them to follow him to the nearby elevator.

"It's only one flight up and I usually take the stairs, but when I have guests I do it the genteel way."

"I probably ought to walk up for the exercise," responded Dr. Hardy, "but it's nice to be treated like a guest. How long have you been here at Palmer, Mr. Andrews?"

"Almost four years. You're probably wondering why I'm not a vice-president or something. Oh, don't protest. Most people think all our research staff are teenagers. But I happen to like to do research, and I hate management. The top brass wanted a research man when they started this center, so they moved me here to be 'research director.' Most of the time we operate as a team. They only need a director when something goes wrong and they have to find somebody to blame."

As they emerged from the elevator and walked down the second floor corridor, Bill pointed out the various laboratory facilities in the area and then led them to a room obviously designed to be a library. Despite the wealth of bookshelves and a handsome reading table surrounded by comfortably upholstered chairs, there was little evidence of a collection of library materials.

Bill turned to Wendy: "And the next question will be 'Where are the books?' Right?"

"I'm afraid you are, Mr. Andrews. It's not too often I see a library without a lot of books or least periodicals lying around."

"Actually this is where the library is supposed to be. I wanted you to see this room first, so you won't be so shocked when you see where the library is right now. Come with me, please."

Bill then led them to an office two doors down the hall. The first look into the room brought a frown to Doris Hardy's face. "I see what you mean," she remarked crisply.

"The room at the end of the hall has just been remodeled," Bill put in quickly. "We'll move the library into it, beginning tomorrow if the men come to move the stuff. As you can see, we've just been dumping everything in here until the new area was finished. By next week, though, we ought to be in much better shape, at least as far as the physical surroundings are concerned."

Dr. Hardy moved back out into the corridor. "Miss Everts said something about your wanting to introduce automation into your library," she remarked.

The change of topic seemed not to bother Bill at all. "When you come right down to it," he responded, "I'm not sure what we need. Jack Roberts—he's a friend of mine who teaches over at Comstock—says he's read a lot of articles about chemistry libraries using computers. I thought maybe we could do something like that here."

"Do you have a regular librarian here at Palmer?" asked Wendy.

"We had a girl for about two years who took care of ordering all the things we needed. George—that's George Miller who used to work here—set up the system for the card file. And he helped Marge catalog the materials. Maybe you remember seeing those four vertical file cabinets in the room we're now using for the library. Most of the documents are in there. We must have well over a thousand by this time. We don't have a very large book collection though—maybe two or three hundred volumes. One of our main problems is what to do about the magazines that keep piling up."

"Then you don't have a librarian at the moment?" Wendy persisted.

"Oh yes, we've hired a new girl. I'll introduce you to her later. She's down doing some typing for the vice-president right now."

"I take it she's not full time in the library then," commented Dr. Hardy.

"Usually she is, but when they have a rush typing job they sometimes call her. She knew that when we hired her."

"What library experience does she have?" asked Doris Hardy.

"Oh, she's not a professional, if that's what you mean. We sent her over to Comstock last week to spend a couple of days with the librarians there. And she can call them for help if she needs it."

Doris Hardy frowned. "I think I'd better be candid with you, Mr. Andrews," she said. "In view of what I've seen thus far, I can't judge whether Wendy or any other of our students would be right for you. It looks as though your main problem is the lack of a trained librarian; but simply on the basis of this visit, I can't make any reliable assessment of your needs. Since I'm pretty rushed right now, I'd like to suggest that Wendy come back when she can spend a little time looking over your files and records. Then maybe she'll be able to make up her own mind about whether she wants to take on this assignment. And you'll be in a better position to decide

whether she can do the job you have in mind. Besides, since the materials
are about to be moved, it doesn't make much sense to try to look at them
today."

"You're probably right," Bill agreed. "I'm sorry things are in such a
mess."

Turning to Wendy, Dr. Hardy asked, "Would it be possible for you to
come back next week?"

"I'd be very grateful if you could, Miss Person," Bill added. "Our researchers are getting pretty impatient with the new girl. She can't seem to
find anything when it's needed, or even figure out how to get it for them."

"I would like to look over the situation a little more," answered
Wendy. "I think I can arrange to come back next week, but I'm wondering
what the 'philosophy' of this library is."

"At the outset, we didn't plan to establish a library at all. We really
need more of a document and information center. We can get most of the
books we want from the university, but we have a lot of specialized material
here—reports, government documents, and such—that isn't available at Comstock. We buy some journals and a few basic books for general purposes.
I'm honestly not convinced that we need a professional librarian."

"I'm sorry to rush away," interjected Dr. Hardy, "but I have to be
back on campus shortly. Maybe we can call it a day for now."

"I understand, but before you go, let me introduce you to Mrs.
Jefferson, our new librarian."

They followed Bill to the opposite end of the hall, where a group of
women were busily typing in a large administrative office area. He showed
them to one of the desks, at which Alice Jefferson was working.

In view of the general office noise, only perfunctory introductions were
made, and Alice returned quickly to her typing. Wendy thought she looked
like a career secretary, but she also noticed that Alice seemed very tired. As
they moved out into the hall, Bill commented, "Alice is a good worker. She
needs the job. Her husband was killed while he was overseas with the army.
And she's got two little kids to look after. That's why she came back
here—so the grandmother could take care of the children while Alice
works."

Wendy made arrangements with Bill to return on the following Thursday afternoon. As she rode back to campus with Dr. Hardy, she commented,
"I don't know whether I can do much good out there or not."

"I don't know either, Wendy," answered Doris Hardy. "But I don't want to influence you unduly one way or the other. I think you'll be able to decide more intelligently when you've had a chance to look over the collection and the records."

When Wendy arrived at the Palmer Lab on the following Thursday, she learned that Bill was out of town attending a conference. He had, however, left word that Wendy was to be allowed to go freely to and from the library. The receptionist gave Wendy her badge and called Alice Jefferson to tell her that Miss Person was on her way up.

A few minutes of conversation with Mrs. Jefferson revealed clearly that Alice had no background to prepare her to take care of the library, although she seemed quite competent as a typist and bookkeeper. Wendy noted that the orders for new materials were being processed adequately, but Alice frankly confessed that she did not know what to do with the materials after they arrived.

"Some of the research men come in the library twice a day to find out whether something has come," Alice complained. "They act like I'm hiding it from them. And when it does come, they snatch it away before I have a chance to do more than check the invoice. I've tried to get them to let me keep it for at least a day, but they say they've got to have it right now."

"Are they *all* that impatient, or only a few?"

"I guess it's really only one or two, but the ones in a hurry never give you any peace."

"How many researchers are there here?"

"About fifteen are served by this library."

"Are there other libraries in the Lab?"

"A couple of small ones. There's a Management Library downstairs and an Economics/Statistics one in the building next door."

"Have they ever talked about combining them into one?"

"Mr. Andrews said they thought about it, but nobody pushed it, so they gave up trying."

"What about Palmer's potential for automation? Is there a computer in the building?"

"I don't think so. They've got some keypunch equipment down in the main office, but I've never heard anyone mention a computer."

"Well, don't let me keep you from doing your work. If it's all right with you, I'll just snoop around for a while."

"Go right ahead, Miss Person. But if you find anything you don't understand, I probably won't be able to help you."

"Didn't the previous librarian leave you any kind of procedure manual?"

"This folder is all I inherited. Take it if you like; it really hasn't done me much good."

The pile of materials which Alice handed over proved to contain a set of procedures for ordering materials for the library, a brief list of what appeared to be subject headings for the collection, and a couple of sample sheets showing the form used in making what Wendy decided were Palmer's equivalent of catalog cards.

Her first examination of the catalog itself revealed a situation much worse than she had expected. While some of the data had been typed on card stock, other records consisted of mimeographed sheets cut to three-by-five-inch size and pasted on cards. Still others were just the cut sheets, often unevenly and imprecisely trimmed.

The concept of main entry had evidently not been familiar to those who had inaugurated the cataloging system. As Wendy thumbed through the catalog, she discovered that some authors' names had been inverted, others recorded in natural order. No attempt had been made to establish a consistent form; she found, for example:

BROWN, J. G.

JAMES G. BROWN

BROWN, JAMES G.

BROWN, JAMES GORDON

J. G. BROWN

All of the Browns so listed seemed to be the same person, and Wendy found that two of the cards actually represented two copies of the same work. A further inspection of the catalog revealed that individual issues of periodicals had been cataloged separately and that each document had been assigned some sort of location number.

"Alice, what do the numbers on the cards stand for?"

"Oh, that's what we file the documents by—over in the file drawers there."

Wendy closed the catalog drawer, but not before she had noticed that whoever had filed the cards was evidently unable to arrange letters beyond the initial one. In fact, even the Ns and Os had become somewhat mixed-up. The file proved to be even more of a shock. As she opened it, she found a 500-page book turned on its side in the drawer, preceded and followed by unbound report literature.

"What's this book doing in the document file?" Wendy asked incredulously.

"Oh, that must be one I missed. I thought I'd pulled all of them out. That's something I was going to ask you about. When I first came here, all the books were in the file drawers with the documents. They caused me so much trouble and took up so much space, I decided to take them out and put them on the shelves. But I don't know whether I ought to mark them in some way and show where they are."

"We could fix them up, I guess, but why were they put in the file in the first place?"

"Search me. Mr. Andrews said Mr. Miller decided to do it that way."

"And I guess Mr. Miller must have also decided to put each periodical issue under a separate accession number. Haven't you ever bound any of your volumes?"

"I really don't know what you mean. All I know is that the only books we have with hard covers are the ones you see on the shelves. Everything else has a paper cover or no cover at all."

"Hi there, Miss Person," came the cheery voice of Bill Andrews. "I got back from the conference sooner than I'd expected, so I thought I'd come by and see how you're getting along. When are you going to start work on automating our library?"

• • • • •

In view of what she has already discovered about the Palmer Library, what answer should Wendy give Bill Andrews at this point?

What procedures can Wendy use to determine the type of library cataloging system which might be most effective for Palmer? How can she find out whether an automated system is either feasible or appropriate for Palmer?

Under what terms, if any, would it be desirable for Wendy to accept a part-time job at Palmer? If Wendy decides not to take the job, what type of person might be recommended to Bill Andrews?

29.
"Make More Title Added Entries, Please"

· · · · · · · · · · ·

Gilmel College had been opened in 1950 with the promise that its curriculum and facilities would be "as contemporary and innovative as the human mind can design." To a large degree, Gilmel had lived up to that promise. Credit hours were abandoned for "course credits"; independent study was encouraged whenever student and faculty could agree upon a plan of investigation; vocational experiences could be substituted for one or more course credits; and the "Pass-Fail" option had been available from the beginning.

Gilmel's library (recently renamed the Learning Resources Center) had been developed to support the "library college" concept. The current 250,000-volume collection reflected careful selection policies and was well stocked with ingredients for independent study and research. Its periodicals collection, with its complete microform versions of back files, was outstanding. As might be expected, Gilmel was also well stocked with audiovisual materials, especially 8mm single-concept loop films.

To complement the collection, the Learning Resources building was designed flexibly, with ample study space both public and private. The students and faculty at Gilmel were obviously proud of the library, as was the administration.

Gilmel's Director of Learning Resources, Arthura Wilton, had been at the college from the time of its founding. As head of the Reference Department at first, and later as director, she had emphasized two aspects of the library: reference service which would provide "information" as well as bibliographic aid, and economical, efficient technical service. Mrs. Wilton had been present when the initial decision was made to classify the library collection according to the Library of Congress system, and she had made every effort, once she became director, to see that the technical services staff took full advantage of the cataloging prepared by the Library of Congress. Proofsheets were purchased to help speed cataloging, and the staff was instructed to "use the LC copy 'as is'; don't tamper with it unless you see an obvious typographic error; don't check everything just on the off chance that it might be wrong."

The cataloging staff at Gilmel included only three professionals. One devoted full time to microforms and audiovisuals. The second was responsible for the original cataloging of monographs and serials and the general supervision of the subprofessionals. The third was the head of the department, responsible for policy development, selection and training of personnel, and problem solving. An excellent corps of subprofessional workers did the bulk of the cataloging. The chief Library Assistant, Wilma Kincade, had been at Gilmel for six years and was a graduate of the college. There were four other staff members at the library assistant level, in addition to the three library technical assistants and the four typists.

Gilmel's reference staff was perhaps the best trained and largest in number of any in the region. Certainly it was outstanding for a college library to boast such a group. There were eight professionals in the department, one of whom served as head. Each had at least a master's degree in a subject field, in addition to the professional degree in librarianship. Four were working on doctorates. Although each staff member tended to concentrate on problems relating to his own speciality, it was not unusual for them to act as a team or to do the "general questions" without regard to area of expertise. The atmosphere in the department was positive and productive—one which pleased the director.

The reference staff had always worked amicably with the Cataloging Department. As sometimes happens in a library with a sizable staff, informal lines of communication had proved to be more effective than the official ones, and it had become common for Bill Regland in reference to take the "cataloging" problems to the chief Library Assistant, Miss Kincade. Since Wilma had been at Gilmel for ten years (including her years as a student assistant), she seemed to know immediately what to do to correct the difficulty.

Bill had been working for a little less than a year at Gilmel. He was not quite sure how he fell into the liaison job with the cataloging people, but he had no objections. He had once been a "searcher" and had always enjoyed solving bibliographic mysteries. He and Wilma got along well, and everyone seemed pleased with the arrangement. If Wilma was not at her desk when Bill had a problem, he simply left a note explaining the difficulty (or asked her to stop by the Reference Desk) and could be sure that the matter was in good hands.

The reference staff had found the cataloging at Gilmel to be quick, accurate, and generally satisfactory. In recent months, however, the various reference librarians seemed to be encountering a difficulty which had not been deemed crucial before. Bill had always been aware that you could not count on finding a title added entry in the card file for every book in the library. He was somewhat vague in his own mind about the policy, but an earlier discussion with the head of the Cataloging Department had elicited the promise that title added entries would be made for all works with distinctive titles, so long as there was not a main entry under title. Bill understood this to mean that titles such as "Works," "Proceedings," and "Poems" would not be represented by added entries, but volumes called, for example, "A History of the Church of England" would be found under title as well as author.

It was the lack of the title card for that "History" which precipitated a crisis. A student had come to Bill with a citation to Robinson's *History of the Church of England*. The reference was incorporated in an old secondary source—the type which does not provide a footnote or a bibliography, just a running citation in the text. The problem was, of course, that the library had dozens of "Robinson" entries in the catalog. A check under title revealed no "History" with Robinson as author, although there was an added entry for R. J. Brown's *History of the English Church*. Bill jokingly asked the student if he would "settle for Brown instead of Robinson," but he knew full well that the Robinson item was needed to document a point in a rather complex argument about the influence of the Church of England upon British society. The student was working on an independent study project and very much wanted to see Robinson's book.

The next step was to try to locate the item through interlibrary loan. But here again, the lack of the author's given names made the task of verification in the Library of Congress Catalog and *National Union Catalog* volumes almost impossible. There was no assurance that LC had even listed it, for the age of the volume was also unknown. On an off chance of success, Bill decided to try the British Museum catalog under "England. Church of England" to see whether a reference to the Robinson work would appear. Fortunately, there was such an entry in the "Appendix" section, and Bill was able to obtain the full bibliographic data.

Before searching the LC and NUC catalogs for a location in the United States, Bill made one last check of the Gilmel catalog. There, under "Robinson, John William," was the needed volume. Quite irritated, Bill muttered a small "damn" and went back to the "H" section to check for the title added entry again. "I'll bet it's filed in the wrong place," he growled, but a full check of the "History of . . ." section revealed no entry for Robinson's work. In distinct annoyance, Bill went back to the author card, checked at the bottom of the LC-prepared copy, and found no indication of a title added entry. "All this time they've been lying to me!" he said to himself with exaggerated hostility. "They said they made title cards for everything except 'Works' and such, but it's obviously not true."

Being a normally sensible person, Bill decided not to rush back to Wilma and demand an explanation. His logic told him that there were several factors which might account for the absence of the title added entry. Perhaps no one was lying to him after all. It could have been just an oversight or something left over from an earlier time when there had been different rules. Feeling much calmer, Bill approached Wilma to try and discover the answer.

Wilma's explanation, however, did not serve to placate Bill. After he had carefully explained the problem to her, she just smiled and said, "Oh yes, that's one of those that we don't make title added entries for."

"What do you mean?" countered Bill. "You told me yourself that you always make title cards for distinctive titles."

"Sure," said Wilma, "that's what I mean. 'History of' isn't a distinctive title, so we don't make a card for it."

"You can't be serious! Why isn't the 'History of the Church of England' considered a distinctive title?"

"The *Anglo-American Cataloging Rules* say that title added entries shouldn't be made for titles beginning with such common words."

Bill was defeated for the moment. He had not been prepared to argue with the *Rules*, but he still felt that there ought to be a title added entry available. Despite Wilma's quite logical explanation, a student and a professional reference librarian had been misled into thinking that the library did not own a needed volume. "And that's just not right," he concluded audibly.

"What's not right?" asked Jean Pilson, his department head.

"Oh, I guess it's not important. It's just one of those 'inscrutable' cataloging policies. I suppose it's not worth getting worked up about."

• • • • •

Bill seems to be at the point of giving up. Should he? Or should he pursue the matter further? If he wants to discuss it further, with whom should the discussion be initiated?

The *Anglo-American Cataloging Rules* seem to place more emphasis than earlier rules upon the use of the title as "main entry" when the authorship is complex or uncertain. Why do the same *Rules* not place more emphasis on the making of title added entries for anything which could be considered by the public to be "distinctive"?

Under what other type of entry might Bill have looked for the Robinson work? Was there anything about the initial search procedure that was erroneous?

Who was "right" in the argument about distinctiveness? What constitutes a "distinctive title," anyway? What does the other literature relating to cataloging and its rules have to say about the question of distinctive titles?

In view of Gilmel's innovative stance as a college and of its Learning Resources director's dedication to good service, could a case be made for inserting such title added entry cards, even when they are not indicated in the tracing on the LC cards? In such a situation, how can the apparent conflict between the two basic library goals of good service and economical cataloging be resolved?

30.
A Plethora of Commercial
Cataloging Services

· · · · · · · · · · · ·

As part of her job description as Supervisor of Instructional Media Centers for the schools of Mountlane County, Madelyn Koster was supposed to "investigate the possibilities for introducing centralized cataloging into the Mountlane school system." She was grateful that the charge had not read "to establish centralized cataloging for the system," for Madelyn had looked carefully at the budget for the media centers and found it not at all padded. To establish a processing center—even to find a place in which to house it—would require capital funds which were certainly invisible at the moment, if not nonexistent.

At the meeting of the County School Board at which Madelyn was interviewed for the position of supervisor, one of the members had raised the question of the high cost of the independent cataloging and processing of materials at each school. "Mrs. Koster," he had said, "we want to know how you feel about putting centralized cataloging into our schools. Are you in favor of it?"

Madelyn had answered forthrightly, but she knew—and certainly the superintendent of the system knew—that she could do little more than indicate that she would favor the move "if, after studying the various possibilities, it looked to be the best choice." She had probably most impressed them by her ability to use the terminology effortlessly: "We would certainly want to consider other alternatives. Our state library has already established a cooperative processing center, through which we might wish to contract for service; then, there are numerous commercial cataloging and processing organizations which might be able to do the job more cheaply than we could do it ourselves. I would want to study all of these and perhaps some others before making a firm decision."

The time to begin a systematic investigation of those various possibilities was now at hand. Mr. Bromley, the Superintendent, had agreed with her that the decision about centralized cataloging should be postponed until she had completed one school year in the system and had had an opportunity to become familiar with the various libraries and media centers operative in the county. She had done that, and the next step was to study the problem systematically.

During the spring, Madelyn had visited the processing center maintained by the state library. It was an interesting visit, but she learned that the center there had not really done much for the school systems and was not particularly enthusiastic about designing a program for Mountlane unless a new staff position could be created specifically for that purpose. Madelyn also learned, discouragingly, how much it costs to start a center—even a small one—and how much time it takes to monitor the center's operations properly. Her first year at Mountlane had convinced her of at least one thing: she could not direct all of her energies toward just one effort, even for a year; there were too many programs that required simultaneous attention.

A few quick calculations brought Madelyn to the conclusion that neither a local center nor the state library center could solve her problem. Each would require the employment of a new staff member, and the negotiations for either arrangement would dominate her own schedule far too completely. Evidently, the only alternative was to look to a commercial cataloging organization for help.

Since it was summertime and her schedule was a bit more flexible than during the school year, Madelyn decided to do her homework on the firms offering centralized cataloging and processing. She spent the better part of a week looking up references to books and articles on commercial processing; most of her daytime hours were consumed in trying to get copies of these materials at the university library fifteen miles away. The experience turned out to be more frustrating than productive, however, for she was unable to locate many of the articles unless she was willing to wait for photocopies through interlibrary loan. Those that she did find in local collections proved to be either outdated or too general to be of much use. What she really needed was a "Consumer Reports" for commercial processors, but none seemed to exist. Of greatest help was the directory of commercial cataloging agents, which at least listed the types of services offered by each company. Although the directory was two years old, it was still valuable to her.

For one moment of wild brainstorming, Madelyn considered writing to every school library system in the country to obtain suggestions about what commerical organization to choose. This she dismissed immediately upon remembering that there were about six such letters addressed to her reposing on her desk right now—all unanswered. Well then, why not write to the American Library Association for help? Madelyn realized that the staff would be sympathetic to her needs, but she also realized that they would be drawing on the same information which she already had at hand. "O.K., kid," she announced to herself, "I guess it's up to you. Make a list of the likely organizations and start going through them, one by one."

From the directory, Madelyn extracted a group of names of companies which had indicated that they could service school libraries and media centers. Then she eliminated those whose headquarters were more than 500 miles from Mountlane, reasoning that the shipping time from firms farther away would be too great. In addition, she discarded the names of those that did not have jobbing services as well as cataloging services, for she believed that it would be a waste of time to buy the materials from one company and ship them to another for processing. It seemed clear to Madelyn that Mountlane should at least aim toward obtaining a product ready for shelving, not one requiring numerous local jobs to be done on it. For this reason, she did not list organizations providing "do-it-yourself" cataloging kits.

The resulting list of firms numbered six. Madelyn was rather pleased with herself for approaching the mattter so precisely and logically. She knew her next step would be to call each of the companies and ask them to send a representative to discuss the possibility of negotiating a contract. A telephone call, she thought, would be preferable to a letter, since letters could be more easily ignored.

Placing the calls was more of a problem than Madelyn had expected. All involved long distance charges, and she really was not quite sure to whom she wished to speak. Still, she thought that the operator at each firm would be able to direct the call properly; thus she placed each call station to station. The results were not entirely satisfactory, however. In two instances, the switchboard operator reported that the sales staff was out of the main office and could not be reached. Madelyn's name and number were recorded for a later return of the call. One company sales supervisor stated flatly that they could not consider taking on any more school systems at the present time. The other three firms each agreed to send a representative within the next week, though none of them could make a specific appointment without consulting with other members of the sales staff. When Madelyn finally hung up the phone, she was much less optimistic than she had been at the outset.

One thing about the procedure that bothered Madelyn a bit was the fact that she hadn't yet consulted with the various school librarians and media specialists in the system. Since it was June, few of them were available—most were either vacationing or taking summer courses. "Still," she thought, "I can get all the details, write them up, and then we can have a meeting early this fall to decide what to do. I know that there are differences in cataloging in the various schools, but we can deal with that problem when I've got a better idea about what's available."

During the next week, two of the sales representatives did call and make appointments to see Madelyn. One wrote to her saying that he would be away on vacation until July but would call her when he got back. (Then she had to write to him and tell him that she would be on vacation in July and would call him when she got back!) A representative from the fourth company appeared without warning on the morning when she had an appointment with an architect to talk about the plans for a new media center. Madelyn managed to talk with the salesman long enough to determine that his firm was really too small to handle the Mountlane contract anyway. From the fifth organization she heard nothing, and she decided that a follow-up call would be useless since the company was rather vague about its services as described in the directory.

Both of the sales representatives who made appointments were prompt and pleasant. Each seemed to know his business and was able to provide samples of the work which his firm could produce. Madelyn was impressed with both of them, though they were not at all alike. Jim Lackland was a genial, joke-making man in his late thirties, while George Carter was a straightforward, no-nonsense professional, thoroughly knowledgeable about his product but lacking even a grain of humor. Madelyn asked both for copies of the literature available on their respective services, but she discovered that Lackland was unable to cite a price for the work which his company would undertake. Carter, on the other hand, quoted a series of prices related to the type of work required and wanted her to set a date on which the service was to begin. Madelyn explained that she first had to consult with her superintendent and with the librarians and media specialists involved. To this Carter replied, "Well, you call me when you're ready to make a decision. But don't wait too long; Wilemsville is talking with us about doing their processing and we can't take on more than one new system this fall."

• • • • •

What should Madelyn's next steps be in this negotiation? Should she reconsider her decision to eliminate the other two "live candidates" (i.e., the one with the salesman on vacation and the one which never returned her call)?

What mistakes, if any, has Madelyn made in her procedures thus far?

What other sources of information which Madelyn might have utilized are available on commercial cataloging and processing—or *are* there any?

What legal considerations might be involved in the negotiation of a contract of this type?

Appendix: Case Analyses

• • • • • • • • • • • • • • •

Written case analyses are, to some degree, always unsatisfactory. The full dimensions of the problems associated with any case study are best revealed within the context of group discussion. In the interest, however, of illustrating different ways in which two of the cases presented in this volume might be viewed, analyses are appended. These show the approach of two graduate students in library science and that of the author of the cases.

The students whose work is reproduced here were enrolled in the School of Library Science at the University of North Carolina at Chapel Hill. Both were new at case analysis. As individuals, they were able to discern and deal with many of the issues raised, but not all of them. Nor does the author's analysis fully exploit the possibilities. Thus, these discussions should be seen as illustrative rather than definitive, as a point of departure rather than as an end.

Case 29:
Student's Analysis

BY ERIC OLSON

• • • • • • • • • • • •

Regland's initial search procedure contained at least two errors. When the item was not located in the catalog under a title entry, before proceeding to the *NUC* or *BM* catalog, two additional searches of the Gilmel catalog would have been more efficient. The conclusions which could be drawn from the title search failure are (1) the title is not in the library; (2) the title was incorrectly cited and therefore may be in the library; (3) there was a filing error in the title entry; and (4) the correct conclusion (though not obvious to Regland)—that there was no added entry. With these possibilities, while he was at the catalog, Regland could have made a quick search of the "Robinsons" and the subject heading "Church of England—History." Even though there are dozens of "Robinson" entries, it would only have taken a few minutes at most to flip through the "Robinson" section. If this procedure seems unlikely, then certainly, in light of the above possibilities, a search under the subject entry should have been made.

While this improved search procedure would have shortened the search time and ended in a successful search, it would not have resolved the Reference Department's problem of when to expect an added title entry. The resolution of this problem involves questions of communication between cataloging and reference and the question of the benefits of additional cataloging versus the cost of that cataloging.

If the Reference Department knew what sort of titles are considered distinctive, then they could structure their search procedures to account for these missing titles. However, although LC obviously considers *History of the Church of England* to be nondistinctive, an examination of the *Rules* does not provide much confidence for predicting what will happen in the future. In fact, the *Rules* do not support Kincade's contention that *History* . . . is not distinctive. Rule 33, paragraph 1, indicates that title entries are not made for titles beginning with common words, but only when "titles

. . . are incomplete or meaningless without the author's name," which does not pertain to this title. Rule 33, paragraph 6, indicates that entries are not to be made where the title is identical with a subject heading under which the work is entered, if the subject heading used has no subdivision. However, *History* . . . and "Church of England—History" are not identical. *(History* . . . is also different from "History, Church" which has a "see" reference to "Church history.") So there is some question as to the basis of LC's decision not to make an added entry, and the librarian is left with the difficulty of trying to determine what to expect from the Library of Congress.

The main argument against making nondistinctive title entries is that they are not helpful to the user, and only tend to confuse him or clog up the catalog with unhelpful cards. They may be confused with subject headings, or there would be so many *Works* . . ., etc., that they would not provide a convenient search path. However, in this case, neither argument is valid in that the title does not conflict with the subject heading structure and is distinctive enough to be located under *History*. . . .

The question, then, is whether to add title entries to the catalog where LC has failed to provide them. This could be done by the nonprofessional staff if they were told to make title entry cards for all items, even when LC does not indicate an added title entry. However, this would likely involve the difficulties mentioned above of clogging the catalog with nondistinctive titles. Items for which LC does not provide an added title entry could be routed to one of the professional staff for review as to the distinctiveness of its title and a decision on whether or not to make the added entry. However, this would also involve a decision of what to do about the present catalog and whether title entries should be added to it.

Although the reference staff seems "to be encountering a difficulty," it would be useful for the chief cataloger and the reference staff to get together informally to try to determine the extent of the difficulty. This would not only indicate to the Catalog Department how crucial this difficulty is and the benefits which might be balanced against the additional cataloging costs, but would also provide an opportunity for the Catalog Department to discuss what types of entry can be expected in the catalog and what this implies for reference search strategy.

In the case at hand, what seems curious is that the informal liaison between cataloging and reference seems to have broken down. It must have been a mighty fit of pique that induced Regland to think that the catalogers were lying to him. And it seems untypically inflexible of Kincade to fall back on the *Rules* rather than trying to explain the situation and informally explore possible solutions. However, this might be explained by the "Monday morning grumbles." At this point, the most useful solution might be for Regland to make an informal survey of the other members of the reference staff to determine whether or not this is a common problem and whether the size of the problem warrants further effort. If the problem is large enough, then Regland could informally approach Kincade and inform her of the nature and size of the difficulty that the reference staff is encountering. It would seem, given the apparent nature of their relationship, that an informal discussion could ensue about whether or not the size of the problem would warrant a change in the cataloging procedures and an investigation of what the reference staff should expect of the catalog in terms of their search procedures.

Unless the difficulty is very large, which seems unlikely, it seems that the most likely solution is to keep the reference staff informed of the quirks in the catalog, perhaps through semi-formal meetings of the reference and catalog staffs, during which difficulties in use of the catalog could be discussed. Also, the informal liaison should be maintained to provide search suggestions by the catalogers and use problems by the searchers.

Case 29:
Author's Analysis

· · · · · · · · · · · ·

In deciding whether Bill Regland should give up at this juncture or carry his concern further, an assessment must be made of the import of the problem. His comment to Jean Pilson suggests that he has charged the difficulty off to "inscrutable" cataloging policies and does not intend to go further. Whether he will think better of this decision later, may depend upon the frequency with which the problem arises again.

Since Bill does not know how many other people have been inconvenienced by the lack of title added entries, one procedure would be to tell his department head and reference colleagues about the experience and ask them to keep a record of all such problems which they encounter during the next month (or other specified time period). This plan would offer the advantage of bringing some evidence of inconvenience in measurable terms. Protocol might suggest, however, that such a plan ought to be initiated by Jean Pilson rather than Bill. Given the acknowledged informal administrative structure, Jean would probably say "go ahead and work out the details," rather than raise objections.

Bill might, on the other hand, merely undertake to keep his own tabulation of similar experiences with the lack of title added entries. This presents the difficulty of not affording an adequate sample of such experience; further, even allowing for a program of gathering all incidents of reference staff needing missing title entries, the problems of the user who does not consult the reference librarian will go unmeasured. At the very least, all of the reference-encountered incidences of needing title added entries should be tabulated.

If Gilmel were more formally structured administratively, the problem should very likely be turned over to Jean Pilson, who would then negotiate the matter with the head of the Catalog Department. Should no solution be achieved at that level, the matter could be referred to Mrs. Wilton, the Director of the Learning Resources Center.

Although the *Anglo-American Cataloging Rules* do indeed place more emphasis upon the use of title main entries in cases of diffuse or confused authorship patterns, the question of whether to make title added entries has not been modified in any particular way by the 1967 *Rules*. The problem of determining what is "distinctive" in a title has persisted for more than a century. The *Prussian Instructions,* for example, utilize a keyword approach to title, alphabetizing under the first substantive word in the title—a policy which often leads to confusion on the part of the user of German bibliographies. The consensus of the cataloging world has been moving toward alphabetization under the first word, not an article, of the natural title, avoiding inversion of titles or selection of keywords that are not the first words of the title.

There is still a problem, however, with the titles that begin with words carrying no information content of significance to the user of the catalog, e.g., "report on," "study of," "history of." The policy of the Library of Congress, viewed inductively, appears to have varied over the years since printed cards were first distributed at the beginning of the twentieth century. Even though the policies have been clearly defined at regular intervals, variations are now discernible in most library catalogs of any age, and the user might reasonably be confused by these unexplained variations. In effect, he will find added entry cards for some *History of . . .* titles but not for others.

From the practicing cataloger's point of view, the staff of the Library of Congress seems to prefer to enter works beginning their titles with *History of . . .,* under subject headings closely resembling the words following the initial title words. Had Bill been aware of this, he would have looked under the subject "Church of England—History" in the catalog. There could be several reasons why he did not follow that plan: (1) He did not think of it, since he was relatively inexperienced as a reference librarian. The variations in use of title added entries were obviously not completely clear to him, as shown by his later discussion with Wilma. He would thus possibly not expect to find the work under a subject heading, since he had concluded that the lack of a title added entry meant that the library did not own the book. (2) He may have learned from his colleagues that subject headings are confusing in their structure and not to be trusted. This attitude is not uncommon among reference librarians, who often find it just as difficult as users do to project the form of a subject heading.

Bill can be forgiven for not wanting to plow through the whole Robin-

son file. This is a tedious process and certainly an embarrassing one to pursue while the student is standing around awaiting your answer. The reference librarian feels a pressure to produce and therefore tends to shy away
from any procedure which might unduly delay a waiting patron. The move
to search another source is fully understandable in this instance. Bill could,
however, have determined at this point how crucial the finding of the book
was to the student and arranged to have him return later to learn of the results of Bill's search. New reference librarians sometimes have a greater urge
to appear competent in their work, thereby looking for shortcuts which actually lengthen the search.

Although no specific information is given to reveal when the student
was released from the search process, it may be assumed that he had already
left by the time the possibility of interlibrary loan was being investigated.
Once the student had left, Bill could then have done a more thorough search
of the Gilmel catalog. But the fact remains that he really did not believe that
Gilmel had the volume and was secure in his conclusion that the lack of a
title added entry meant the lack of the book.

Bill's decision to look in the British Museum catalog seems strange at
first. It is probably not especially unusual, for reference librarians whose
previous experience has shown them the value of a particular bibliographic
search strategy may return to that strategy in a similar instance. In one
sense, it was unfortunate that the use of *BM* proved successful, for the
chance of finding another title there, under new circumstances, is not very
great. Bill was lucky that time; he might not have been again. On the other
hand, a tedious search through the LC and NUC catalogs under "Robinson"
is a horrendous prospect. Given Bill's situation, recourse to *BM* does not
seem too bizarre; for if he were lucky, as he was, it would save perhaps hours
of time. If *BM* did not pay off, then he had wasted only a few minutes.

The literature of cataloging is not at all clear about the matter of what
constitutes a distinctive title. Discussions of distinctiveness, in the context of
periodical and serial titles especially, may be found in Semour Lubetzky's
works on the cataloging code and in the report of the 1961 Paris Conference on Cataloguing Principles.

A more pertinent question may be whether the library's public has a
commonsense concept of distinctive titles. Observation of library use suggests that specific citations are searched under the information provided;
thus, if a library patron encounters a citation beginning "A History of" or
"A Report on," he will look it up that way. If, however, he receives the ci-

tation orally or calls it up from his memory, he may produce only the content-carrying words of the title. The library must, therefore, decide whether it will try to cover for all user approaches or merely for those based on one of these approaches.

Because Gilmel has set itself up as an innovative school and its Learning Resources Center is expected to aid the students in their self-directed study programs, a case could be made for developing a catalog facilitating self-help. On the other hand, the presence of a large and specialized reference staff could argue for streamlined cataloging and the consequent greater emphasis upon direct assistance to patrons. In the latter case, the "finding list" philosophy of the catalog would presumably supersede the "bibliographic" concept.

The assumption of the "finding list" stance, however, logically implies that known information be fully indexed by the library, that is, that headings be inserted to represent the author, title, and specific subject(s), under the assumption that the patron has some sort of written citation when he approaches the catalog. Imprecise information of the hearsay variety will not lead quickly to the library's holdings, under this philosophy. The user with the most accurate citation will be best served by such a catalog.

The deletion of title added entries would appear to be in conflict with a "finding list" theory, although it might well be in harmony with a "bibliographic" one. In the "bibliographic" approach, the user is expected to think more in categorical terms than in specific title word terms. Thus, he can find what he wants through the categorical (i.e. subject) headings provided by the catalog rather than through content-devoid title words such as "history of."

The Learning Resources Center thus seems to face a dilemma of sorts. If it adopts the finding list theory, a program of review of title added entries must be inaugurated. If the correction is to be thorough, all previously-cataloged materials must be examined to determine where title added entries have not been inserted. Obviously, this would be a very costly process. If, on the other hand, the present practice is continued in the interest of economy and serving the bibliographic function, the reference staff (and all future members added to it) must be fully informed about the rules governing the making of title added entries.

Again, it may be noted that the degree of inconvenience caused patrons and reference staff members ought to be assessed. There is danger here of attacking a gnat with a machine gun—of generalizing prematurely on the basis of what may be one atypical instance.

A final comment may be made about the problems associated with "informal" administrative and communication lines. Bill Regland is certainly operating at a higher level in the library hierarchy than Wilma Kincade, although their communications have been from colleague to colleague thus far. In this crisis, Wilma is put on the defensive and apparently falls back on the "Rules" as a means of avoiding censure from a colleague/superior. Although cataloging staff members are often noted for their defense mechanisms, these devices are sometimes adopted because a worker comes into controversy with someone who has been acting as his equal but in point of power is not. At such times, the informal lines of communication may evaporate or be severely impaired. Working up and down through the "proper" lines of authority can prove slow, but these lines serve a protective function which should not be overlooked.

SELECTED BIBLIOGRAPHY

Anglo-American Cataloging Rules. North American Text. Chicago: American Library Association, 1967.

International Conference on Cataloguing Principles, Paris, 1961. *Report*. London: Organizing Committee of the International Conference, 1963.

Jackson, Sidney L. *Catalog Use Study*. Chicago: American Library Association, 1958.

Lubetzky, Semour. *Code of Cataloging Rules: Author and Title Entry*. Chicago: American Library Association, 1960.

Perrine, Richard H. "Catalog Use Difficulties: Causes & Cures." *RQ*, VII (Summer, 1968), 169–174.

_____. "Catalog Use Study." *RQ*, VI (Spring, 1967), 115–119.

Case 30:
Student's Analysis

BY EVELYN M. BEDARD

• • • • • • • • • • •

Since Madelyn's personal telephone calls were not too effective in accomplishing a meeting with the salesmen, I would recommend her making use of secretarial time in some letters. Her telephone calls should also have been followed by letters to the individuals as a reminder and record of the contact with the company and its representative.

If the two salesmen contact her, she should make a definite appointment, but on the basis of the service or of answers received from the two who did visit her, this does not really seem like it would be a profitable expenditure of time.

Initially, Madelyn should have begun some background reading before the summer. There does not seem to be a tremendous amount of literature in the area, but she could have scanned *Library Literature* and *Library Resources and Technical Services*. In the latter, she would have found in the Spring issue of 1969, a quite comprehensive article and directory of companies offering services, by Barbara M. Westby. Using this, and assuming she has a secretary, she should have sent letters to a number of companies, even to some beyond her 500-mile range. There is no assurance that companies close by will meet shipping dates any better than those some distance away. In the letters she should have asked for any information pamphlet or packet available for prospective customers and also asked about the availability of librarian consultant services to school systems initiating a central processing service provided by the company. Her letter could have asked if the company provided a list of school systems using their services. Such a list, if provided, might have been one of satisfied customers, but it would have had some potential for personal contact by mail.

Using both the directory article and information received, in her free moments Madelyn could have reviewed the companies in terms of services offered, and made notes which would help her compare and then come to a decision as to which contacts she should follow up with either a telephone call or a letter or both.

It seems to me that, administratively, she had made a management error in not sounding out the various school librarians and media specialists with regard to the venture into a centralized processing system. This could have been accomplished in her familiarization visits and staff visits. (I presume a supervisor does that as part of her administrative functions.) The bringing up of the issue would allow them time to give some thought to what they would like to see offered and also prepare them, like it or not, for the need of some compromise in trying to standardize the system. When Madelyn negotiates ultimately, she is going to need to present her plans with some idea of standarization, for the processing will be far too costly to customize for each school. From a meeting with the staff as a group, she could have elicited questions which might have helped her in formulating questions when she either met with a librarian consultant or talked with the salesmen. Also, it is possible that some of her staff might have had some knowledge about commercial processing or of some school systems that did. Fall seems rather late for a preliminary meeting with the staff.

While writing to every school system in the country would have been out of order, she could have written to the state boards of education to see if they had information on school systems within their purview which utilized commercial companies for centralized processing in their instructional media centers. Again, some would have responded, and letters could have gone out or person-to-person telephone calls could have been made. There is an address list contained in "Centralized Processing: A Directory of Centers," by Donald D. Hendricks in *Library Resources and Technical Services,* Spring, 1970. The *School Library Journal* may have offered some help in this direction.

In "Commercial Processing Firms: A Directory," by Barbara Westby (Spring, 1969 *Library Resources and Technical Services)* one has the beginnings of a "consumer report" in that either Miss Westby or colleagues of hers visited some of the companies. It would seem that *Library Technology Reports* would offer services in this direction. The American Library Association has a responsibility in this direction, and certainly members of the Resources and Technical Services Division of the Association should be supportive of critical evaluation of services purchased.

There seems to be need of consultation with the school superintendent with regard to how extensive a program the centralized cataloging should be;

that is, does Madelyn have the right to assume both the processing and the purchasing can be done with the same company, or must the book purchasing be done with the present jobber(s)? Also, she should be informed as to whether the negotiations are going to have to go out on a bid. This will influence her justifications if she has to ultimately narrow down from three companies, yet wants the company which best meets her requirements. She also needs to know if a contract has to be renewed on a yearly basis, and this may well be so because of annual budgets. Because of contractual arrangements, the legal adviser to the school system will have to be consulted, and he will want to review the document. This would be necessary to be sure that the services to be purchased, along with any limitations or warranties by the company, are incorporated in the contract. Stipulations with regard to recourse which the purchaser of services will have and provisions for termination of services by either party to the contract should be clearly stated. Madelyn is going to need to read the fine points carefully.

At this time, I would like to suggest an alternative for Madelyn if she has an extensive system to control. An administrative assistant with a business background would be of help to her. Maybe I am dreaming, but in view of the many duties of a supervisor of instructional media centers, it would seem that such an assistant could be of tremendous help in attending to details, while leaving the professional needs to be met by Madelyn. Sometimes, however, this kind of work can be incorporated into the function of an executive secretary.

Case 30:
Author's Analysis

· · · · · · · · · · ·

Although Madelyn feels herself to have been quite systematic and logical in her steps thus far, she has, it seems, almost reached an impasse. One salesman is pushing for a beginning date of service, while another can provide her with no price information. Following through in the pattern of her earlier steps, she can "logically" merely accept the offer of the salesman—Mr. Carter—who has presented specific price and product data.

There are several reasons, of course, why Madelyn should not go to her superintendent to try to see that Carter's firm is given a contract. In the first place, she herself has already recognized that she can only recommend, not let a contract: but she has also noted that there is as yet no consensus from the school librarians under her supervision about what kind of centralized cataloging or processing is desired. Her earlier decision was merely to obtain the needed information and present it to the librarians and media specialists at a meeting in the fall. In the second place, the interviews with the salesmen were far from satisfactory. While Lackland was unable to cite prices—possibly because the price schedule was too complex to be quoted without more information about the needs of the school system—Carter displayed characteristics reminiscent of high pressure salesmanship, e.g., "Willemsville is talking with us. . . . and we can't take more than one new system this fall."

Madelyn might go back and attempt to talk with the salesmen for the other two companies thought to be good possibilities. Given her experience with Lackland and Carter, however, she could reasonably conclude that a similar interview would result in the other two cases. The failure of the Carter and Lackland interviews should suggest to her that her basic approach is faulty.

If Madelyn has not technically made "mistakes," she has certainly proceeded unwisely at times. Given her newness to the job of supervisor and her unfamiliarity with the field of commercial processing services, her questionable judgment is understandable. It may be charged that she should have started much earlier in her consideration of the problem, but her superintendent had encouraged her to postpone making any decision until the end of her first year on the job. Her guilt feelings about the postponement may be pushing her into frantic activity over the summer; but, looking closely at what she has actually done and why, Madelyn's critic must admit that she was not aware that she was making premature or hasty decisions. Her only acknowledged guilt feeling relates to her failure to consult with her school librarians and media specialists.

What then has she actually done wrong? Her problems in finding relevant, up-to-date literature are common. Few public and academic libraries have research-level collections in library science. It is not at all unlikely that she would have to order photocopies of materials which seem from their titles to be relevant to her need. Madelyn, like many college students, could be reminded that she should have started her literature search earlier; but she did not have the blocks of time necessary to do this type of search during the school year.

She might have ignored the literature altogether, but she was conscientious enough to try to find some help in an acceptable research fashion. Whether hers was the most effective approach might be questioned; in any case, it certainly was not a fast one, as she eventually discovered. Writing to some individuals or the staff of a library organization such as the American Library Association would have been simpler; however, there is no assurance that they would have answered promptly or at all. She might, nonetheless, have launched a two-pronged attack with better odds that at least one might produce something of use to her.

Madelyn's visit to the state library's center produced results which are not surprising but of which she could hardly have been certain in advance. Although the center might have been able to take on her county schools without adding another staff member, despite what they told Madelyn, the fact that the center's staff was not enthusiastic about the prospect would suggest that she might encounter all kinds of roadblocks if she tried to overcome their objections. This would no doubt require more time than she had to give to the project.

Her reasoning that the cost of an independent center for her county schools was prohibitive may be correct, but she has relatively little evidence on which to base her conclusion. She has done no local cost study, nor has she fully investigated the possibility of getting authorization from the Mount-lane County School Board to establish a new position for a head of the processing center. Thus, some further consideration might be given to the development of a local center for Mountlane. If and when Madelyn finally does meet with her librarians and media specialists, she might present the alternative of pushing for money and staff to do the job locally, rather than contracting with a commercial processor. Should she decide to move in this direction, her next step would be to obtain some realistic cost estimates based on information from other school-oriented processing centers. Her review of the literature should have revealed that there are few centers which try to combine processing for different types of libraries, which, in turn, may suggest that costs and requirements related to a state processing center for public libraries may not be fully transferable to school libraries in a single county.

Madelyn's desire for a "Consumer Reports" kind of help in selecting a processing firm is understandable. Librarians have, however, been rather cautious about going into print to reveal the inadequacies of a particular firm. Some companies which serve one type of library poorly may perform quite well for another; or it may be the peculiarities of a library's requirements that make it impossible for certain firms to do satisfactory work. Directories can be compiled from documented factual information; evaluations necessarily involve some subjective judgments for which the customers may not be able to produce adequate proof. Without proof, the librarian who maligns a company in print may find himself the subject of legal action. Even a voiced negative evaluation could be viewed as slanderous. For this reason, library associations have tended to avoid publishing uncomplimentary evaluations of companies offering vending and processing services.

The procedure which Madelyn followed of weeding out and making contact with likely commercial processors is based upon a number of possibly faulty assumptions: (1) that shipping time is dependably related to distance; (2) that companies not shown as jobbers in the directory would not be able to purchase materials; (3) that processing kits would not be a viable alternative to contracting with a firm for complete processing. Each of these assumptions should have been examined more carefully. Shipping time may be a relatively small consideration, when contrasted with service time connected with other parts of the processor's work (e.g., pulling of books from stock, securing books not in stock, performing the processing routines, packing for shipping). Since the directory that she was using was two years old, some companies might have added a jobbing service not previously recorded there. Whether it would be worth inquiring by letter or telephone call, on the chance that their service had been augmented, is a moot question; however, she might have included one or two whose processing services were particularly attractive as related to Mountlane's requirements. The matter of substituting processing kits for full processing should have been examined along with the possibility of establishing an independent center for Mountlane, and subjected to the same kind of procedure and cost analysis.

If Madelyn made a truly major mistake, it was probably in not consulting her librarians and media specialists before all this began. Despite her busy schedule, she could have called a meeting in the spring to discuss the matter. Had she done so, she might not have ruled out kits or a separate center, and her tedious negotiations with the various sales representatives might have been made unnecessary. She is actually in no position to evaluate the services offered because she does not know what custom processing may be demanded by her colleagues. To criticize her as being somewhat inept in negotiating with the salesmen is perhaps to waste time, for she is not at this point ready even to talk with them.

There is, nonetheless, a school of administration which might argue that Madelyn, as supervisor, has the privilege and the obligation to look at the situation and decide what is right for her library system. She has, though, shown no particular expertise in the matter of cataloging or processing and has already recognized that she needs input from the librarians and media specialists. It would appear that she ought to stop sales negotiations at this time and prepare for the fall meeting with her colleagues. Even if she did have cataloging skills, the morale of the librarians and media specialists might be badly lowered if she elected not to consult with them about an activity so vitally related to the well-being of the library system.

If Madelyn is an active member of a library association, she might be able to tap, informally, the expertise available among the membership associated with school library systems. It is doubtful, however, whether there is an easy way to select a centralized processing plan for any library. The tedious process of analysing and comparing the work available from the various firms probably must be undertaken eventually. A trial period of six months or a year may be negotiated to lessen the danger of unwittingly contracting with an unreliable company, providing that the school system is legally permitted to secure such an arrangement.

The question of legalities involved in letting a contract is an important and complex one. In the few systems still requiring bids, the possibility exists that cost factors will be rated more important than quality of performance. If disaster is to be prevented, some quantified measures of quality must be devised and written into the contract. A fairly complete discussion of these considerations is found in the Hensel volume listed in the following bibliography.

SELECTED BIBLIOGRAPHY

Hensel, Evelyn, and Veillette, Peter D. *Purchasing Library Materials in Public and School Libraries*. Chicago: American Library Association, 1969.

Piercy, Esther J., and Talmadge, Robert L., eds. "Cooperative and Centralized Cataloging." *Library Trends*, XVI (July, 1967), 1–175.

Westby, Barbara M. "Commercial Processing Firms: A Directory." *Library Resources and Technical Services*, XIII (Spring, 1969), 209–286.